The Blind Man and the Loon

THE BLIND MAN AND THE LOON

THE STORY OF A TALE

CRAIG MISHLER

Foreword by **ROBIN RIDINGTON**

UNIVERSITY OF NEBRASKA PRESS

LINCOLN & LONDON

An earlier version of chapter 5
was presented as a paper entitled
"Folk Art Meets Folk Tale: The
Blind Man and the Loon," at
the American Folklore Society
Annual Meeting in Louisville,
Kentucky, on October 25, 2008.

An earlier version of chapter 7 was
originally published as "Diving
Down: Ritual Healing in the Tale
of the Blind Man and the Loon" in
Arctic Anthropology 40.2 (2003):
49–55. © 2003 by the Board of
Regents of the University of Wisconsin System. Reproduced courtesy of
the University of Wisconsin Press.
The work was first presented as a
paper at the International Congress
of Arctic Social Sciences (ICASS
IV) in Quebec City, May 18, 2001.

Library of Congress
Cataloging-in-Publication Data
Mishler, Craig.
The blind man and the loon:
the story of a tale / Craig Mishler;
foreword by Robin Ridington.
p. cm.   Includes bibliographical
references and index.
ISBN 978-0-8032-3982-1
(cloth: alk. paper)
1. Indians of North America—
Folklore. 2. Loons—Folklore. I. Title.
E98.F6M56 2013
398.2089'97—dc23   2012043318

Set in Charis by Laura Wellington.
Designed by Nathan Putens.

Contents

List of Illustrations vii

Foreword ix

Preface xiii

Acknowledgments xv

Introduction: The Story of a Tale xix

1 The History and Geography of the Tale 1

2 The Writing of the Tale 27

3 The Tale Behind the Tale 49

4 The Telling of the Tale 67

5 The Art of the Tale 93

6 The Mediated and Theatrical Tale 119

7 The Power of the Tale 135

  Conclusion and Afterword 153

Appendix A: Paradigm of Tale Traits 157

Appendix B: Annotated Bibliography
of Variants 163

Appendix C: Knud Rasmussen's
Greenlandic Variants 191

Appendix D: The Steenholdt Text
and Additional Variants from
Hinrich Rink's Collection 211

Notes 217

References.................................... 223

Index 239

Illustrations

MAPS

1 Regional oicotypes of "The Blind
  Man and the Loon" with hypothetical
  diffusion routes 9

2 Inuit communities with artworks
  depicting the Blind Man and the Loon 98

FIGURES

1 Dena'ina Chief Affanasi with dentalium
  shell necklace, ca. 1900–1904 15

2 The migration of written texts of
  "The Blind Man and the Loon" 28

3 First page of Wittus Frederick Steenholdt's
  manuscript story No. 25a, 1827 31

4 First page of the Blind Man and
  the Loon story from Hinrich Rink's
  Danish collation, 1866 35

5 First page of Sylvain Vitoedh's Loucheux
  Gwich'in variant from Petitot, 1888 38

6 Dandy Jim and wife Susie, ca. 1902 53

7 Ivaluardjuk 59

8 Netsit 59

9   Nâlungiaq 60

10 Ikinilik 60

11 Kibkârjuk and Huwakzuk 61

12 Amaunalik, ca. 1937–38 63

13 Peter Kalifornsky 66

14 Maggie Gilbert with her first
    husband's family, 1927 68

15 Woodcut from Rink's *Tales and
    Traditions of the Eskimo*, 1875 95

    Following page 98

16 Annie Blue, 2009

17 James and Maggie Gilbert, 1973

18 Kenneth and Caroline Frank, 2008

19 Kenny Thomas Sr., in performance, 2000

20 *Aulajijakka: Things I Remember
    #5*, by Kananginak Pootoogook

21 *Blind Man and the Loon* (bronze
    sculpture), by Jacques and Mary Regat

22 *The Loon Gives Lumaq His Sight*,
    by Germaine Arnaktauyok

23 *Blind Man Sees Loon*, by Robert E. Sebastian

24 *The Old Man and the Loon*, by Carla Rae Gilday

25 *Lumak*, by Davidialuk Alasua Amittuq

26 *The Legend of the Blind Boy*, by Toonoo Sharky

27 Old Hamilton loon mask, artist unknown

28 *Blind Man and the Loon* (wood bas-
    relief), by Jacques and Mary Regat

29 *The Loon's Necklace* film pamphlet cover, 1949

Foreword

From a distance of miles and centuries, stories in the oral tradition seem to have an independent existence, drifting from place to place like species of animals over time and territory and gradually evolving from one form to another. Indeed, early folklorists and anthropologists sought to dissect and classify them in the same way that anatomists and taxonomists dissect and classify groups of animals. Later, Swedish folklorist Carl von Sydow (also known as the father of actor Max von Sydow) coined the term *oicotype* to describe local forms of a widely distributed folktale. His idea was that stories evolve and adapt to local conditions over time.

The Blind Man and the Loon is a remarkable work that traces a single story through Inuit and Athabaskan variations. It is clearly a labor of love. Craig Mishler has collected and told the story himself. At the same time, he also traces the contexts in which the story has been told, collected, adapted, and sometimes appropriated. While he uses the terminology of academic folklore, he does not rely exclusively on this rather hermetic language. He takes the reader on a shared journey of discovery and places himself within the narrative to do justice to the people he cites, both historical figures and ones he knows or has known personally. His comments on field technique reflect his own experience as storyteller and collector as well as his encyclopedic knowledge of the relevant literature. Knud Rasmussen comes out as exemplary. Franz Boas doesn't do as well. Mishler is also forthright on the issue of cultural appropriation and doesn't hesitate to point out the failings of the popular and often praised film *The Loon's Necklace*. He tells a cautionary tale for outsiders contemplating the use of Native American oral narratives as "children's literature."

Mishler is a self-confessed collector who early on made the switch from coins to folktales. From there it was just another step to start collecting stories about storytellers and stories about the collectors of stories. He is also a gifted storyteller in his own right. He is schooled in the traditions of distributional and typological folklore, but he is also and perhaps primarily sensitive to the poetic values of storytelling.

Not every collector has been so sensitive. Some even failed to give the names of the people from whom they heard a story. This is unfortunate and indeed disrespectful, for as the author says, "The storytellers who have performed and recorded the story of the Blind Man and the Loon are the unsung poet laureates and Nobel prize winners for literature of their times. . . . They are diverse and fascinating people who need to be honored and remembered, and what follows here is a nod to an illustrious pantheon of voices, names, and faces."

Oral stories live only in the moment of their telling. At least before the advent of electronic communication, stories have been sustained by face-to-face personal contact. They are creatures of breath and ears and voices, and take place in settings like the ones Knud Rasmussen described for his encounters with Inuit storytellers in the 1920s. These settings have recently been vividly recreated by the Igloolik Isuma film cooperative in their feature film *The Journals of Knud Rasmussen*. Actor Pakak Inukshuk delivers a masterful rendition in Inuktitut of a story the shaman Avva told Rasmussen about acquiring his spirit helpers. His performance honors Rasmussen, his friend Avva, and the Inuit people who told him a wealth of stories, including that of the Blind Man and the Loon.

Stories span generations of living people before they jump into the realm of tradition. A story lives and is reborn each time a storyteller makes it his or her own and passes it on to an attentive audience. As Dane-zaa elder Tommy Attachie told anthropologists Robin and Jillian Ridington, "When you sing it now, just like new." Storytellers make stories new with each telling. They assemble traits and motifs wafted to them from distant times and places and construct coherent narratives from them. Stories are cultural (what Alfred Kroeber called "superorganic"), but they are enacted as individual creations in the way that Edward Sapir, in his critique of Kroeber, said all culture is individually enacted.

As a story gradually moves from one cultural and geographic area to another through countless tellings, it evolves into distinctively adapted *oicotypes*. In his collecting adventures, Mishler has recorded versions of the Blind Man and the Loon from a variety of oral poets in several different areas. One of these is Maggie Gilbert, a Gwich'in Athabaskan elder, whom we meet in chapter 4. Unlike most versions of the story, which have come down to us as mere plot summaries or at best as stilted prose, Maggie's story, recorded in Gwich'in, transcribed in that language, and translated into English using a line-for-line poetic form, preserves a sense of place, of context, and of voice. From the original audio document, the author has crafted a written document that does justice to the performance event.

Beyond recording and researching multiple versions of the story, the author looks at himself as a collector and sees in the mirror a reflection of all the other collectors who engaged in one way or another with the story of the Blind Man and the Loon. Like the storytellers themselves, each collector "has left his or her mark on the text." While some collectors, like Franz Boas, at times failed to name the people from whom they heard a story, the names of folktale collectors are almost always known. Chapter 2 is a journey through the archives of collected versions of the Blind Man and the Loon, looking for the stories of the collectors themselves and thereby shedding light on the marks they made on the texts they produced. Written documents do not change over time, although readings and interpretations do evolve in parallel to the way stories themselves evolve. As Thomas King has said, "There is no truth; there are only stories." Mishler gives the reader a gift by recounting the truth behind the myriad versions of "The Blind Man and the Loon" that his own passion for collecting has uncovered.

Robin Ridington

Preface

This book tells the story of a tale, a folktale familiar to thousands of residents of the arctic and subarctic. To understand this book, it is important for readers to be familiar with the basic elements of the tale, even though it has been told hundreds if not thousands of different ways. The following text, collected in the early nineteenth century by Moravian Brethren missionaries in Nunatsiavut or northern Labrador, but never published until now, represents the basic story line.

The text undoubtedly comes from an oral performance in Inuttut, the Eskimo language of Labrador, but was first hand-written in German. The storyteller and the collector remain anonymous. It was eventually collected by Hinrich Rink, a Danish scholar who actively sought out and compiled traditional tales in Greenland and other Inuit areas (see Rink 1866, 1875, and appendix D).

The Blind Man and the Loon

They also tell about a man called Kimungak [Kemongak], that two common loons made him recover his eyesight. He had a sister called Inukviak. The three of them, he, his mother, and his sister, lived in a place among people with extremely long fingernails and without good thoughts.

At the time the three of them were together in the winter house, a polar bear came to the window, and then the mother in a hurry handed her blind son a bow and arrow and helped him take aim, and thus he shot the bear, which fell down. And he said to himself, "Because you hit the creature so well, it fell right down."

But instantly his mother screamed, "No, no, not the bear, only the frame beneath the window did you shoot." As soon as the bear was dead, the mother and her daughter went right to the tent and left Kimungak behind alone in the winter house. While they lived off the bear, the daughter, without her mother knowing, often brought her brother something in the winter house. Because the mother who wanted him to starve would not allow that, she [her daughter] fearing her mother, hid it inside her clothing and brought it to him in that way.

xiii

When she then told her mother something, her mother often said, "Have you already finished that big hunk of meat I gave you?"

"I just don't economize" was her usual answer.

While now Kimungak always stayed alone in the house and often heard the cries of the common loon, he often exclaimed with great urgency, "Would that they, who so often cry, come to me and restore my eyesight."

And see, soon afterward, at night, two common loons came to him and talked to him with a human voice, and they brought him along to a pond, leading him by his arms. And there they ducked him into the water several times, asking him if he was about to be suffocated.

The first time they made him breathe they asked if he saw anything, and he faintly saw the glimmer of something. Once again they dove together with him, and when again they let him breathe, they asked, "What do you see now?" Looking around, he said, "I see [the] land."

Again they ducked him under the water and when again they let him breathe, they asked him if his sight was still unchanged. At that point he saw mouse holes on the other brink of the bay and the stretched skin of the bear he had killed in his blindness.

Thereupon he went home, and because his relatives did not know he had come back, he, feigning blindness, crawled into the house [on hands and knees]. His mother, they say, did not give him anything to eat before she found out that he could see.

When now they left the house and went to the shore and came to a place with a lot of belugas, Kimungak used his mother as a hunting float when he harpooned a beluga. "Which one do you want me to harpoon?" her son asked. The mother answered, "Now, now, now, the dark one" [because the dark ones are not so strong]. And he harpooned that one.

Being now [dragged] in the sea, she said, "Why did my son make me into a float-luk [voice of the beluga]? I, the only one who nursed him. Please let me get out, back up on smooth and dry ground-luk luma." These were her last words and thus she became completely transformed into a beluga. In the North she can still be seen from time to time.

Source: Hinrich Rink Collection, NKS 2488, III, 4°: No. 303, Danish Royal Library, Copenhagen. Translated from the German by Birgitte Sonne

Acknowledgments

Over a forty-year project, there are many folks to thank for assistance. I should begin rather than end with my wife, Barbara, who has patiently encouraged my work throughout, never complaining when I came home from the library and announced that I'd found still another version of the tale of the Blind Man and the Loon, though she heard this repeated dozens if not hundreds of times over the years. My research and writing have benefited enormously and continuously from her engagement and interest and her ever-loving smile.

My efforts have also benefited enormously from the assistance of international colleagues and consultants. Just as folktales are linked by oral transmissions between storytellers, so too are scholarly adventures linked socially. Here is part of the trail. My fascination with the published Greenlandic variants of Hinrich Rink led me to look for his papers in Denmark. After locating them online in the Danish Royal Library archives in 2001, I began to look for a Danish folklorist who might be familiar with Greenlandic traditions and with the Danish documents.

In 2007, during a chance conversation, my colleague Owen Mason, former editor of the *Alaska Journal of Anthropology*, happened to mention his recent fruitful trip to Copenhagen, where he conferred with the Danish archaeologist Hans Christian Gulløv. Owen shared Gulløv's email address, and Gulløv duly referred me to two other Danish scholars, one of whom was Kirsten Thisted. Thisted in turn referred me to Birgitte Sonne, which quickly led to a most productive fruitful correspondence and friendship. I hope someday to shake the hand of Hans Christian Gulløv, who also recently led me to the Erik Holtved photo portrait of Amaunalik, the lively Greenlandic storyteller, which appears in chapter 3.

Since providing his original lead, Owen has provided important comments on my discussion of the Blind Man and the Loon's connection with the archaeological record and the development of Thule culture, so I am greatly indebted and grateful to him on two fronts. He is a fellow detective of the first magnitude. Claire Alix is another archaeologist who thoughtfully commented on chapter 1 of the manuscript, helping me to understand the prehistoric development of bow and arrow technology.

Most especially, I thank Birgitte Sonne, in Denmark, who steered me to and through her Sonnesbase to find additional Greenlandic variants of the tale and make sense of them. This text database, compiled in Danish, is freely available for downloading on the Web. Each Greenlandic tale text or tale summary has a unique number, assigned by the askSam viewer. Whenever referring to these Sonnesbase numbers, I employ the abbreviated prefix SB.

One text not in the database (because it comes from Labrador rather than Greenland) was most graciously translated by Birgitte and appears here in the preface. Birgitte also pointed me toward the unpublished papers of Knud Rasmussen and also kindly invited me and my wife to visit her by train at her home near Glumsø, where she gave us a daylong drive through a part of the Danish countryside we would never have discovered on our own. We truly enjoyed her hospitality and that of her husband, the distinguished poet Jørgen Sonne. Without Birgitte's expert assistance, the scope and shape of this book would have been vastly different.

Through Birgitte I was able to contact Lucy Ellis, a student at the University of Copenhagen, who translated numerous Sonnesbase documents from Danish to English, and Liv Trudsø, who skillfully guided me through the archives at the Danish Royal Library (DRL) in 2007. An additional nod goes to Ivan Boserup, head archivist at the DRL, for granting permission to photograph and reproduce the image of Wittus Frederick Steenholdt's historic manuscript. Arnaq Grove, whom we also met at the Arktisk Institut in Copenhagen, dutifully referred me to Birgitte Jacobsen, who in turn referred me to Karolina Platou Jeremiassen in Nuuk. Finding time between her university studies and her young children, Karolina has provided new transcriptions and translations of three unpublished Greenlandic texts collected by Knud Rasmussen as well as the 1827 Wittus Frederick Steenholdt text, the oldest known variant of the tale (see appendixes C and D).

My interview with Maggie Gilbert, the blind Gwich'in storyteller, which forms the centerpiece of chapter 4, was made possible by the ad hoc translation skills of Ernest Erick of Venetie, who took a keen interest in traditional storytelling way back in 1973. Ernest did not translate the story itself but helped me elicit it. His grandmother, Myra Roberts of Venetie, was another one of my favorite storytellers.

Here in Alaska I also wish to thank my Gwich'in collaborators. Fanny Gemmill transcribed a first draft of Maggie Gilbert's variant, reproduced in chapter 4; this draft was subsequently proofread and refined by Maggie's grandchildren, Lincoln Tritt and Caroline Frank, and Caroline's husband, Kenneth Frank (Drizhuu).

Kenneth, especially, showed great patience in helping me match up the Gwich'in and English translation, line for line, with numerous annotations on Maggie's performance and style. He is the truest of friends and a close partner in the preservation of Gwich'in language and culture. Also, a tip of the hat to Maggie's daughters, Naomi Tritt and Florence Newman, and Maggie's son, Trimble Gilbert, whose blessing made it possible for me to include their mother's story in this book. I treasure their friendship over the years.

Ingrid Kritsch of the Gwich'in Social and Cultural Institute has been most diligent in sending me published materials and assisting in the procurement and processing of digital recordings in the Northwest Territories. She also introduced me to the art of Carla Rae Gilday, included in chapter 5. The eminent linguist Michael Krauss, an old-time friend and fellow collector of the tale of the Blind Man and the Loon, was especially helpful in guiding my thinking about the antiquity and precise wording of the tale.

For the portrait photos that accompany chapter 3, I profusely thank Amy Carney and Patricia Linville of the Seward (Alaska) Community Library, the staff at the British Columbia Archives, Bent Nielsen of the Arktisk Institut in Copenhagen, M. Scott Moon of the *Peninsula Clarion* newspaper, Leon Unruh of the Alaska Native Language Center, and Todd Paris of the University of Alaska Fairbanks.

For permission to reproduce the wonderful art illustrations that accompany chapter 5, I am most grateful to the artists Germaine Arnaktauyak, Toonoo Sharky, Carla Rae Gilday, and Robert Sebastian. Their work has given me a heightened appreciation of the tale and its importance to Native people. And I am especially grateful to Jacques and Mary Regat, of Anchorage, who allowed me to interview them about their two elegant sculptures, one in wood and one in bronze, and how they see the story. A quick wink goes to my cousin Clark for his excellent photo of the Regats' wood bas-relief hanging in the Fairbanks North Star Borough Public Library.

Leslie Boyd Ryan and Donna McKie of Dorset Fine Arts, Michelle Anne Olsen of the Inuit Art Foundation, Angela Linn of the Alaska Museum of the North, Caroline Riedel of the University of Victoria Maltwood Art Museum, and Tanya Anderson and Vincent Lafond of the Canadian Museum of Civilization all helped me secure digital images and permissions.

I am deeply thankful to Matthew Bokovoy and the staff of the University of Nebraska Press for their unflagging editorial support and advocacy. I am also extremely grateful to my devoted cartographer, Carol Belenski, who has so patiently helped me develop the beautiful maps for this volume and most of my other books. And I will be forever indebted to my colleague Gary Holton for assistance in setting up a much-needed companion website for this book: http://www.uaf.edu/loon/.

I have benefited greatly from the free use of several archives, notably the British Columbia Provincial Archives in Victoria, the Glenbow Museum Archives in Calgary, the Alaskan and Polar Regions archive in the Rasmussen Library at the University of Alaska Fairbanks, the Danish Royal Library and National Archives in Copenhagen, and the Northwest Territory Archives in Yellowknife. I am grateful for staff assistance at each repository. The international dimensions of "The Blind Man and the Loon" have encouraged me to travel and see more of this magnificent, exciting world. I have followed the story to many places, and it has become an essential part of my life.

Introduction

The Story of a Tale

Although there is almost no district which is completely devoid of folklore
or stripped of it, nevertheless, it is provincial towns rather than big cities;
and villages rather than provincial towns; and among the villages, the ones
which are most of all quiet and impassable, located in the forests or in the
mountains, it is these which are most endowed and blessed with folklore.

—JACOB GRIMM, 1815

Of the many thousands of stories recorded in Native North America by folklorists, linguists, ethnographers, and amateur enthusiasts, perhaps none have received as much attention as Raven Brings Daylight (Oosten and Laugrand 2006) or the Star Husband Tale, the latter now well-known through the classic studies made by Gladys Reichard (1921) and Stith Thompson (1953). The most recent study of a single tale known across the arctic is Kira Van Deusen's *Kiviuq* (2009), written from the perspective of a professional storyteller. Still, there are other widely diffused oral narratives or "diasporic folktales" (Haring 2003) actively circulating in oral tradition begging for scholarly attention.

Most notable among these is "The Blind Man and the Loon," also well-known under such titles as "The Blind Boy and the Loon," "The Lumaaq Story," "The Origin of the Narwhal," or "The Loon's Necklace." Permutations of this intriguing paleo-tale have circulated in small villages over a very large part of Greenland, Canada, and the United States in the form of at least ninety-four published oral variants, sixteen unpublished archival manuscripts, three unpublished archival recordings, twenty or more literary and semi-literary renderings, a ballet, a theatrical concert, three films, three audio compact discs, an LP vinyl record, numerous works of folk art, and a myriad of virtual texts floating about on the Internet, including two on the official government web site Nunavut. com. These formal reincarnations and pathways demonstrate how the story continues to renew and reproduce itself. Despite its ancient roots, it is very much a living thing.

Reflexivity

My own involvement with this tale is that of a collector, but I also see myself to some extent as its curator, biographer, interpreter, and friend. Sometimes I have been asked or have volunteered to perform the tale, especially to audiences who are interested in my research but who are unfamiliar with Native American oral tradition. This has led to open conversations about its significance, its distinction as a repository of values and beliefs, its dissemination, and its totally remarkable life history.

In my own field work I have collected three oral variants in Alaska—a Gwich'in version told to me in 1973 by Maggie Gilbert, a blind woman in Arctic Village; an English version told by Abraham Luke of Dot Lake on July 10, 1983; and a videotaped performance in English from Kenny Thomas Sr. of Tanacross on October 30, 2000. Maggie Gilbert's variant is published here for the first time ever (chapter 4). The other two have already been published elsewhere (Mishler 1986; Thomas 2005). The compelling voices of these performers remain in my head. Hearing and telling the tale has allowed me the luxury to live inside of it. I am part of its habitat, especially now that my own eyesight is weakening.

My father, Clayton Mishler, was a tremendous storyteller, and as a child I was regaled with tales of his many adventures as a young man and as a sailor in the U.S. Navy. He was shipped off to China for three years during World War II and never forgot a single moment of it. My father's brother, Edward Mishler, was another great influence. Uncle Ed was a superb joke teller and always had us bent over in stitches. He worked for many years at Great Lakes Steel in Detroit, which must have been a joke factory as well as a steel plant. During holiday get-togethers and other Sunday afternoons, there was nonstop storytelling, joking, and magic tricks between my father and Uncle Ed.

One of my boyhood hobbies was coin collecting. I recall spending hundreds of hours going through rolls of coins from the bank to find nickels from every mint and every year, which I then carefully inserted into a handsome folder. After three or four years I managed to collect every American nickel except two. My bubble burst when I went to a coin show in Detroit and was told by a dealer that without those missing two nickels my collection was basically worthless. I soon got rid of the nickels.

This same impulse, I suppose, led to my professional interest in collecting songs and stories. I now have folders bulging with printed copies of the Blind Man and the Loon story. I also have cases and cases of original field recordings on cassette tape, most of them stories told by Alaska Natives. Nevertheless, the analogy between collecting nickels and collecting folktales or folk songs is not a good one. It is not necessary to collect all the variants of a tale or a song to gain a good understanding of it or to appreciate its true value. Two missing variants of a story, unlike two nickels missing from a coin collection, will not substantially affect our grasp of its beauty and its power. For every variant collected, there are probably hundreds or thousands more that are transmitted orally without documentation.

For forty years, while collecting and studying this story, I have been in my reverie. But the psychology of collecting folklore is a bit hard to understand. Perhaps it is the same impulse that prompts wealthy people to collect rare paintings, or compels celebrities such as Jay Leno and Chuck Berry to collect vintage cars. The popularity of antique stores, auctions, garage sales, and television programs such as *The Antiques Roadshow* and *American Pickers* illustrates the fundamental appeal of collecting material culture. As Wikipedia says, "Collecting includes seeking, locating, acquiring, organizing, cataloging, displaying, storing, and maintaining whatever items are of interest to the individual collector." To this list of gerunds I should hasten to add "interpreting" and "sharing."

But do we become what we collect? Will we be remembered for what we collect? In the process of collecting do we become larger than ourselves? Certainly we expand our experience and find a lifetime of adventure by doing so. The annual meeting of the American Folklore Society essentially brings together collectors of folklore so that they may compare, admire, and critique each other's findings.

My earliest educational training at the University of Michigan was in English and American literature, although I started out as a wide-eyed astronomy major. At Michigan I also became intrigued in anthropology by taking lecture courses from Marshall Sahlins and Leslie White. After stints at the University of Colorado and Washington State University, I immigrated to Alaska as a Vista Volunteer in 1969, to work with Native youth from broken families and with recovering alcoholics in Fairbanks. The next year I met my wife Barbara and started a family. I began my first fieldwork working with the Gwich'in, Koyukon, and Han Athabaskans in the early 1970s, while I was teaching at Anchorage Community College, now part of the University of Alaska.

After five years of college teaching, I returned to graduate school in 1976 to study folklore and folkloristics at the University of Texas at Austin. There I learned many of my analytical skills from the late Américo Paredes, my dissertation supervisor. I also studied under the beneficial tutelage of Roger deV. Renwick, Richard Bauman, Marcia Herndon, Annette Weiner, and Joel Sherzer.

Following graduate school I found employment as a historian with the Alaska Division of Geological Surveys and the Alaska Division of Parks and worked side by side with field archaeologists. Then, in my ten-year stint with the Alaska Department of Fish and Game, Division of Subsistence, I was fortunate to work with coastal Alutiiqs, especially on Kodiak Island, and with the Aleuts in the Aleutian and Pribilof Islands. However, as often as I asked, I never found the tale of the Blind Man and the Loon circulating among elders in these culture areas.

The emphasis during my studies at Texas was always on folklore as performance and as verbal art. With additional studies in cultural anthropology, I have augmented this approach with a concentration on ethnography and ethnohistory. My inclination has never been toward grand theoretical matters as much as fieldwork and field methods. With humanistic motives, my first goal has been to honor and recognize the people I study and learn from.

Some readers will be aware that there are two major traditions of folklore scholarship, both of which began in northern Europe. Ethnopoetics, which comes from the Finnish philological tradition, is a modern form of literary criticism, where "The Text is the Thing" (Wilgus 1973). In chapter 4, I adopt this approach to a great extent in my analysis of Maggie Gilbert's Gwich'in language variant. I cast her transcribed Gwich'in language oral performance in lines, as poetry rather than prose paragraphs, and my analysis dwells on the relation of individual lines to one another and to the overall dramatic structure of the tale. I owe this exercise to the pioneering work of Dell Hymes and Dennis Tedlock.

The other major tradition in folktale method and analysis, represented in chapters 1, 2, 3, and 7, is grounded in ethnography and areal studies and was first championed by the Swedish scholar Carl Wilhelm von Sydow. From this perspective, folklore gets its power and meaning from our understanding of its many contexts and uses, including the identity of the storyteller and the social dynamics of his or her community.

Archaeologists repeatedly tell us that artifacts must be understood in situ. Artifacts have certain intrinsic properties, which need to be delineated, but their fuller significance is discovered by learning their location and relationship to other artifacts and to the soils in which they are embedded. The same is true for stories. Stories are embedded in people, in repertoires, in performance and discourse, in media, in cultures, and in history.

Each of these scholarly traditions is well-founded and carries great merit, and this book demonstrates the benefits to be gained from combining them. As Linda Dégh wrote so perceptively in her book *Folktales and Society*, "We can hope to advance only if we succeed in uniting the two directions, in putting the textual analyses on the right socio-cultural basis" (Dégh 1969, 46).

The more I have studied the corpus of the Blind Man and the Loon, the more my sense of wonderment over its creation and replication has grown. In a very real way, it embodies the history and anthropology of the entire western arctic, a history reflected in its wide geographic distribution across two continents, an anthropology that involves nearly every major scholar who has ever worked there.

One of my methods has been to examine the table of contents of every available published anthology of North American Indian folk tales to look for texts and translations of the Blind Man and the Loon. To do this I browsed through countless libraries and used bookstores and spent many hundreds of hours doing various keyword searches on the Internet. Much of this effort, to be sure, proved fruitless, but sometimes newly found texts have emerged from misleading titles. I did not compile variants that I did not see with my own eyes, even if they were referenced online or in print. The result of these decades of searching is the Annotated Bibliography of Variants in appendix B.

A key argument in this volume is that the tale of the Blind Man and the Loon is not only found in many archives, it is in itself an archive of late prehistoric and early historic Indian and Eskimo cultures, packed tightly with a commonwealth of ethnographic data, world views, beliefs, early technologies, and values. It is a grand repository for the knowledge and wisdom of antiquity. The Finnish folklorist Kaarle Krohn (1999, 45) said it well when he wrote, "And just as little of our culture is derived from a single nation, from a single race, so, similarly, few folktales come from the creative genius of a single people, be they Indian or Egyptian; they are, rather, common property, achieved by a joint effort of the entire world, more or less civilized, and are thus a part of international science."

I have long had an interest in plotting the distribution of this international tale type and in comparing its manifold morphemic variations region by region and trait by trait, evidenced by an unpublished paper I first presented at the American Anthropological Association meetings in 1988. This paper was called, "The Loon's Necklace: A Native American Tale Type." However, today I am more eager to understand its significance to the people who tell it. To do this it is important to know the storytellers as well as the story. For non-Natives, this significance is lost not so much in the mistranslation of texts, but in the non-translation of contexts, especially its in situ oral performances. One of the goals of this book is to reopen the story to its many ethnographic, linguistic, and biographical contexts.

The motif that seems to endear non-Natives to the tale is the way the blind man rewards the loon for restoring his eyesight by decorating him with his dentalium necklace, an artistic touch of reciprocity and respect, bonding man with nature. Unfortunately, this element is absent from about 95 percent of the published oral variants, including almost all of the Eskimo variants collected from oral tradition, so I am extremely skeptical that the power and longevity of the story lies in telling us how the loon got its distinctive and beautiful white markings. However heartwarming, this is simply a regional trait found only in a handful of British Columbian and Alaskan variants belonging to the Indian subtype. Still, it gets a lot of attention because this single regional trait has been framed and highlighted and then popularized in children's literature, music, and film.

Book Overview

In chapter 1, "The History and Geography of the Tale," I have defined the paradigms of thirteen selected traits (see appendix A) found within the tale's two major subtypes. For simplicity's sake I call these the Eskimo or Inuit subtype and the Indian subtype. They are like the ventral and dorsal sides of a fish or the proximal and distal ends of a bone, two views of the same thing. These major subtypes are cognates and are logically subdivided into eight regional groups called oicotypes, and the eight oicotypes are in turn subdivided into individual oral variants. A map of places where the tale has been recorded displays its huge territorial range and regional distribution (see map 1, p. 9).

Or, to draw an analogy, the variants of the Blind Man and the Loon story are spread out and grouped like Darwin's finches, each species with a peculiar bill adapted to a different Galapagos island environment. However, this book is not intended to be a detailed, technical study of all the variants or of all the subspecies of the tale. Nor is it a search for origins or ur-forms. Rather, it looks broadly at the genera, the grouping of regional oicotypes, moving fluidly across the continents of North America and Greenland like gigantic herds of caribou.

In chapter 2, "The Writing of the Tale," I look at its dissemination and replication in various Native and European languages, including Danish and English, during historic time. Judging from its wide geographic distribution and the relative isolation of the peoples among whom it was found during the nineteenth century, it seems safe to presume that the tale of the Blind Man and the Loon traveled orally across two major continents via what Alaskans affectionately call "the mukluk telegraph."

The story's written texts, as documented in numerous Eskimo and northern Dene languages, are almost certainly descendants of those told orally in much earlier times, even though no oral recordings emerge until the 1930s, when the Danish scholar Erik Holtved began using an early disc recorder in Greenland. Since the early documentation of oral texts, the written record has also produced many semi-literary works, imaginative recreations, and abridged retellings targeted at children. There has been a great deal of interplay between oral and written tradition; they are closely entwined, especially in the new digital age.

Chapter 3, "The Tale Behind the Tale," tells the story of the storytellers and the collectors of the Blind Man and the Loon. The rock star singer and guitarist John Mayer has said, "When you hear a great song, you trace it back to who the singer is." The same thing is true with a great story. It has a thousand faces. Although visibly missing from so many recorded variants, the lives and personalities of some of the collectors and performers of the Blind Man and the Loon have occasionally been documented, and they are fascinating in themselves.

In chapter 3 I have included a few biographical sketches and anecdotes about the storytellers, and have sought to add their photo portraits. There are also some references to their published biographies, where known, in appendix B, the Annotated Bibliography of Variants. In this appendix I have listed the storytellers rather than the collectors of the tale as the primary "authors," although in fact it was nearly always the result of a close collaboration. Where the storytellers were left anonymous or where multiple storytellers were recorded by a single scholar such as Knud Rasmussen, I have listed the texts by their collector.

In chapter 4, "The Telling of the Tale," I present the Native language text of one variant which I recorded from a blind woman I met in 1973. Maggie Gilbert came from the small Gwich'in community of Arctic Village, remotely located off the road system in the Brooks Range of northern Alaska, although much of her life was lived nomadically outside of the village. I present here what I know of Maggie's life for context and describe details of the performance setting. Then I explicate the many voices in the text to open up subtleties of form and meaning, offering clues about its position as a subtle masterpiece of performance narrative.

"The Blind Man and the Loon" embodies a wealth of verbal art. But the Inuit or Eskimo subtype of the tale, in particular, has inspired a palpable wealth of modern visual art, in prints, tapestries, and sculpture, from many different artists, presented and discussed in chapter 5, "The Art of the Tale." The scenes represented in these artistic pieces are the embodiment of selected subtraits, intertwining the genres of folk tale and folk art.

In the late twentieth century up to the present day the story of the Blind Man and the Loon has also been newly interpreted through films, audio recordings, ballet, classical music, radio, and other media. It has even been adopted into the repertoires of some professional storytellers. And it may be found all over the Internet, under a host of evanescent titles. Chapter 6, "The Mediated and Theatrical Tale," explains how the story has been modified and manipulated through these mass media articulations.

In Native North American oral tradition, there are many stories with power. From a semiotic and ethnographic perspective, chapter 7, "The Power of the Tale," attempts to answer the question of why this one narrative is so potent and so widespread, crossing so many linguistic and cultural barriers. A cherished kind of power, concentrated and embedded in both major subtypes of the Blind Man and the Loon, is the power of healing.

I wish to alert readers that there are two bibliographies herein. The first one, containing primary sources for the tale texts, both written and oral, is found in appendix B. The second one, addressing secondary and critical sources, is found in the References section. This rule of thumb should make it easier to find sources as they are cited.

Finally, as we fly together across the landscape, I should add that one reason the tale of the Blind Man and the Loon has traveled east across three countries from Alaska to Canada and Greenland in one direction and south to the Northwest Coast and the Great Plains in another is because of its direct links with medicine power, witchcraft, shamanism, and healing. In a philosophical way, it is also a study of kinship and the nuclear family, and its simultaneous existence in so many places testifies to a vast social network. It has flourished cross-culturally and internationally among two large disparate language families, the Inuit and the Na-Dene, and it has proven its durability and popularity in print and other media for a minimum of 185 years. Then too, we must not overlook the tale as a collective parable about the importance of subsistence and sharing—the highly portable flash memory of ancient cultures and modern ways of life.

The Blind Man and the Loon

CHAPTER ONE

The History and Geography of the Tale

Morphology and Geography

Some years ago I presented a paper attempting reconstruction of the archetype of the Blind Man and the Loon (Mishler 1988). At that time I defined paradigms for thirteen selected traits found within each of its two major subtypes (see appendix A). I called these the Eskimo or Inuit subtype featuring the Blind *Boy* and the Loon and the Indian subtype featuring the Blind *Man* and the Loon. With these two major ethnic subtypes the tale behaves like a double helix. Its DNA gets passed on from generation to generation, reproducing itself much like genetic information being transmitted from storyteller to storyteller. To extend the metaphor, the trait sequences of each variant function like genomic sequences, so that studying the morphology of the tale is equivalent to studying its molecular structure. In a manner of speaking, the combination and sequencing of traits and subtraits constitutes each variant's signature DNA.

There is also some congruency between the trait sequences of these major subtypes and their geographic distribution, which calls to mind the linguistic area hypothesis. That is, the Eskimo subtype largely corresponds to the high Arctic, while the Indian subtype corresponds largely to the Subarctic and the Northwest Coast, with some fragments found in the Plains and Great Basin. This affords a rough-edged but convenient basis for our typology.

In its inferred migration eastward across the Canadian arctic coast and then north toward Greenland, collected variants of the Eskimo subtype follow a path virtually identical with maps of the eastward Thule tradition diaspora constructed by archaeologists (see McGhee 1996). But while it was moving eastward along the North Slope of Alaska in what is today the Inuit homeland, it was also presumably moving south into what are today the Yup'ik and Alutiiq homelands. The Eskimo subtype is represented by variants in three primary language groups: Iñupiaq/ Inuktitut/Innuinaqtun/Kalaallisut, Central Yup'ik/Cup'ik, and Alutiiq (marginally), as well as multiple dialects.

Bypassing the Aleutian Islands, the Alaska Peninsula, and Kodiak and following essentially a linear southeasterly pattern, the tale eventually reached the Dena'ina of Cook Inlet and went south along the Northwest Coast, where it apparently turned east and entered the interior of the continent. When it moved inland it seems to have turned north into the homeland of northern Dene peoples and simultaneously south into the Great Basin and Great Plains (see Dumond 1969 and map 1).

The Indian subtype, then, is represented through the languages of Dena'ina, Gwich'in, Tanacross, Dogrib, Ahtna, Upper Tanana, Lower Tanana, Chipewyan, North Slavey, Chilcotin, Sekani, Eyak, Carrier, Tagish, Tahltan, and Kaska. In Alaska, the tale is conspicuously absent from the repertoires of Ingalik and Koyukon storytellers, leaving some significant white space in map 1 (p. 9). Also, the tale is found hardly at all among Algonquian-speaking people.[1]

On the Northwest Coast it has been found in Kwakiutl, Tlingit, Bella Coola, and Haida. In perhaps one of its most recent historic manifestations, the tale has also been incorporated into Assiniboine, Ute, and Arapaho. Hypothetically, Oklahoma signifies the story's farthest expansion to the south (Dorsey and Kroeber 1903, 282–85).

Carl von Sydow ([1932] 1999, 145–48), the great Swedish folklorist, maintained that identifying and understanding regional oicotypes is even more important than reconstructing hypothetical archetypes or ur-forms. I agree. Each of this tale's two major subtypes has four regional groups or oicotypes embedded within them, thereby helping us understand from a cross-cultural perspective the stability and the range of variation that jointly characterize the tale's morphology and its environmental adaptation.

To better understand what an oicotype is, I might attempt to explain it as akin to ecotype, a term commonly used in evolutionary biology. Following this analogy, an oicotype describes a distinct regional geographic variety within a tale type, which is adapted to specific cultural, linguistic, and environmental conditions. A tale type in turn consists of a group of stories, called versions or variants, with the same basic plot or dramatic situation.[2] Each variant constitutes a separate telling.

I shall advance the hypothesis that these oicotypes of the tale of the Blind Man and the Loon emerged in their modern forms well after the tale migrated eastward along the Arctic Coast to Greenland, southward along the Bering Sea and North Pacific Coasts, north again into the interior boreal forest, and south into the Great Plains. Each oicotype represents an adaptation that may be best understood by studying a region's subsistence economies, cultural history, and ethnography.

While I recognize the value of trait comparison and variant comparison, I have purposely detached myself from the Historic-Geographic method pioneered by Finnish folklorists Julius and Kaarle Krohn (1971). The Historic-Geographic method was an attempt to isolate and compare the traits of a folktale in order to reconstruct its hypothetical archetype or ur-form, determine its point of origin, and map its historic routes of dissemination across the landscape. The method was very rigorous and widely used by folklorists in the first half of the twentieth century but later came under heavy criticism because it ignored aesthetic and stylistic elements and the lives and personalities of the storytellers.

My principal objection is that this method, when properly executed, becomes a tedious statistical exercise with little to show in the end except a hypothetical ur-form. For me, the larger questions are not the birthplace of the story or even how the story has traveled and changed across time and space, but rather, who told it and who recorded it under what circumstances, and what is its underlying power and its appeal to the people who tell it? Can we reconstruct their world view and values? Can we understand the tale as an art form and as performance? This is something I discuss at length in chapters 4–7.

The Eskimo Subtype

"The Blind Man and the Loon" belongs to a genre of stories variously known in Inuktitut as *unikkausiq* or *unipkaat*. Such stories are set in the distant past when humans could transform themselves into animals and vice-versa. *Unikkausiq* are distinguished from *unikkaatuaq* or *quliaqtuat*, the latter being legendary stories set in the more recent past featuring characters who are directly related to present-day people (Dorais 1990, 201; MacLean 1990, 163).

The Eskimo subtype is partly identifiable on the basis of the motif of the cruel mother or stepmother blinding her son at the very outset, although occasionally this motif is replaced by a cruel grandmother blinding her grandson. Either way the woman's aggression is accomplished either through sorcery or through chemicals thrown on the boy's eyes while he is sleeping. Her motive is selfish—she is too lazy to process all of the meat and skins her son or grandson brings home.

A second distinguishing trait of the Eskimo subtype is the identity of the game animal hunted and shot with an arrow by the young man, which is always a bear and usually specified as a polar bear. However, in Central Yup'ik versions this trait is usually absent (see for example, Charlie 1997). A third trait in the Eskimo subtype is the presence of a friendly sister who prevents him from starving to death by secretly giving him morsels of her own food, but this trait too is missing in the Yup'ik variants. The fourth and final trait that marks the Eskimo subtype is the means by which revenge is carried out by the young man against his wicked mother or grandmother.

In nearly every Inuit variant, the blind man takes her hunting; harpoons a whale, walrus, or narwhal; and arranges for her to be dragged to sea helplessly attached to his harpoon line. In many cases, she is magically transformed into a beluga whale or a narwhal, whereupon she often becomes known as the Luumajuq. Is this matricide or something more benign? In some variants the young man is haunted by guilt for murdering his own mother.

Another important structural feature of the Eskimo subtype, especially those encountered in Groups A and B, is the presence of sequels to the basic story line. These sequels are highly suggestive of the basic grammar of Eskimo languages, which is polysynthetic. That is, sentences are formed by adding a series of suffixes to single stems. "The Blind Man and the Loon" itself frequently behaves like a stem or free morpheme (with its core set of characters and the acts of betrayal, healing, and revenge), while various optional sequels (the shadow people, the people with long claws, the people without anuses, the Sun and the Moon, etc.) act like suffixes or bound morphemes attached to the stem, piece by piece.[3] This is how the basic story line is often built up and stretched into a longer episodic narrative. We rarely encounter this kind of structure in the Indian subtype: when the evil wife is killed, end of story.[4]

In a rather remarkable way, the fate of the wicked mother or grand-mother in the Eskimo subtype resembles the fate of Captain Ahab in Herman Melville's epic novel, *Moby Dick*. Nonetheless, there doesn't seem to be any substantive connection between the novel and the folktale. We know, for example, that Greenlandic oral variants of "The Blind Man and the Loon" were recorded several decades before *Moby Dick* was published in 1851. It may be just a coincidence that in chapter 135 of the novel we read Melville's description:

> The harpoon was darted; the stricken whale flew forward; with igniting velocity the line ran through the grooves;—ran foul. Ahab stooped to clear it; he did clear it; but the flying turn caught him round the neck, and voicelessly as Turkish mutes bowstring their victim, he was shot out of the boat, ere the crew knew he was gone. Next instant, the heavy eye-splice in the rope's final end flew out of the stark-empty tub, knocked down an oarsman, and smiting the sea, disappeared in its depths.

The Indian Subtype

The Indian subtype of "The Blind Man and the Loon" is not so easily categorized by genre. In Gwich'in, for example, there is only one word, *gwandak*, for stories and for news. The really old stories are sometimes referred to as *denaadai' gwandak*. No categorical or generic distinction is made between ancient and more recent tales.

The major bifurcation that distinguishes the Indian subtype from the Eskimo subtype is most obvious within the dramatis personae. While the Eskimo variants (with one exception) all have a young man and his mother and sister, or a boy and his grandmother and sister, making up the nuclear family unit, the Indian variants without exception portray a fully grown man and his wife in these roles. In the Indian subtype the protagonist is usually elderly and is frequently recognized as a medicine man.

Also, in the Indian variants, the wife is seldom responsible for causing the man's blindness. The blindness is most often a given at the beginning of the story. But the wife greedily takes the meat of the animal he shoots and abandons him to suffer and die. In the Indian subtype the blind man usually does not have a helpful confidante, such as a sister, to feed, console, and sustain him. The Indian subtype also shows more regional variation in form than the Eskimo subtype, encompassing four separate culture areas: the Northwest Coast, the Western Subarctic, and in fragmentary fashion, the Plains and the Great Basin. Accordingly, the game animal hunted by the blind man varies from brown bear to moose to caribou to buffalo.

A final distinguishing feature of the Indian subtype is the very prompt slaying of the wicked wife by the blind man after his vision has been restored. This sudden outburst of anger and matricide contrasts sharply with the Eskimo subtype, in which the healed boy or young man returns and patiently bides his time for revenge, waiting days, months, or as long as a year to even the score—what we might call a "slow burn." Moreover, the blind Indian protagonist does not usually get any cooperation from the natural world in exacting his revenge, such as the Eskimo young man receives from the harpooned whale or narwhal. In some cases the Indian wife is transformed into a tiny ant, a kind of humiliation.

The Full Tale Type

It is clearly evident from so many shared traits and other structural correspondences that the two major subtypes have a common ancestor. They are close cognates. The Aarne-Thompson tale type index (Aarne 1964) does not recognize "The Blind Man and the Loon" as a single Native American tale type, although it should. However, Stith Thompson's *Motif-Index of Folk Literature* registers what closely approximates such a type in motif K333.1: "Blind dupe. A blind man's arrow is aimed for him by his mother (or wife) who deceives him into thinking that he has missed his aim. She eats the slain game herself" (1955, 271). This motif alone, nevertheless, does not define the full tale type.

Part of my purpose here is to test the infrastructure of this basic motif against the corpus of texts and distinguish it from the more complex tale type of which it is a part. Some other motifs that commonly occur in the story have been conveniently listed by Edwin Hall in his book

The Eskimo Storyteller (1975, 246–47), following the variant he collected from Paul Monroe in Noatak, Alaska. These motifs are: B211.3, Speaking bird; B450, Helpful birds; B516, Sight restored by animal; F952, Blindness miraculously cured; K2210, Treacherous relatives; Q261, Treachery punished; Q411, Death as punishment; and (for Eskimo variants only) D2060, Death or bodily injury by magic; and F952.S12.1, Cruel mother blinds son. To summarize: the tale type of "The Blind Man and the Loon" is a complex sequence of motifs.

What unites the Eskimo and Indian subtypes are four fundamental elements that distinctively mark the narrative as a single tale type. These are not as specific as tale traits but are a necessary precondition for the story's narrative syntax. The first element of the syntax is that the central character is a man or boy who is blind at the outset or becomes blind, sometimes as a result of cruelty. The second element is that he is lied to and mistreated by a close woman relative (a wife, mother, step-mother, or grandmother), after shooting a game animal with his bow and arrow. Third, his vision is restored due to magic performed by birds (usually in the form of loons diving under water, but also sometimes by licking his eyes or by touching his eyes with feathers), and fourth, he takes revenge on the evil woman either by killing her directly or by arranging for her death and transformation into another creature (a narwhal, beluga, ant, or owl).[5]

My first impression was that without the presence of these four elements set in exactly this order the story is not recognizable as "The Blind Man and the Loon." The four elements of this story line, so I thought, were its generic signature.

But there are some variants that defy this signature and which are still recognizable as the same tale type. The Selawik, Alaska, Eskimo variant told by Nora Paaniikaaluk Norton (Anderson and Sampson 2003), for example, strays from this formula or template. This Group C variant is different in that the blind boy does not shoot an animal with his bow and arrow. He is mistreated by his mother giving him spoiled berries and dirty water and takes revenge by dumping her overboard from a boat rather than tying her to a harpoon line. She is not transformed into anything at all.

Likewise, the Dene variant told online by elder George Blondin (n.d.) as "Regarding a Blind Man" lacks the fourth basic element, the revenge taken by the blind man on the heartless woman who mistreats him. It seems possible that Blondin's story was edited before being posted on the Web, since the violent ending may not have been deemed suitable for the audience of children the story was intended to reach. So I have come to realize that the four core elements are present in most but not all variants. If two or more of these four elements are missing, all we have left is a fragment of the tale.

Traits

In addition to these four elements or motifs, eleven to thirteen traits are generally manifested on the syntagmatic axis or story line (see appendix A). By *trait* I mean the smallest element of a story that is subject to variation. Unlike the four basic or core elements, these traits vary considerably and may be easily configured into trait paradigms. Some are visible by their absence. These traits are: (A) the cast of characters; (B) the special identity of the blind protagonist; (C) the cause of his blindness; (D) the species of animal he kills; (E) the betrayal behavior of his woman relative; (F) the identity of a helpful confidante (usually his sister); (G) the number and kind of bird(s) who help restore his sight; (H) how his vision is restored; (I) the reward given to the bird, if any; (J) the final insult given to the hunter by his woman relative after he returns to her; (K) the kind of revenge he takes against her; (L) the fate of the woman; and (M) sequels which follow, if any.

Regional Group Variants

Altogether, eight regional groups or oicotypes can be loosely identified, based on geography and on a combination of selected traits in the known variants (map 1). Half of these groups belong to the Eskimo subtype and the other half to the Indian subtype, and approximately half of all oral variants belong to each major subtype. Not all of the recorded oral variants fit neatly into these eight oicotypes, but most do. Each regional group is marked to varying degrees with respect to one another and with respect to the other variants. For each regional group I suggest one variant as a representative of traits held by other variants in the group. In nearly every case I have selected a published

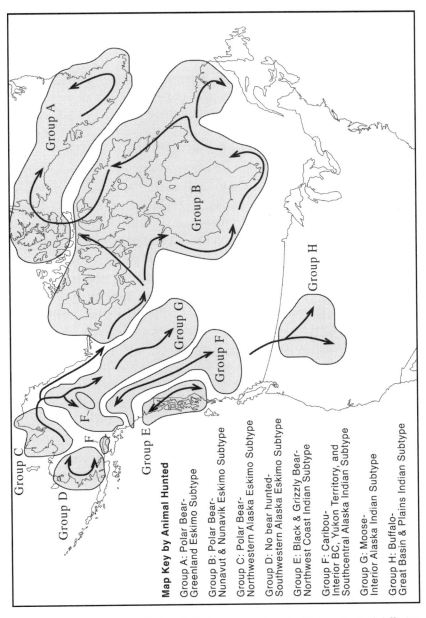

Map 1. Regional oicotypes of "The Blind Man and the Loon" with hypothetical diffusion routes.

Native language variant for this purpose because it is much less likely to be redacted or abridged.

Eskimo Oicotypes

Three regional groups of northern Eskimo texts emerge from a comparison of major traits, two of them in the eastern and central Arctic, primarily around Baffin Island and Greenland (which I call Group A), one in the vast Nunavut/Nunavik region (Group B), and the third in the area ranging from Kotzebue Sound south along the Alaskan coast of the Bering Sea to the western tip of the Seward Peninsula (Group C).

In Regional Group A, located in Greenland, the blind boy or young man is almost always named Tutigak or Uluak. This group is also largely identifiable on the basis of near-unanimity of Traits D, E, F, and K. That is, the hunted animal is a bear, and the cruel female figure betrays the boy by lying about his killing of the bear and by withholding the bear's meat from him but does not abandon him. In this group also, the blind boy has a helpful sister who secretly provides food for him against his mother's or grandmother's wishes. The blind young man's vision is usually restored by birds (oftentimes geese rather than loons) who drop excrement onto his eyes, or they wipe his eyes with their wings. To gain his revenge, he ties his mother or grandmother to a harpoon line and harpoons a whale or narwhal, which drags her out to sea. In the Greenlandic variants the disloyal mother or grandmother is not only carried away by a narwhal, she is often transformed into a narwhal. A number of Greenlandic variants also have sequels attached (see appendix C, #3). A good representative of Group A variants is the story of Uluak (Sonnesbase Document [SB] 2176) collected by Knud Rasmussen at Nuuk in 1902 (see text in appendix C, #2).

Two unusual and interesting Greenlandic variants (SB 324 and SB 767) identify the blind man's mother as a lesbian who covets the blind man's wife. The mother then uses her stone lamp's wick-trimmer as a dildo. The storytellers (Jonasine Nielsen and Hans Lynge, respectively) clearly regarded this behavior as a great vice. But such a trait is aberrant since it is not found anywhere else within the wide distribution of "The Blind Man and the Loon" and does not enter into other Greenlandic variants. Consequently, these two variants do not fit neatly into Group A.

Regional Group B is the Lumaaq group, geographically based in the eastern Canadian territory of present-day Nunavut, the Nunavik region of Northern Quebec, and Labrador. The Lumaaq group is the group most likely to have sequels attached after the wicked mother or grandmother is killed. The most famous of these sequels is the Sun and the Moon story, in which the blind man and his sister are guilty of incest. The name Lumaaq, or its variants (Luumaq, Lumaa, Lumak, Lumaag, Lumiuk, Luumajuq, or Lumaajuuq), is sometimes given to the blind man and is sometimes attributed to his mother. The online Inuktitut Living Dictionary (http://www.livingdictionary.com/) defines Luumajuq as "the cry of a harpooned whale." "Lumaa" is also frequently associated with the wicked mother's dying words as she is pulled out to sea by the harpooned beluga, walrus, or narwhal. One storyteller, Lucassie Nutaraaluk of Iqaluit, actually heard her voice once while he was surrounded by a pod of whales. Nutaraaluk maintains that "It is only when the world will come to an end that Lumaajuuq will die. . . . She is still alive today" (Nutaraaluk 2001, 66).

In this oicotype the blind man is more likely to be healed by diving with a loon or loons rather than having his eyes touched by their wings or filled with their excrement (see map 1). And as is the case in many Group A variants, his mother is frequently transformed into a whale or narwhal. An excellent example of Group B is Arnaitok Ipellie's "Lumajuuq" (1997). Ipellie was from Iqaluit, Nunavut.

Regional Group C, collected from Northwest Alaska, displays unanimity in five traits, A, C, D, G, and I: the cast of characters includes a mother, her son, and daughter; the blindness inflicted on the young man is a cruel act performed by the mother; the hunted animal is specifically a polar bear; and a talking loon restores his sight with the use of water but receives no reward for doing so. The cruel mother or grandmother is punished by being dragged out to sea, but she does not holler "Lumaa" or anything similar as she is towed away. A second difference from Groups A and B is that there are no sequels.

In comparing the Eskimo variants in Regional Groups A and B with Regional Group C, we quickly discover that an essential difference exists between the degrees of cruelty inflicted by the wicked woman. Those in Regional Groups A and B underscore her lying and withholding of meat while those in Regional Group C underscore her infliction of blindness.

In roughly 60 percent of the versions in Groups A and B, from the eastern arctic, the cause of the boy's blindness is accidental—meaning only one crime is committed against him. Snow blindness, to be sure, is a major occupational hazard for arctic sea ice hunters, a hazard that gave rise to the prehistoric invention of snow goggles (Ford 1959, 146–47). In Group C, from the western arctic, however, about 75 percent of the versions show the blind man in the story to be a victim of *both* offenses—he is blinded and then starved. In several of the Group C variants, the blind boy lives alone with his mother or grandmother and does not have a sister. This makes for a simpler storyline.

This compounded crime, as it were, corresponds in turn with the greater variety of violent acts meted out by the blind hero to gain revenge. In other words, Group C narrators apparently feel free to impose more extravagant nonstandardized retributions, such as chopping off the woman's fingers as she hangs onto the side of the umiak, dumping her overboard, setting her adrift on the open sea where she will die of thirst and starvation, or choking her to death by stuffing roots in her mouth. These retributions are made only for the compounded crime. A worthy Native language representative of Group C is the version told by Nora Paaniikaaluk Norton of Selawik, Alaska (Anderson and Sampson 2003, 175–86).

Group D variants come from the Central Yup'ik Eskimo area of Southwestern Alaska. This group is somewhat aberrant from the others in its nil option for Trait D: Animal(s) hunted. For the Yup'ik, the blind man does not shoot a threatening bear with his bow and arrow. Also, Group D lacks the K2 trait, which is characteristic of Eskimo groups A, B, and C. That is, the blind man takes out his revenge, but he does not do it by tying his mother or grandmother to a harpoon line. A high quality bilingual text representing Group D is elder Annie Blue's "Blind Boy and the Arctic Loons" (Blue 2007, 2–17). Blue's book also includes a CD recording of the story in Central Yup'ik. At the end of Blue's variant the blind boy himself turns into a loon, becoming one with the animals who restored his eyesight. This ending is unique.

There is one very condensed English language variant of the story collected by Kaj Birket-Smith (1953, 151) from an Alutiiq elder named Makari, of Prince William Sound, Alaska. Makari demonstrates that the story was formerly known to the Alutiiqs or Pacific Eskimos, but I have

been unable to find other elders in Kodiak and the lower Kenai Peninsula who know it, and there are no known Alutiiq (Sugpiaq) language
texts. All in all, this single Alutiiq variant by Makari represents a kind
of cul-de-sac for the Eskimo subtype, an isolate.

Indian Oicotypes

The major bifurcation that distinguishes the Indian subtype form
the Eskimo subtype is most obvious within the realm of the dramatis personae. While nearly all the Eskimo variants have a boy and his
mother and sister, or a boy and his grandmother and sister, composing
the nuclear family unit, the Indian variants without exception portray
a man and his wife in these roles. In the Indian variants the man is
frequently identified as a medicine man. Also, the female villain in
Indian variants is seldom responsible for the hero's blindness, but she
inevitably abandons him, and the blind man usually does not have a
helpful confidante, such as a sister, to sustain him.

A second distinguishing feature of the Indian subtype is what I call
"the final insult" (Trait J), when the cruel wife offers her long-lost
husband a drink of bug-infested water. This is in turn followed by "the
Aha! moment" when the blind man lets her know that he can see again
and then kills her.

This contrasts sharply with the Eskimo subtype in which the young
man returns and patiently bides his time for revenge, waiting days,
months, or as long as a year to even the score—referred to earlier in this
chapter as "a slow burn." And the Indian blind man does not usually get
any cooperation from the natural world in seeking his revenge, such as
the Eskimo boy receives from the harpooned beluga whale, narwhal,
or walrus.

Within the Indian subtype it is also profitable to distinguish between
four regional groups. The Indian regional groups are notably earmarked
by ecological area adaptations, as specified in Trait D: Animal(s) hunted.[6]
These groups are quickly identified by different keystone subsistence
species. In Regional Group F, the Interior of British Columbia, the southern Yukon Territory, Central Alaska, and Southcentral Alaska, the blind
man hunts a caribou; in Regional Group G, Interior Alaska, the northern
Yukon, and the western part of the Northwest Territories, he hunts a

moose. In Regional Group E on the Northwest Coast of Alaska and British Columbia he hunts a grizzly bear or black bear, and in Regional Group H, the Plains and Great Basin, his target animal is a buffalo. Each of these regions is shown in map 1, and each is marked in respect to the Eskimo subtype, in which the hunted animal is described as or implied to be a polar bear.

The traits for Indian regional groups F and G (northern Athabaskan) overlap a great deal. Group G (the moose group), for example, may be the youngest group of variants in the entire corpus for the simple reason that moose have only emerged as a large game species in the Interior of Alaska and the Yukon Territory within the last 125 years or so, apparently moving north and extending their range out of British Columbia between 1875 and 1900 (see McClellan 1987, 33). A Gwich'in language variant that elegantly represents Group G was told to me by Maggie Gilbert of Arctic Village in 1973 (see chapter 4).

Group F, the caribou group, is represented by several published variants but has become celebrated in the popular film *The Loon's Necklace* (chapter 6). Only texts in Group F (Morice 1892; Farrand 1900; Kalifornsky 1991; Thomas 2005), besides the filmmaker's own renderings (Leechman 1931, 1942, 1956), provide a template for the loon being rewarded with the blind man's dentalium shell necklace (see fig. 1). Such necklaces are handmade by stringing the shells into parallel rows, separated by strips of tanned moosehide and alternating strands of red tube beads, trade beads, or seed beads. Some dentalium necklaces are larger and more lavish than others, and there are stylistic differences between tribal groups.

Dentalium shell necklaces are traditionally worn only by Dene chiefs or medicine men, so this reward, like a potlatch gift, symbolically confers leadership, power, wealth, and prestige on the loon (see Simeone and VanStone 1986). The Kaska language version told by Charlie Dick of Frances Lake, Pelly Banks, and Ross River, Yukon Territory, where the loon is rewarded with the blind man's multicolored coat rather than his necklace, is a good example of Group F (Moore 1999, 310–29).

There are two curious anomalies in Group F. First, while Group F is geographically contiguous in British Columbia, it is discontinuous in Alaska. The Dena'ina and Lower Tanana variants, for example, stand in isolation and contrast to those of their next-door neighbors, the Ahtna,

Fig. 1. Dena'ina Chief Affanasi with dentalium shell necklace, ca. 1900–1904. Sylvia Sexton Collection, Album 6. SCL-1-804. Reproduced with the permission of the Seward Community Library, Seward, Alaska.

Tanacross, and Upper Tanana, whose variants all belong to Group G, the moose group. Also, the two Eyak variants recorded by Krauss are split. One, told by Lena Nacktan of Cordova, belongs to Group F, while the other, told by Anna Nelson Harry of Yakutat, belongs to Group G. Krauss (1982, 85n) carefully notes that Harry uses "Deni·gih", the Ahtna word for *moose*, rather than the Eyak word, suggesting that she may have learned the story from an Ahtna storyteller. Other than this, there is no easy way to explain the diffusion and discontinuity of these anomalies.

Group E, the grizzly bear and black bear cluster on the Northwest Coast, displays one trait more commonly found within the Eskimo sub-type—that is, in most of the variants the woman lies and withholds meat from her blind husband. This, along with the presence of a bear as the target animal, helps us see Group G as a transitional form between the Eskimo subtype (in Regional Groups A, B, and C) and the Interior Dene variants in Regional Groups F and G. Another trait (L) that distinguishes Group E from the other Indian oicotypes is the presence of some kind of sequel. As a result, the texts in Group E are among the longest found anywhere. A faithful Native language text and translation from Group E is the one told by Walter McGregor in Skidegate, Queen Charlotte Islands, British Columbia (Swanton 1908). In this variant, the blind man uses the loon's medicine power to kill his wife and gain revenge, instructing the dead grizzly bear's head to bite her face.

Regional Group H (the buffalo group) includes those texts collected on the Plains and in the Great Basin, excepting the Blackfoot aberrant. Boas (1916, 825, 828) includes an Osage text in his list of variants, but this cannot be considered a true variant because it omits the tale's quintessential defining traits—a man's state of blindness followed by female betrayal and the magical restoration of his sight. Variants in this group have been recorded among the Assiniboine, the Utes, and the Arapaho.

The variants in Group H stand out particularly in their omission of the loon as an agent for restoring the man's sight. In the Great Basin, the blind man borrows one or two eyes from an owl and other creatures, and in the Plains versions, he cures himself by rubbing some kind of dirt or powder into his eyes. This makes ecological sense considering that this western region has no loons at all except for a few Common loons wintering at Lake Tahoe. There are no published Native language texts for Group H, but a strong representative is the full-length English language version told by the Southern Arapaho storyteller Cut Nose to George Dorsey in western Oklahoma (Dorsey and Kroeber 1903, 282–85).

Diffusion

What then can we say about the origin of the full tale type and its subsequent transcontinental diffusion? It would be tempting indeed to declare that Hinrich Rink's Greenlandic sources, the ones he used for his published Danish and English "collation," are the oldest, dating in manuscript form from 1827, but this hypothesis is suspect on several grounds. First of all, there are some other fairly early western Canadian Hare and Gwich'in language versions from Émile Petitot (1886, 1888) and one from the Carrier collected by Father Morice (1892).

And Rink's redacted Danish version, titled "Den Blinde, som fik sit Syn igjen," the earliest ever published (Rink 1866, 1875), presents us with a distinct challenge. His Danish text, he writes in a preface, "has been collated from eight copies, among which two have been received from Labrador, the rest from different parts of Greenland, three of them having been written down before 1828" (Rink 1875, 99; see also appendix D). The morphology of Rink's synthetic variant generally reflects the morphology of variants in Group A, but it does not reduplicate the narrative syntax of any one of them.

While it is certainly possible that the tale diffused west and southwest from Greenland and underwent dramatic regional transformations during this short sixty-year period after Rink's and before Petitot's fieldwork, the very slow and limited means of transportation and face-to-face oral communication in the Arctic and Subarctic during the nineteenth century make this east to west explanation of the story's movement rather improbable. And Rink's book *Eskimoiske Eventyr og Sagn* (1866, 1875) certainly would not have broadcast the tale into rural areas of the western arctic and subarctic.

Moreover, the dates of the tale's collection variant by variant should not be confused with the true age of the tale itself. It does not even seem very profitable to speculate on the relationships between oicotypes, even though they may be imagined and inferred, as shown in map 1.

We know, for instance, that there was sustained historic contact in the late nineteenth and early twentieth centuries between the arctic slope Iñupiat Eskimos (Group C variants) and Gwich'in Indians (Group G variants) at places such as Old John Lake in northern Alaska (see especially Sarah Frank's recollections in Mishler 2001, 588–605; also Burch 1979). These gatherings, ostensibly for trading caribou skins, also featured social dancing and games, and surely storytelling did not lag far behind. Several Gwich'in, including Old John Vandeegwizii, spoke fluent Eskimo, and Johnny Frank was known to sing Eskimo songs (J. Gilbert 1991). The Gwich'in also have a long history of hostile and friendly relations with the Inuvialuit Eskimos in the lower Mackenzie River valley of the Northwest Territories. So ultimately, it proves much more worthwhile to look at the regional history and prehistory of the peoples from whom the story has been collected.

Archaeological and Linguistic Dimensions: Dating the Tale

Although recorded in written form by Steenholdt as early as 1827 (see chapter 2), "The Blind Man and the Loon" seems to be a much older story than that, extending well back into late prehistory. We know from text evidence that it is at least 185 years old, although it may in fact be well over a thousand years old.

There is both archaeological and ethnographic evidence to suggest that Group C in Northwest Alaska constitutes a very early development of the tale, perhaps the earliest of all. In an important article on symbolic archaeology, Phyllis Morrow and Toby Volkman (1975) discuss the excavation of a single loon skull whose eyes were carved out of ivory. This skull was found associated with a human burial at Ipiutak (Point Hope, Alaska) by Helge Larsen and Froelich Rainey (1948). The radiocarbon dating of the Ipiutak loon skull to the first few centuries AD suggests a fairly ancient origin.[7]

Morrow and Volkman (1975, 150) argue quite convincingly that this artifact, with its symbiotic ties to the tale of the Blind Man and the Loon, was vitally connected with Eskimo shamanism and played the role of a supernatural guardian with great visionary powers: "We suggest that the ivory eyes of the Ipiutak loon skull represent the loon's supernatural and actual clear-sightedness, qualities vital both to the shaman, who must see in the other worlds, and to ordinary people, whose success in hunting depends to a large extent on acute vision."

There are no motifs within any of the oral texts to suggest that the tale was in any way influenced by white contact either directly or indirectly. Early European and East Asian trade goods such as tea and tobacco are not mentioned in any of the variants. Cultural descriptions within the story, for instance, are minimal. The blind man and his family live in a tent or igloo, sometimes illuminated by an oil lamp. Their food is boiled over a driftwood fire. Their hunting technology includes only a bow and arrow, a knife or women's ulu, and, in the Inuit versions, a harpoon with a line and float attached. Today ulus are made from steel, but during the Thule expansion they were fabricated from chipped stone or slate, with handles of bone, antler, wood, or ivory (Frink et al., 2003, 116). These features make the cultural landscape of the story decidedly prehistoric in flavor even though all the recorded variants and storytellers come from the historic era.

Archaeological theorists maintain that the ancestors of today's Greenlanders migrated east along the arctic coast from Alaska and then Canada about 1000 AD to 1500 AD, a period known as the Thule expansion (see McCartney 1980; McGhee 1996; Gulløv and McGhee 2006). By this token, the ancestors of the modern Inuit may well have brought the Blind Man and the Loon story with them as they moved east across North America during the Middle Ages. It was in their backpacks, so to speak, along with their ulus.[8] This is one plausible general theory about how the story traveled so far across the Arctic.

Another plausible explanation, of course, would be that the tale of the Blind Man and the Loon slowly diffused through oral contact between neighbors and trading partners sometime after the great eastward Thule migration and diaspora were complete. By this reckoning, the tale moved only a few kilometers at a time, absorbed band by band until it became part of a large social network.

Either way, it is paradoxical that the oldest recorded variants (from Group A) are found at the extreme eastern end of its distribution, near the very limits of its assumed migration, in Greenland. Nevertheless, it is well documented that in the early 1860s, a powerful shaman named Qitdlarssuaq and his band of some forty to fifty followers traveled north from their homeland in northern Baffin Island to Devon Island. From

Devon Island they crossed Ellesmere Island and ended up in northern Greenland, where they joined that country's Polar Eskimos (see Mary-Rousselière ([1980] 1991). It was just a few decades before this historic migration that Danish missionaries and Hinrich Rink began writing down variants of "The Blind Man and the Loon."

There are just a few internal clues linking the story to early Thule culture. The Thule were the ancestors of all modern-day Inuits. They developed their culture in northern coastal Alaska before AD 1000 and then started migrating eastward across present-day northern Canada, reaching Greenland and northern Labrador about three centuries later. Thule culture was based on whaling, an ice-edge hunting economy clearly manifested in the Eskimo subtype of "The Blind Man and the Loon," where the blind man's mother, while standing on the ice, is either deliberately attached to or accidentally caught up in a harpoon line and pulled into the sea by a large narwhal, beluga, or walrus.

Knud Rasmussen was quick to notice that the blind man's use of his sister and mother as a bladder float reveals an ancient marine mammal hunting technique, a technique that changed with the introduction of iron and steel: "At that time, when they did not know how to hold a large animal by fastening the line to an ice-pick stuck in the ice, the hunter would use his companion as a 'harpoon bladder', i.e. the line was tied round his [or her] waist, and then one had to find a hummock on the ice, against which he [or she] set both feet; when there were two of them they were able to hold the powerful animal" (Rasmussen 1932, 206).

Of course, this is exactly what happens in the story. We are told in many versions that the mother or grandmother was used as an *avatuq* or *avataq* (known in English as a drag float, harpoon-float, seal poke, or inflated seal bladder). The buoyant avataq, connected to a long line, acts as a drag that tires out the animal as it attempts to escape. The drag float or avataq technology that was essential to successful marine mammal hunting goes back at least as far as the Punuk, Birnirk, Okvik, and Old Bering Sea tool assemblages, dating collectively from 200 to 900 AD. These tool assemblages mark the early stages or phases of Thule culture before the great eastward migration (see Ford 1959, 238–42; Dumond 1987, 118–50; Owen Mason pers. comm.). Birnirk sites, for example, have been found in northwest Alaska at Cape Nome, Cape Krusenstern, Cape Prince of Wales, and Barrow.

Accidents experienced by walrus hunters with long coiled lines attached to their harpoons are still remembered by Siberian Yupik Eskimo elders on St. Lawrence Island, Alaska. There the walrus was hunted with a simple set of tools: a harpoon shaft, a toggle head point, a coiled line, and an inflated seal poke or float. The site of the fatal accidents was a walrus breathing hole some distance offshore in the sea ice. It was not uncommon for men to get tangled up and pulled underwater and under the ice to their deaths (Hughes 1960, 103; Silook 1976, 30; Kiyuklook 1987, 183–84). One hunter, named Kiiwaq, died this way near Savoonga in the 1950s or 1960s, and his body was never found (Oozeva 1987, 129–33).

When struck with the harpoon, a walrus or other large marine mammal will immediately dive under water, often with great force, pulling on the coiled line, which was from 100 to 150 feet long. If the hunter was not careful in releasing the harpoon shaft from the toggle point, the rapidly unraveling line could wrap around his arm or leg or neck and pull him violently into the water. One Savoonga hunter said it was safest to loop the harpoon line around a chunk of solid ice for an anchor (Kiyuklook 1987, 183). A Gambell hunter advised keeping the coiled line downwind from the hunter (Oozeva 1987, 129).

The story of the Blind Man and the Loon has not yet been recorded among the Eskimos on St. Lawrence Island, but the harpoon and float technology used there in historic and prehistoric time mirrors the same technology used by marine mammal hunters throughout the arctic until the introduction of the rifle. Many Eskimo variants of the story are therefore cautionary, reminding hunters of the mortal dangers they face if they are careless.

Examples of Western Thule–era harpoon heads made of caribou antler may be seen in photos accompanying a field report of a burial exposed at Point Barrow (Jensen 2007, 121), but in the Canadian arctic such harpoon heads are also known to have been made from ivory or sea mammal bone (McGhee 1977, 142–43).

As recently as 1998 one South Baffin storyteller (Nutaraaluk, in Saladin d'Anglure 2001, 96) remembered a time when onshore sea mammal hunting was accomplished by attaching a harpoon line to a rock. The technique was called *pitungniaqtut*. In Hinrich Rink's time, during the early nineteenth century, Greenlanders generally hunted marine mammals from kayaks using toggle-pointed harpoons attached to inflated seal bladders. Today Inuit hunters still use kayaks or umiaqs and harpoons attached to seal bladders, but when an animal is struck with the harpoon, it is followed until it surfaces, whereupon it is shot with a rifle.[9]

Thule culture also featured the bow and arrow, a trait not found in the earlier Paleoeskimo Dorset complex, and obviously this technology is well represented in the blind man's shooting of the polar bear (see Kankaanpää 1996, 71). The hunters of Point Barrow (Nuwuk), for example, were still using bows and arrows as late as 1883, when John Murdoch collected a variety of them for the Smithsonian. Murdoch (1892, 202–7) observed that a special kind of "bear arrow" was employed for hunting polar bears. His collection included two bear arrows with flint points, one barbed bear arrow with a steel point, and six bear arrows with iron points. Presumably the blind man in the Barrow variants of the story used flint-pointed arrows (Spencer and Carter 1954; Spencer 1959, 396–97).

Birket-Smith observes that "the bow must in consequence be regarded as one of the very oldest elements in Eskimo culture" although it largely fell out of use before the year 1894 (1918, 3, 8), when guns became widely available. He also notes its prominence in the Blind Man and the Loon story he collected from the Alutiiq storyteller Makari in Prince William Sound during the 1950s. Although the prehistory of bows and arrows is fairly complex and still being developed with new evidence, the French archaeologist Claire Alix says that these tools were acquired or developed by Arctic Paleoeskimos as early as 4000 BP, while Subarctic peoples (early Dene or northern Athabaskans) acquired them potentially around 3600 BP and certainly no later than 1100 BP (Alix pers. comm.; Hare et al., 2004).

According to Susan Crockford (2008, 123), "Thule archaeological sites, as well as those of earlier Bering Sea people . . . contain these distinctive elements of their material culture: large toggling-type harpoons, lances, pottery, stone lamps, dog-harness components and sled parts, fine bone needles with very small eyes, elaborately carved ivory, and faunal assemblages containing the remains of dogs, bowhead whales, walrus, bearded seals, and ringed seals." From his excavations across the arctic, Therkel Mathiassen (1927, 60–63) observed very early on that whips, sledge bindings, and dog harnesses were major technological developments that allowed for the expansion of Thule culture from Alaska to Greenland.

One reason to conclude that the tale emerged from a very early phase of Thule culture is that none of the variants makes any mention of dog traction. That trait of Thule culture is conspicuously absent from oral tradition. In fact, the only dog ever mentioned in the tale is a single animal, which emerges in a few variants when the wicked mother lies and tells her son that he missed the polar bear with his arrow and mistakenly killed their household pet. In the Netsilik variant collected by Knud Rasmussen, for example, the blind man and his sister "left their village and wandered in over the land, ashamed at having killed their mother. . . . They walked and kept on walking in over the land" (Rasmussen 1931, 234).

Curiously, Eskimo variants of "The Blind Man and the Loon" also include no mention of other Thule culture traits, such as pottery, bone needles, or carved ivory. The animals hunted by the blind man, across multiple Eskimo variants, include the polar bear, walrus, beluga, ringed and bearded seal, and narwhal. None of the variants portrays the hunting of bowhead whales, a signature trait of Thule subsistence in its later stages. And there is also no indication in these texts of skin boats or umiaks, another pivotal component of early historic Inuit marine mammal hunting, although a kayak appears in one Greenlandic variant (SB 2274, appendix C).

Importantly, stone lamps emerge prominently in three Greenlandic variants of the Blind Man and the Loon story, these being SB 167, SB 324, and SB 767 (see appendix B). Women's curved knives or ulus are also prominent in many variants of the tale, and these were an integral part of the Thule tradition, although they are also found much earlier, in the Kachemak phase of Ocean Bay culture (Dumond 1987, 66). The wicked mother's famous last words in many variants, as she seeks to sever the harpoon line that is pulling her under water, is "My ulu! My ulu!" (see appendix B, part 4: SB 23, SB 167, SB 168, SB 207, SB 324, SB 548, SB 1375, SB 1544, and SB 1608; also Rasmussen 1908).

Turning now to the Indian subtype, it is important to state that the Blind Man has never been recorded among Pacific Coast or Southern Athabaskans (Apache and Navajo). If the tale had been part of proto-Athabaskan language and folklore, one would think it would still be found in one form or another among Northern, Southern, and Pacific Coast branches of the Na-Dene language family. However, because it is only found today among Northern Athabaskans, we infer that they must have composed it or learned it sometime after the Pacific Coast and Southern Athabaskans split off and migrated south, probably as the result of volcanic eruptions in the St. Elias mountains of eastern Alaska that fell over the Yukon Territory about 1,400 years ago (see Workman 1974).

Such geological and archaeological studies are in line with estimates of linguistic differentiation among northern Athabaskans taking place before 500 AD (Krauss and Golla 1981, 68). All of this means that the story of the Blind Man and the Loon was either composed or acquired by northern Athabaskans sometime after that split, that is, after AD 500–600, and possibly just before or during the Thule migration just a few centuries later. It would seem that the most likely homeland for the proto-Athabaskans was "in eastern interior Alaska, the upper drainage of the Yukon River, and northern British Columbia, or some part of this area" (Krauss and Golla 1981, 68).

Nevertheless, Michael Krauss (pers. comm.), a senior specialist in Athabaskan languages, believes the story is considerably older. The punch line of the story, according to Krauss, comes when the blind man returns to his wife and she calls him "my dear husband" (*siqa'kih* in Eyak), a taboo kinship term that is normally reserved for only the most intimate and private moments. This term is found in both Eyak and Lower Tanana variants of the tale, demonstrating that both the kin term and the story in which it is embedded are from proto-Athabaskan and therefore more than 2,000 years old. The wicked wife's use of this kinship term is apparently the trigger or final straw that prompts the blind man to kill her.[10] In Anna Nelson Harry's Eyak text, Krauss (1982, 88) calls it "the climactic line of the story, masterfully delivered." As mentioned earlier, this is indeed the "Aha!" moment in which she realizes that her husband now knows everything about her lies and deceptions.

Folklorists often wish for some means of dating folktales akin to those used by archaeologists for dating artifacts, a kind of carbon-14 that will help link them to a distant cultural horizon. In a fundamental symbolic way, a tale such as "The Blind Man and the Loon" may be viewed as "timeless." But as we have just seen, the tale can also be dated to some degree by its own internal references to early subsistence technologies associated with Old Bering Sea, Punuk, Okvik, Birnirk, and Thule material culture; by its linguistic earmarks; by its areal distribution; and by its affiliation with the histories and prehistories of the people who continue to tell it. Within this wide framework, it now seems entirely reasonable for us to estimate the age of "The Blind Man and the Loon" as at least 1,000 to 1,500 years old and possibly quite older than that. It is truly the voice of antiquity in the arctic.

CHAPTER TWO

The Writing of the Tale

It is regrettable to report that efforts to write "The Blind Man and the Loon" over the past century and a half have been less than diligent. Philologically speaking, there are many ways to write a folktale found in oral tradition and many, many ways to represent and misrepresent it. For better or worse, each collector and editor has left his or her mark on the text. If we compare the earliest recorded oral variants with those recently recorded in Native languages, the basic narrative thread has survived reasonably intact, but the stories have often been heavily damaged, twisted, and corrupted after being transposed into written form.

There is a tremendous amount of variation in the written record both in longhand and in print. Some scholars have used translations; others have gone with Native language transcriptions and transliterations. Too many have been satisfied with summaries, and a few have severely edited the tale to please children and their parents. "The Blind Man and the Loon" has appeared in Danish, English, French, German, Inuktitut, Kalaallisut, Ahtna, Dena'ina, Eyak, Kaska, Slavey, and now Gwich'in (see chapter 4). It has appeared in interlinear, parallel column, back-to-back, and facing-page translations, in prose and in verse. While we can be thankful there are a number of authentic variants based on indigenous language performance, these are *not* the ones that have reached a wide reading audience.

The tale also circulates widely on the Internet, giving it many reincarnations and new threads, yet the vast majority of Web variants derive

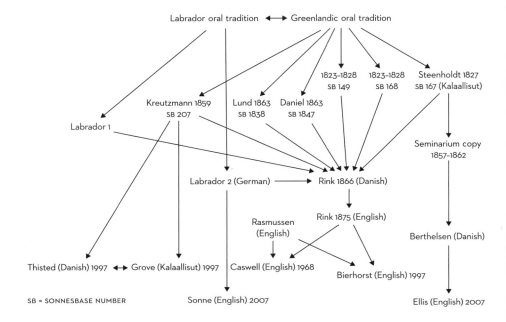

Fig. 2. The migration of written texts of "The Blind Man and the Loon," Labrador and Greenland variants.

from previously printed hard copy editions. I want to begin by discussing the first written forms of the tale as they appeared in the nineteenth and early twentieth centuries. There is a paper trail.

The earliest known texts of "The Blind Man and the Loon" come from Greenlandic Eskimos, some of whom were taught to write their own language by Danish missionaries or who dictated their stories to missionaries. These texts begin to appear in manuscript in the late 1820s and then in printed form in Danish starting in 1866. I do not mean to argue or even suggest that the story first originated in Greenland, although that is certainly in the realm of the possible. But because the first recorded transcripts and dated variants of the story come from that continent, they quickly attract our attention. The swiftest guide to these early Greenlandic variants is the readily accessible Sonnesbase.[1]

Besides the migrations of Thule and Na-Dene peoples in historic space, there are the migrations in historic time of written texts of "The Blind

Man and the Loon." These migrations can be understood by examining the multiplicity of handwritten and published texts (fig. 2) plus those now posted on the Internet.

A. The Hinrich Rink Collection

After Greenland became a colony of Denmark in the eighteenth century, it was through the efforts of the early nineteenth century Danish Lutheran missionary Peder Kragh (1875) that some of the earliest Greenlandic variants of the tale have been preserved to the present day. Kragh's predecessors, Otto Fabricius and the Norwegians Hans and Paul Egede, were responsible for designing an orthography for Kalaallisut and for teaching that orthography to the Greenlanders. Paul Egede's Greenlandic-Danish-Latin dictionary was published in 1750. But Kragh, who arrived in Egedesminde, Greenland, in 1818, and remained there for ten years, also became fluent in Greenlandic. As a result, he translated much of the Old Testament into Kalaallisut, and in the process of doing so, developed a strong interest in Greenlandic oral traditions, encouraging his literate catechists, converts, and associates to document those traditions. These catechists were "writing storytellers."

Why would Kragh want to document Inuit traditions? His fascination with oral tradition was probably based on the notion that the old stories provided a window into Eskimo religious belief and spirituality, especially the practice of shamanism. In order to convert the Greenlanders to Christianity, it was important for the early missionaries to point out the "errors" in heathen beliefs and world view. Kragh and his cohorts were probably not interested in Greenlandic stories for their own artistic merits. It is unmistakably clear that Kragh's predecessor Hans Egede believed that Greenlandic Eskimo stories such as the Sun and Moon were silly and full of superstition (Egede 1818, 207–8).

Whatever the motivation, one of Kragh's students, Wittus Frederik Steenholdt, authored a small booklet of handwritten stories, dated 1827, which can now be found among Hinrich Rink's papers at the Black Diamond, the central branch of the Royal Library in Copenhagen, Denmark (NKS 2488, folio VI, pp. 40h–43h, story no. 25). The title of Steenholdt's unpublished booklet is *Samling de Grønlandske Fortællinger* (Collection of Greenlandic tellings).

According to Birgitte Sonne (pers. comm., 2007),

> Steenholdt was ¾ Danish, brought up in Greenlandic and some Danish, in which he also became completely fluent. He was taught privately by missionary Peder Kragh into a catechist (clerk + teacher), into an organ player by some Jacobsen, and became employed as both catechist and organist in 1827—in his home settlement, the colony and mission of Aasiaat/Egedesminde. He was a most highly appreciated literate Greenlander who served the changing missionaries with great competence. He did translations of Old Testament texts, taught the children to read and write, and taught for a while at the teachers' college in Jakobshavn, Ilulissat (established in 1845).

Steenholdt was born in 1808 and died in Jakobshavn in 1862. He was raised in Greenland as the son of a Danish merchant, and he had three different wives, remarrying after the deaths of his first two.

Steenholdt's untitled story No. 25a in this 1827 manuscript booklet is the earliest known recorded variant of "The Blind Man and the Loon" and also one of the longest, just over six handwritten pages and containing several sequels (see fig. 3; also appendix D, Sonnesbase [SB] Document 167). The inclusion of these sequels gives it fairly close affinities with variants in Group B in the Nunavut/Nunavik region of eastern Canada. Rather than showing only a bare skeleton of the basic story line, the Steenholdt manuscript represents an extremely full-fledged and detailed account of the events in the tale and contains a fair amount of dialogue between characters. Even at this early date in its written history, the tale is quite robust.

The text is monolingual in Greenlandic (Kalaallisut), without any Danish translation. It has been translated into English for this volume by Karolina Platou Jeremiassen (see appendix D). In this paleotext, as well as in most of the other variants collected in Greenland, the blind man has the name Tutigaq. The person Steenholdt collected the story from, however, is not identified. Steenholdt's pamphlet was later recopied in longhand by students in a Danish seminarium sometime between 1857–62, and this Kalaallisut variant also has also been preserved. The students' copy is not an exact duplicate of Steenholdt's but rather a fair copy, with some changes in orthography and phrasing.

On April 22, 1858, Hinrich Johannes Rink sent out an historic invitation

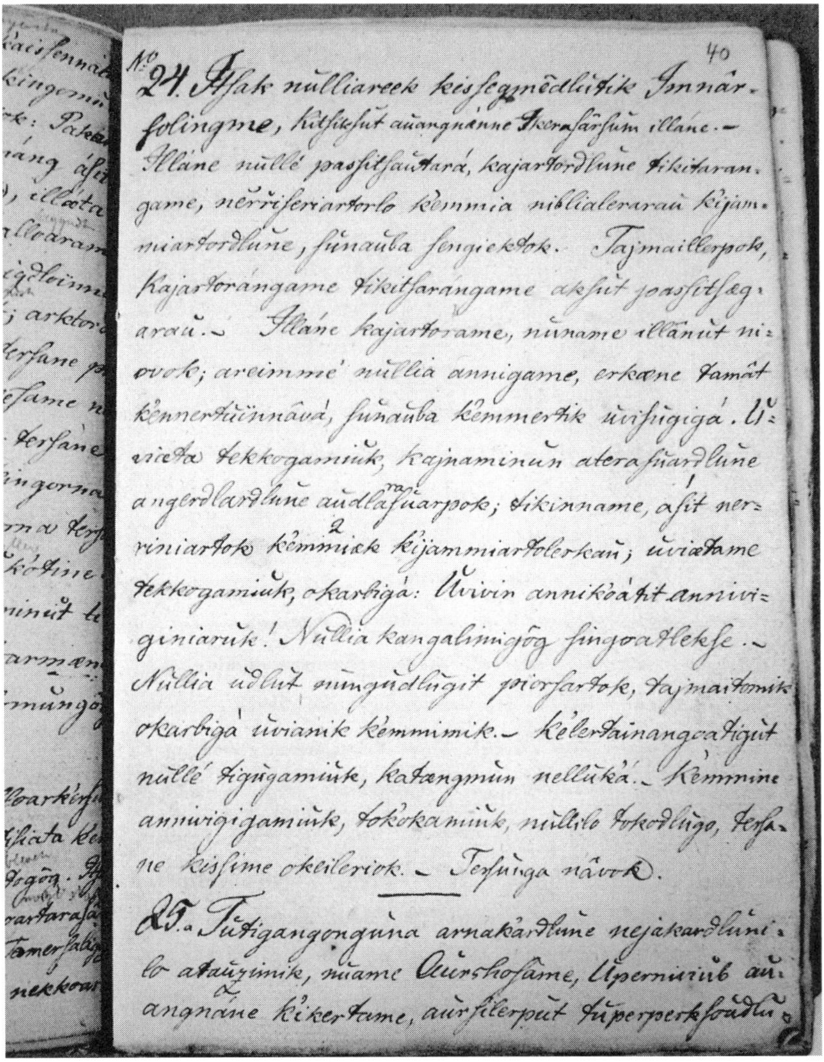

Fig. 3. The first page of Wittus Frederick Steenholdt's manuscript story, No. 25, photographed from the 1827 manuscript booklet *Samling de Grønlandske Fortællinger* (Collection of Greenlandic tellings). NKS, 2488, II, 4°. See translation in appendix D. Courtesy of the Danish Royal Library archives (the Black Diamond), Copenhagen. Photo by Craig Mishler.

in both Greenlandic and Danish for Greenlanders to send him their stories (see Thisted 2001). Rink was a Danish geologist and government administrator in Greenland, and Peder Kragh was one of those who supplied him with his collections, sending him more than ninety stories (Thisted 1998, 208). Along with the Steenholdt variant of "The Blind Man and the Loon" (SB 167), Kragh gave him two others (SB 149 and SB 168) from the period 1823–28.

The original handwritten text of SB 168 has been lost altogether, and only a student copy of the original survives. And one problem with SB 149 is that it borders on being a fragment, lacking the essential motif of revenge by the blind man against his stepmother. It is also an aberrant text, in that it is told in the first person. This use of the first person point of view for such an ancient tale is rather unique in Inuit storytelling and in all other variants of "The Blind Man and the Loon."

But Rink was not satisfied with simply publishing the early stories Kragh gave him. During the period 1857 to 1863 Rink received or recorded five additional variants of "The Blind Man and the Loon." Three of these were attributed to specific individuals: Jens Kreutzmann of Kangaamiut (SB 207), the catechist Jakob Lund (SB 1838) of Pamiagdluk, and Amos Daniel (SB 1847). The other two came from Moravian missionaries in Labrador (see preface and appendix D).

Kreutzmann, who lived at Kangaamiut, credits "okalugtuan Avdla" (the teller Avdla) for his variant of "The Blind Man and the Loon" (SB 207), the first oral performer of the story to be named and recognized. Birgitte Sonne (pers. comm., 2007) says, "Kreutzmann's father was a Danish trade manager, his mother half Greenlander. He considered himself a Greenlander, was trained in hunting, was a good friend of Aron [of Kangeq], was literate also in Danish, and helped Rink send out the call to catechists and missionaries all along the coast to collect stories in 1858." Sonne sees Kreutzmann's texts as "more acculturated than most of the others from that period."

Kreutzmann (1997a and b), who lived from 1828 to 1899, was also a major talented artist, recognized for illustrating as well as recording folktales. Along with Aron of Kagnek and several others, he was instrumental in developing something one art historian now calls "narrative pictorial art" (Kaalund 1983, 173). However, for all of the art Kreutzmann produced to illustrate traditional tales, including ink sketches, paintings, and wood carvings, it appears that he did not illustrate "The Blind Man and the Loon."

It is not known for certain whether Jakob Lund and Amos Daniel were tradition bearers and wrote down their own vernacular traditions or whether they simply recorded those of others whom they met and knew. The Lund variant (SB 1838) appears under the title, "Nerdlerit tagpigssitânik" (The geese which gave him back his sight). Only in Greenland are birds other than loons identified as healing the man's blindness, although loons are the magical agents in at least some of the Greenlandic variants. The Daniel variant (SB 1847) survives in manuscript but is preserved in handwriting which remains largely illegible and unusable.

Of the two Labradoran variants, one of them was recorded in German and has been translated into English by Birgitte Sonne (see preface). The other is in Inuttut and still remains untranslated. Neither of them has been published until now. So of the eight variants collected and used by Rink in his published "collation," only six are currently available for study in English, and one of those six (SB 149) is just a fragment.

The result of Rink's 1858 solicitation was a tremendous manuscript compendium of Greenlandic stories written in Greenlandic, and today they occupy two large volumes in the Rink collection at the Danish Royal Library in Copenhagen. The first of these is found in NKS 2488 II and consists of 962 handwritten pages. The second is in NKS 2488 III and consists of 712 handwritten pages. The number of texts and the amount of material Rink accumulated is simply staggering. It is most certainly a great cultural legacy for all Greenlanders and begs for an editor and publisher.

Rink's motivation for collecting the tales was quite different than the one pursued by the early Greenland missionaries. Kirsten Thisted (2001) believes that Rink wanted to preserve and understand the old stories so that they would foster pride in the heritage of the Greenlanders. Yet at the same time Rink was eager to translate them all into Danish, and then later on into English. In hindsight, it is now difficult to understand how Greenlanders would ever take pride in Danish and English versions of their tales. It is true, the Kalaallisut variants have all been preserved, but many of them remain in manuscript form and are hidden away in archives. Only Rink's first book, *Kaladlit Okalluktualliait: Kalâdlisut kablunâtudlo* (1859), is in a bilingual Danish and Kalaallisut edition.

Well ahead of his time as a folklorist, and anticipating the later work of Antti Aarne and Stith Thompson, Rink isolated tale motifs in a reflective essay, saying, "The main material of which the traditional tales are composed consists of what we may call Elements of the Folklore, namely events, animate beings or persons, properties of the same etc., more or less reiterated in different tales. They are combined in various ways, and such compilations can be taken out of one story and inserted in another" (1887b, 17). Two such "elements" he picked out from "The Blind Man and the Loon" were the wicked mother using "witchcraft" to blind her son and the son's exile from society after he murders his mother in revenge. Such an exile is generally known as a *kivigtok*.

Rink's Edits and Notes

In his introduction, Rink felt he was providing a "nearly literal rendering of the verbal narratives, *with only the omission of the more arbitrary reiterations and interpolations*" ([1875] 1997, 91, emphasis mine). He does not specify what these "arbitrary reiterations and interpolations" are, but it is a good guess that they are the stylistic devices known today as "reporting speech." Phrases equivalent to "they say" or "it is said" or "it is told" permeate Native American folk narratives. In Inuktitut such phrases take the form of -*guuq* or -*njuuq* suffixes; in Kalaallisut they take the form of -*gɔq* or -*gɔr* suffixes. These serve an important ethnopoetic, rhythmic function and constantly remind listeners that that the performer of the tale is not its author (see Mishler 1981; also chapter 4), yet editors and many readers find these phrases tedious and redundant, so they are systematically chopped out, especially in translation.

In my own collaborative work transcribing and translating Gwich'in texts with reporting speech, I often get a vociferous complaint from Gwich'in translators on the order of, "She's just repeating herself." Regrettably, many Native scholars expunge this reporting speech. The oral style markers are lost in the process, reminding us that writers and readers have a separate set of expectations for narrative than speakers and listeners.

But Rink's effort to eliminate redundancies from the stories was only the first step. At some point he made an editorial decision to combine all the known variants of each tale type so that they would be as full and as complete as possible, "such as might agree best with the supposed

Steen.« Idet han sagde dette viste han den sorte Steen frem, og klemte den, men han magtede den ikke, den blev blot lidt smallere. Kagsagsuk kom saa hjem til sin Boplads og skal senere aldrig mere være reist ud, for at kappes med andre.

2. Den Blinde, som fik sit Syn igjen.

En Enke, siges der, havde en Søn.og en Datter. Da Sønnen var voxet til og begyndte at fange, havde hun Gavn af ham. Engang først paa Vinteren fangede han en ung Remsæl. Da han bragte den hjem, vilde Moderen have den til Brixeskind, men han havde udseet sig den til Fangerem. Derover blev Moderen vred, og da hun nu beredte Skindet og afhaarede det, hexede hun over det og sagde: »Naar han skjærer dig i Strimler, naar han kløver dig, skal du briste og træffe hans Ansigt.« Og hun tænkte ikke paa andet, end at det skulde træffe hans Ansigt. Da det nu var færdigt og han havde skaaret det til en Rem, spændte han den ud og strammede den, og da han derpaa skrabede den med en Muslingeskal, bristede en lille Blære paa den, og traf begge hans Øine og han blev blind. Da nu Vinteren kom, manglede de Føde og begyndte at leve af bare Muslinger, og den Blinde indtog sit Leie paa Brixen og gik ikke mere ud. Saaledes levede de til midt paa Vinteren. Da viste der sig en Aften en stor Bjørn, der gav sig til at gnave af Vinduesrammen, og derpaa stak Hovedet ind igjennem Vinduet. Moderen og Søsteren flygtede forfærdede hen paa Brixen, men den Blinde sagde til Søsteren: »hent mig min Bue!« Da hun havde bragt ham Buen, spændte han den og sagde, at hun skulde sigte for ham. Derpaa holdt hun den i Retningen af Bjørnen og gav ham Tegn, derpaa skjød han og Pilen ramte Dyret, som vendte Ryggen og styrtede til Jorden. Da sagde Moderen: »du traf Vinduet.« Men Søsteren hviskede: »du har skudt en Bjørn.« De havde den nu til Vinterforraad, men naar Moderen kogte Kjød, og det var færdigt, gav hun Sønnen blot lidt Muslinger, og lod ham ikke smage af sin Fangst, men holdt den hemmelig for at udsulte ham. Men naar Moderen var ude, gav Søsteren ham i Smug af Kjødet, som han derpaa i Hast nedslugte, førend Moderen kom ind. Hele Vinteren over gjorde Søsteren saaledes; endelig bleve Dagene lange, og henad Foraaret sagde hun engang til ham: »dengang du endnu kunde see og da du fangede, naar vi saa vandrede sammen langt omkring paa Landet, hvor var det dog fornøieligt!« Broderen sagde: »Velan da, lad os gaae, jeg følger efter dig og holder dig ved Ryggen.« Dagen efter, da det blev lyst, gik de paa Vandring sammen,

4*

Fig. 4. The first page of the Blind Man and the Loon story from Hinrich Rink's Danish collation, as it appears in *Eskimoiske Eventyr og Sagn* (1866, 51). Photo by Craig Mishler.

original and most popular mode of telling the same story" ([1875] 1997, 91). In the case of "The Blind Man and the Loon," he "collated" eight different variants, six of them from Greenland and two of them from Labrador, melding or welding them together under the single title "Den Blinde, som fik sit Syn igjen" in his book *Eskimoiske Eventyr og Sagn* (1866; excerpt in fig. 4). Rink says, "The text of this story has been collated from eight copies, among which two have been received from Labrador, the rest from different parts of Greenland, three of them having been written down before 1828" ([1875] 1997, 99). We know all this from his own prefatory notes and endnotes.

Here are Rink's notes to his first edition, translated from the Danish by Lucy Ellis and edited by Birgitte Sonne:

> The Blind Man Who Regained His Sight. Eight versions of this legend were gathered, namely, two from Okak and Hebron in Labrador,[2] three in Kragh's collection and moreover from Amos Daniel, Jens Kreutzmann and Jakob Lund; that is, as with the former, both in older and newer versions, and from Labrador as well as from the northernmost and southernmost Greenland. The addition of the "flight inland" is only found in two of them and is also mutually aberrant. Likewise, some are extremely reduced/abridged, namely those from Labrador, but on the whole they are remarkably similar to each other. In a couple of the Greenlandic variants, the son is called Tutigak. In one of the Labrador variants, he is called Kemongak. The birds that heal him are loons: Red-Throated Loons in some variants and Common Loons in others. In the Labrador variants they heal the Blind Man by telling him to dive down into an inland lake. In the same variants, his mother cries out, "I was the one who breastfed you!" after she is thrust into the water. But in the Greenlandic variants, she cries, "I was the one who wiped up your pee!" On the other hand, there are curious word-for-word parallels in other sections of the variants told by different storytellers. (Rink 1866, 355–56)

Consequently, the first published text of "The Blind Man and the Loon," "collated" from Greenlandic and Labradoran sources, is a semi-literary redaction, appearing as it does with many other stories in the volume, *Eskimoiske Eventyr og Sagn*. Eleven years later, Rink published the same volume in English as *Tales and Traditions of the Eskimo* (1875).

In this English edition, the story of the Blind Man and the Loon emerges under the title "The Blind Man Who Recovered His Sight." This volume is still in print and widely available in English paperback, and the original Danish edition is available for downloading online.

It is an interesting task to examine exactly how Rink created his redaction. By redaction I mean the conscious merging of several older written variants into something new and synthetic. Censorship may play a role in the redaction process, but there are other things going on as well. What elements did Rink borrow, cut, and paste from each of the eight early variants into his one semi-literary creation? This is a separate exercise and cannot yet be fully studied since we currently only have six of the original eight variants at hand (see the preface and appendix D).

In schematic form (fig. 1), it becomes easier to explain how the oldest Greenlandic variants of "The Blind Man and the Loon" came to be read and understood by Europeans and Americans.

B. The Émile Petitot Collection

The French Oblate missionary Émile Petitot (1838–1916) was the first to record Dene language variants of "The Blind Man and the Loon." Working in western Canada, Petitot recorded only two variants of the story, but they are important for establishing the Indian subtype as something quite distinct from the Eskimo one. Petitot's tales, recorded from the Loucheux (Gwich'in) and the Hare around 1870, were published first in French in 1886, and then republished with Loucheux (Gwich'in) and Hare (North Slavey, Sahtu) language texts in 1888, under the same title, *Traditions Indiennes du Canada Nord-Ouest*. The Gwich'in text finally became available in English translation under the title *The Amerindians of the Canadian North-west in the 19th Century, As Seen by Émile Petitot*, edited by Donat Savoie (1970, 2:176–80). Savoie (1996) has also published a brief biography of Petitot, and a fuller one has been written by John Moir (2000). In theological terms, Petitot (1876/1878, 57/278) saw the Dene as descendants of the ancient Hebrews, and he looked at their stories and customs for clues to their Asiatic origin.

In his comparative study *Accord des mythologies* Petitot (1890, 447–52; also fig. 5) saw a resemblance between the Gwich'in story of the Blind

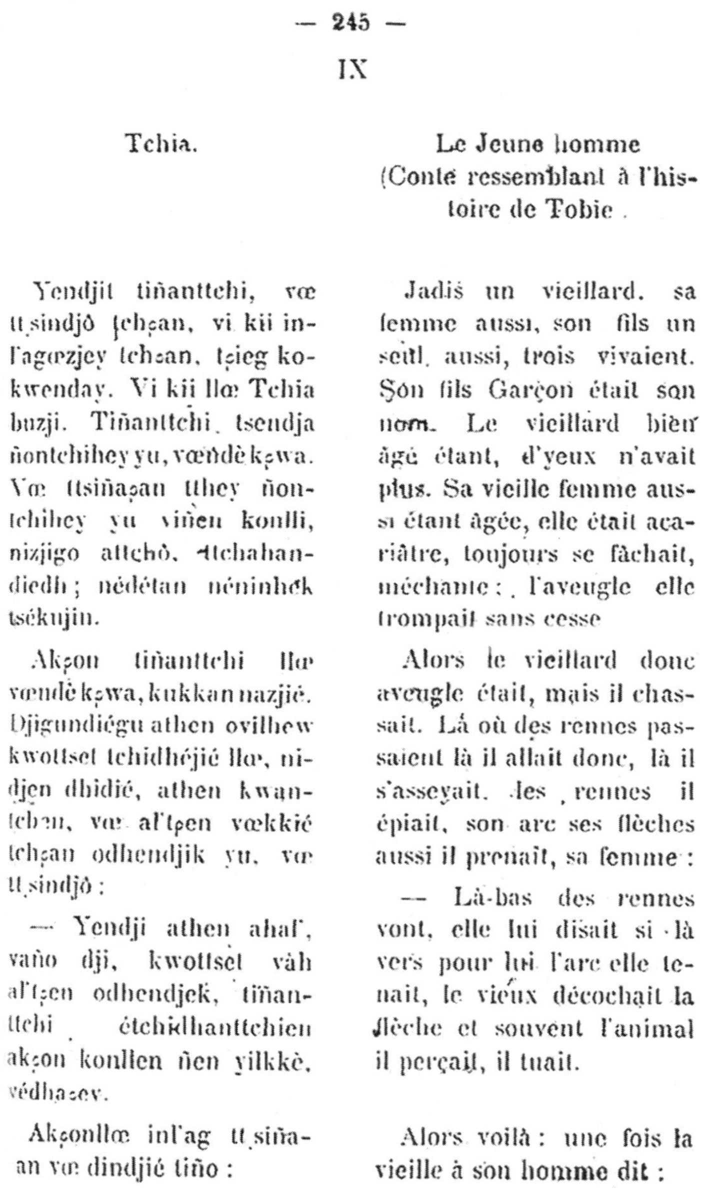

IX

Tchia.

Le Jeune homme
(Conte ressemblant à l'histoire de Tobie .

Yendjit tiñanttchi, vœ tt sindjô ʃchɛan, vi kii in-l'agœzjey tchɛan, tɛieg ko-kwenday. Vi kii llœ Tchia buzji. Tiñanttchi tsendja ñontchihey yu, vœñdè kɛwa. Vœ ttsiñaɛan tthey ñon-tchihey yu viñen konlli, nizjigo attchô, ᵈtchahan-diedh ; nédétan néninhɛk tsékujin.

Akɛon tiñanttchi llœ vœñdè kɛwa, kukkan nazjié. Djigundiégu athen ovilhew kwottset tchidhéjié llœ, ni-djen dhidié, athen kwan-tchɛu, vœ al'tɛen vœkkié tchɛan odhendjik yu, vœ tt sindjô :

— Yendji athen ahaʃ, vaño dji, kwottset vàh al'tɛen odhendjek, tiñan-ttchi étchiᴋlhanttchien akɛon konllen ñen yilkkè, védhaɛev.

Akɛonllœ inl'ag tt siña-an vœ dindjié tiño :

Jadis un vieillard, sa femme aussi, son fils un seul, aussi, trois vivaient. Son fils Garçon était son nom. Le vieillard bien âgé étant, d'yeux n'avait plus. Sa vieille femme aus-si étant âgée, elle était aca-riâtre, toujours se fâchait, méchante : l'aveugle elle trompait sans cesse

Alors le vieillard donc aveugle était, mais il chas-sait. Là où des rennes pas-saient là il allait donc, là il s'asseyait. Les rennes il épiait, son arc ses flèches aussi il prenait, sa femme :

— Là-bas des rennes vont, elle lui disait si là vers pour lui l'arc elle te-nait, le vieux décochait la flèche et souvent l'animal il perçait, il tuait.

Alors voilà : une fois la vieille à son homme dit :

Fig. 5. First page of Sylvain Vitoedh's Loucheux Gwich'in variant, collected by Émile Petitot at Fort Good Hope in 1870 and published with a French translation in Petitot's *Traditions Indiennes du Canada Nord-Ouest* (1888). Photo by Craig Mishler.

Man and the Loon and the canonical Roman Catholic book of Tobie, Tobit, or Tobias, a Jewish holy man. In chapter 2 of that Old Testament book, Tobias is blinded by a swallow's dung falling in his eyes, a test by God of his patience. He is then scolded by his wife Anna, much as the Loucheux blind man is harassed by his shrewish wife.[3] The resemblance between the two stories actually ends there, but it was enough to persuade Petitot that there was a strong link.

The text in figure 5 is recognizably Gwich'in, even though Petitot's peculiar orthography is quite a departure from that used today. The title, "Tchia" (Boy), would now be written as *Chyaa tsal,* a fairly congruent phonemic spelling but minus the important adjective. Petitot's word for blind man, *nédétan,* is fairly close to the modern orthography, written *dinjii ndee ehdan.* Petitot even got the formulaic ending correctly, the final word *Ettet* being equivalent to today's *It'ee* ending (see Maggie Gilbert's tale in chapter 4). Whatever his linguistic shortcomings and theological bias, Émile Petitot needs to be fully credited as the first scholar to actually publish a Native language text of "The Blind Man and the Loon."

C. The Franz Boas Collection

Franz Boas has the distinction of being the only scholar who personally collected both Inuit and Northwest Coast variants of "The Blind Man and the Loon." He first recorded a variant among the Central Eskimo on Baffin Island in 1885 (1888) from an anonymous storyteller and then later found the story circulating among the Kwakiutl (1895, 1910) and the Tsimshian (1916). This was an important and no doubt surprising discovery, which eventually led him to do an extended comparison of all known variants in his notes to *Tsimshian Mythology* (1916, 825–29).

After presenting an English variant of Henry Tate's "The Blind Gitq!ā°da", Boas identifies in his notes eighteen separate variants of the tale. He summarizes several of them but does not speculate about their diffusion. At the same time, Boas also recognized that the story had reached the Great Plains (Group F). He cites texts from the Assiniboine, the Arapaho, and the Osage which are closely related.

It is ironic that Boas, for all of his interest in documenting and preserving American Indian languages, neglected to publish Native language variants of many of the tales he and his students collected, including the tale of the Blind Man and the Loon. For example, even though translations of the tale appear in *Kwakiutl Tales* as "The Blind Man Who Recovered His Eyesight," the tale does not appear in the more comprehensive three-volume set, *Kwakiutl Texts*. And while it appears prominently in *Tsimshian Mythology* as "The Blind Gitq!ā°da," it is noticeably absent from *Tsimshian Texts*.

Indeed, Boas recorded many of his Northwest Coast texts in Chinook Jargon and then translated them into German or English. Chinook Jargon, a kind of lingua franca, presented him with a host of problems since often it was inadequate for expressing the complexities of the fifteen Native languages he was mediating with it. Despite these limitations, Boas may have been one of the first to compensate Native storytellers for sharing their texts, from time to time offering them money, tobacco, and cotton (Bouchard and Kennedy (2002, 24–27).

D. The Knud Rasmussen Collection

The master collector of "The Blind Man and the Loon" was Knud Rasmussen (1879–1933), the son of a Danish missionary and a Greenlandic mother. Rasmussen was raised in Greenland where he learned to speak Kalaallisut fluently. He was formally educated in Lynge, North Zealand, Denmark, and later attended the University of Copenhagen but never graduated. However, at the end of the Fifth Thule Expedition, which lasted from 1921 to 1924, he was awarded a PhD from that institution.

Rasmussen collected at least fifteen variants of the Blind Man and the Loon story, ten in Greenland and five in northern Canada. I say "at least fifteen variants" because this many have already been discovered, but there may well be more variants in his many journals and manuscripts, preserved in Danish (see Søby 1988). Unfortunately, Rasmussen did not think it important to publish any of his collected variants in the original Inuktitut or Kalallisut, and until now only two of his nine Greenlandic variants have been printed, one of them in English (SB 1375) and one in Danish (SB 1544). Thanks to the efforts of Karolina Platou Jeremiassen of Nuuk, I have attempted to rectify this by repatriating three more of them here: texts SB 1496, SB 2176, and SB 2274 are all in the current Kalallisut orthography (see appendix C).

The five Canadian variants, all of them published, come from the epic Fifth Thule Expedition, when Rasmussen and his crew traveled by dog team from Greenland to Alaska. It appears that Rasmussen did not collect any variants of the tale when he visited Alaska, despite the fact that it is well known in villages all over northern Alaska, and especially in the Barrow area (see Spencer and Carter 1954).

There is a gap of about fifty years between Rink and Rasmussen. The primary difference between Rink and Rasmussen is that Rasmussen recorded details about the storytellers, providing their names, biographical notes, and often taking their photographs. In one case he even gives details of the performance context. Disregarding the conventions of the time, Rasmussen did not see the stories as ends in themselves but took a strong interest in the storytellers and occasionally documented their lives (see chapter 3).

One of the travesties of Rasmussen's legacy is found in the way that one of his Iglulik texts has been butchered by modern scholars. The Iglulik variant told by Ivaluardjuk in 1921 was first translated and published in English as "How the Moon Spirit first came" (Rasmussen 1929, 77–81). In 1983 the same story was used to support an interpretive essay written by Jarich Oosten (1983). Oosten rewrote and summarized Rasmussen's English translation without acknowledging that he had done so and without crediting Ivaluardjuk as the original performer.[4] Oosten even retitled it as "The myth of the sun and the moon" (the sequel L2). This misappropriation of Ivaluardjuk's story seems to have been largely ignored and forgotten, even though it was published in a leading scholarly journal, *Études/Inuit/Studies*. But the collateral damage did not end there. It was subsequently picked up and republished in a book called *Northern Voices: Inuit Writing in English*, edited by Penny Petrone (1992, 14–16).

Petrone took Oosten's summary and passed it on uncritically as the real thing but coined still another title, "Origin of the Sun and Moon," which further distorted Ivaluardjuk's original. This treatment might not have been so bad if Petrone had only taken the time to check Oosten's version against Rasmussen's translated original. But in her introduction, she vouches for the authenticity of her entire anthology, saying, "Except for correcting obvious printing errors, I have not altered any text. Each piece appears with its own stylistic devices, peculiarities of spelling, grammar, syntax, and punctuation, preserved to show development in the use of language" (1992, xv). So while scholars often pay lip service to sacred texts, the exigencies of publication lead them to manipulate these texts to suit other purposes.

E. Semi-Literary Variants

Accordingly, and with all due carelessness, the next level of writing the story thrusts it into the realm of creative writing. Although Rink was the first to do this openly and with a free hand, this kind of treatment has primarily flourished in the late twentieth century.[5] I define *semi-literary variants* of "The Blind Man and the Loon" as imaginative recreations of the oral variants, generally composed by combining several manuscript oral variants (as in Rink 1866 and 1875) or several previously printed variants, and then "adapting," "retelling," or "improving" them. Such variants are generally distinguished by being targeted to a reading audience of children, although there are exceptions such as Lynch (1978), who has written a small book for adults in basically the same form as one usually designed for children. That is, it has fairly large print and line drawings on every page.

By *semi-literary*, I follow Lauri Honko's (2000) identification of epic forms that are transitional between the oral and the literary. Honko's notion of semi-literary is a text that is "tradition-oriented." The text essentially comes from oral tradition but has then been altered and "improved" by the collector/editor to make it appeal to a wider reading audience.

The semi-literary variant tries to retain the principal elements of the story (characters and story line) but deletes dramatic elements that may deemed offensive. It may also summarize the oral or combine several oral variants into one. It falls short of being either fully based on the oral (accurately recorded in the Native language, closely translated, or in the vernacular with minimal editing), or, on the other hand, completely literary (in which the collector/editor rewrites or retells the story from his or her imagination). Good examples of semi-literary variants of "The Blind Man and the Loon" are those found in Rink (1866, 1875) and Leechman (1931, 1942, 1952, 1956, 1964).

Rink's edition had a profound and lasting effect on Greenlandic folklore, and it has influenced several modern American writers who have popularized "The Blind Man and the Loon." Two of these writers, Helen Caswell (1968) and John Bierhorst (1997), have acknowledged their debt to Hinrich Rink, Knud Rasmussen, and to others such as Franz Boas, in creating their own redactions. Alice Mills (2003, 471) has also combined four sources, admitting that her mixed version of "The Blind Boy and the Loon" is a "retelling" based on those of Norman (1990), Hall (1975), Rink (1875), and Nungak and Arima (1969). Bierhorst, Caswell, and Mills are pure popularizers in the sense that they have essentially produced redactions of redactions, so far removed from oral texts that they should be regarded as simulacra.

After Hinrich Rink's landmark compilation (1866, 1875), the real flowering of semi-literary variants of "The Blind Man and the Loon" occurred in the late 1960s and 1970s, with those produced by Caswell, Ramona Maher, and William Toye. This reflects a new kind of treatment of oral traditions, one in which they are viewed as a common-pool resource, as part of the public domain. Virtually all of the semi-literary variants are based on the Eskimo subtype. In fact most bear a generic relationship to the oral variants from the eastern Arctic. Caswell, for instance, admits up front that her tale is "retold" but does not acknowledge her source. It is readily apparent, nevertheless, that she modeled her version closely after the Central Eskimo variant collected by Boas in 1885. A notable exception to this borrowing pattern is the Kiowa-based variant included in N. Scott Momaday's *The Way to Rainy Mountain* (1969, 58). Momaday reconstructs the tale as heard from his grandmother, giving it poetic qualities.

Some examples of common-pool resources include irrigation systems, public lakes, fishing grounds, pastures, and forests. When oral traditions begin to be viewed as common property, they are no longer recognized and respected as the private property of the storyteller, of the community, or of the indigenous tribal group they came from. So it is easy for non-Native authors to make money publishing books of folktales such as "The Blind Man and the Loon" by appropriating them and processing them in such a way that they no longer closely resemble their original form. Even when they are false, inaccurate representations of oral tradition, they still sell.

A cynical view of this intertextual process is that these semi-literary variants of folktales are a devious way around copyright protections. That is, the traditional storyteller does not need to be paid a royalty because he or she freely gave it up to a collector long ago. And from a western perspective, it is clear that individuals do not own stories unless they are clearly copyrighted. So oral poets can be easily exploited. While the true motives of semi-literary writers of folktales remain unknown, it is clear that not only have they have escaped copyright infringement, but through the process of redacting they have profited from the marketing and sale of traditional knowledge through their books.

Citing Clark Wissler's early twentieth century renditions of Blackfoot tales, the poet and essayist Robert Bringhurst decries such manipulations and concatenations. Reducing all the variants of a traditional story into a single stereotypical version, he writes, destroys "the *reality and power*" of the story, along with its history and content. "Textual standardization," he continues, "like political and doctrinal and commercial standardization, is the antithesis, not the culmination, of culture" (1999, 337). Of course this exact same charge can be leveled at Hinrich Rink, even though Rink must be credited with recognizing the importance of the Blind Man and the Loon as a distinct Inuit tale type.

A more sympathetic view is that this is the way oral storytelling has always operated, by combining multiple variants into other variants. Stories are modified as they are retold. One Native American storyteller who happens to be a close friend of mine, Kenneth Frank of Arctic Village (fig. 18), says that he has learned traditional stories told in his own Gwich'in language this way, by listening to selected elders tell the same story and then putting them all together to make the fullest and most complete variant. This is particularly true for Gwich'in story cycles such as Vasaagìhdzak and Ch'iteehawęę, which contain numerous loosely connected episodes (see McKennan 1965; Mishler 2001).

A case in point is Johnny Frank, Kenneth Frank's grandfather, the master storyteller who came up with the unique episode of Vasaagitsak and the King (Mishler 2001, 70–75). This episode is clearly influenced by European tradition but remains unknown to other Gwich'in tradition bearers, including Kenneth. So it is not too much to say that both oral and semi-literary traditions make heavy use of such recombinations and imaginative additions. Tradition bearers such as Kenneth Frank, who embody oral tradition in their cultures, see themselves as storytellers rather than plagiarists, collecting various pieces of the tale from others and then adding their own touch, extending and elaborating. They know full well that audiences get tired of hearing the same story performed the same way, over and over.

A key difference between oral variants and semi-literary variants of "The Blind Man and the Loon," however, is that the shamanistic and violent parts of the story tend to drop out in the literary process. The cruelty of the blind boy's mother, who either blinds him intentionally using witchcraft or lies to him and tries to starve him, flies against the sanctity of motherhood and parental love. Then the cruelty of the blind man killing his own mother, grandmother, or wife flies against the sanctity of filial and marital love. From this perspective, the writer of semi-literary folktales is adapting and filtering tales from other cultures for members of his own culture, to suit what he or she perceives is a more ethical set of norms.

The themes and raw actions found in the Blind Man and the Loon and other Native American tales are not considered savory for young Anglo-American juveniles, the intended reading audience for most popularizers. Accordingly, the tales are censored and abridged as they are rewritten. Such treatment is in keeping with the popular misconception that all folklore is intended for children and, consequently, that it is trivial.

We could view the semi-literary variants more sympathetically if they preserved the key elements, motifs, dramatic acts, and themes of the tales they recreate. But in many cases they do not. While the story of the Blind Man and the Loon may indeed be delivered unvarnished to Eskimo and Indian children, the harsh reality is that it sometimes gets completely whitewashed of its violence before it is presented to non-Native children.

And so it is that we find William Toye and Elizabeth Cleaver's *The Loon's Necklace* (1977) winning the Imperial Order of Daughters of the Empire (IODE) Children's Book Award in 1977 and the Amelia Frances Howard-Gibbon Illustrator's Award from the Canadian Association of Children's Librarians in 1978. This slim twenty-four page volume was recently named in a list of "Native American tales every child should know" (Polette 2006), and Wal-Mart suggests it for children ages four and up. Cleaver maintains that it is "a famous Tsimshian legend."

A comparison of Toye's retelling with the variant Boas collected from Henry Tate (Boas 1916) reveals their close similarities. One major difference is that Toye's text introduces an "old hag" with magical powers who does the dirty work of the wicked and selfish wife in the Boas and Tate variant. Another, almost purely literary, version by Corrinne Dwyer (1988) invents Owl-Woman as the evil character, making the blind man's wife and son, as well as the blind man himself, innocent victims. Such treatments totally sidestep the betrayal by close kin that makes the oral variants so powerful and so tragic.

Helen Caswell's *Shadows from the Singing House* (1968) is still found in nearly every community and school library in Alaska and Canada, and Ramona Maher's long out-of-print book *The Blind Boy and the Loon and Other Eskimo Myths* (1969) is recommended for all children ages eight and older and classified as "juvenile nonfiction."

In his book, *Why the Man in the Moon Is Happy and Other Eskimo Creation Stories*, reteller Ronald Melzack says that "Because Inuit life is so different from our own, it was necessary to retell the stories in a way that would appeal to children of *our* culture" (emphasis mine, Melzack 1977, 64). To his credit, Melzack leaves in the violent elements of "The Origin of the Narwhal," but he comes up with two traits absent from any other oral tradition: (1) the wicked old woman is portrayed as a stranger and no relation to the blind boy, and (2) the blind boy kills the polar bear with a spear instead of a bow and arrow.

In Raymond Jones and Jon Stott's more recent anthology, *A World of Stories: Traditional Tales for Children* (2006), we find an unexpurgated orally-based variant of the Blind Boy and the Loon. The Native American tale is fittingly placed side by side with violence-infused European Märchen, folktale classics such as "Snow White" and "Hansel and Grethel." In their introduction, Jones and Stott candidly admit that "Although most traditional stories were not created specifically for children, young listeners no doubt paid attention to those that interested them and were within their range of understanding" (2006, xii). To be sure, in oral cultures, children can usually eavesdrop on adult-to-adult storytelling performances, while in literate cultures children rely much more heavily on books adults read aloud or make available to them.

Reflections

All of this demonstrates how, and to a certain degree why, most published versions of "The Blind Man and the Loon" stemming from Rink and other popularizers diverge sharply from variants still actively circulating in Native oral tradition.

In review, I have identified several salient layers of distortion, simplification, and loss: one from the process of linguistic translation (eliminating reporting speech), one from the process of semi-literary redaction (both expansion and abridgment), and still another from the process of editing and censorship. All judgments aside, however, it is through Hinrich Rink's redaction and the work of other popularizers such as Douglas Leechman and Toye and Cleaver that this tale has fully entered the consciousness and the imagination of the wider world.

CHAPTER THREE

The Tale Behind the Tale

The saddest part of folklore scholarship has always been the lack of recognition of the storytellers. Many collectors did not even tell us the names of the persons from whom they recorded their texts. But it's not just the stories themselves that are important: it's the lives of the stories, and the lives of the stories are deeply embedded in the lives of the storytellers. And it's time to recognize that the lives of the storytellers also become texts if they are documented.

We know this is true, especially with classical authors. Just think about how much has been written about the lives of William Shakespeare, Jane Austen, Charles Dickens, Emily Dickinson, Mark Twain, and Ernest Hemingway. We are interested in them not just for what they wrote, but for who they were, for their humanity, their life histories. Usually there is no way to connect the social lives of the storytellers directly to characters or dramatic actions in a given tale, or to know one performer's influence on another, but without individual personalities continuously engaged in daily face-to-face listening and talking, there would be no oral traditions.

In the words of Hungarian folklorist Linda Dégh (1969, 182):

> The narrator weaves his own person into the tale, he imparts his own point of view when he tells the tale. His own fate is involved in all the situations of the tale; he identifies himself with the tale action; and he interprets all the life expressions of his people. Every narrator does this, but the means depend on his personality.

The storytellers who have performed and recorded the story of the

Blind Man and the Loon are the unsung poet laureates and Nobel prize winners for literature of their times. For not only did they pass on this special tale to collectors and to the world, but in their heads and hearts they accumulated an entire repertoire of other traditional stories, as well as their own life stories, to communicate. They are diverse and fascinating people who need to be honored and remembered, and what follows here is a nod to an illustrious pantheon of voices, names, and faces. We might call it a virtual chain of custody, with many missing links.

When we look at a list of the collectors of "The Blind Man and the Loon," it reads like a Who's Who of Danish and North American arctic anthropology. Among the distinguished Danish collectors are Hinrich Rink, Knud Rasmussen, Gustav Holm, Kaj Birket-Smith, and Erik Holtved. French as well as French-Canadian scholarship is well represented by Émile Petitot, Paul-Émile Victor, Jean Malaurie, and Bernard Saladin d'Anglure. North American anthropologists and linguists who have recorded texts include Franz Boas, George Dorsey, Alfred Kroeber, Frederica de Laguna, Diamond Jenness, Robert Lowie, Livingston Farrand, Catharine McClellan, John Swanton, James Teit, Robert Spencer, Edwin Hall, and Michael Krauss, along with many others.

"The Blind Man and the Loon" has captured the attention of so many scholars in different places and times because it is at the very foundation of Greenlandic, Canadian First Nations, and Native American culture. Collectively, these folklorists and ethnographers have provided the treasury of texts that underlie this book (see appendix B). Their work has inspired me greatly.

This chapter looks at selected tradition bearers of "The Blind Man and the Loon" and the ethnologists who worked with them to record the story. Obviously we cannot survey every storyteller and every collector, or every encounter between them to establish the sequences of oral transference, but we can look selectively at a handful of them to get a fuller understanding of what their lives and their characters were like.

Franz Boas's Sources

There are villains as well as heroes among the collectors of "The Blind Man and the Loon" because the names and identities of many Native storytellers have already been forgotten while the collectors' fame and place in history lives on. All too often collectors did not think their storytellers' names or their lives were important enough to record. For Franz Boas and many of his students, oral traditions were to be collected much like harpoon points, spruce root baskets, or carved wooden spoons, no different from items of material culture. As a result, nearly all of his texts are disembodied from personal, cultural, and performance contexts. In *Tsimshian Texts*, he identifies storytellers only by their English first names. Robert Bringhurst, in looking at Boas's *Tsimshian Mythology*, complains that "this vast comparative enterprise pays no attention to individual authorship and makes no allowances for individual artistry, intelligence or style" (1999, 136).

From a contemporary perspective, Franz Boas is indeed one of the guilty, seeming to feel that individual variation was insignificant and that a standardized text was more important than the context. The Central Eskimo variant of "The Blind Man and the Loon" that Boas published comes from an anonymous source. His Kwakiutl text is attributed to a person named NEg·é, and his Tsimshian translation came from the hand of his trusted assistant, Henry Tate (Boas 1916, 2: 246–50). Unfortunately, the accuracy of Boas's translations from Tate have also been called into question (see Maud 1989, 2000). It turns out that Tate, a Native author from Port Simpson, British Columbia, actually wrote down stories in nonstandard English and then back-translated them into Tsimshian.[1]

Boas was clearly more interested in where the story had been recorded than in who told it under what circumstances. Initially, he considered the Central Eskimo version of "The Blind Man and the Loon" to be "a creation story" because it seemed to explain the origin of the narwhal (1904, 4), but this assessment greatly oversimplifies the tale and misses the mark.

Familiar with the writings and research of Hinrich Rink, Boas soon realized that the tale of the Blind Man and the Loon had traveled great distances across the continents: "Here we have an excellent example of a very complex story in two widely separated regions. We cannot doubt for a moment that it is actually the same story which is told by the Eskimo and by the Indian" (1891, 17). Finally, in *Tsimshian Mythology* (1916, 825–29), Boas includes a detailed comparison of the story's Northwest Coast and Eskimo variants, identifying eighteen printed sources and summarizing several of them. This comparison is the result of Boas's wide reading of folkloric texts.

James Teit's Source: Dandy Jim

James Teit was a young Shetlander who immigrated to the small railroad community of Spences Bridge, British Columbia, to work as a clerk in his uncle's store in the winter of 1884. Gradually, he made friends with the local Interior Salish Indians and eventually married one of them. Then he became fluent in their Nlaka'pamux language and began to make ethnographic and folkloric collections, some of them under the patronage of a wealthy Chicago businessman, Homer Sargent. Later on he was mentored by Edward Sapir and Franz Boas and hired by them to do additional research, some of it while traveling on horseback in remote mountainous areas.

Teit's field work along the upper Stikine River in northwestern British Columbia began in September 1912, when he met and worked closely with Dandy Jim, a middle-aged member of the Nahlin clan of the Raven Phratry "noted for his affability and intelligence." Teit, one of the first white supporters of Indian land claims in British Columbia, was attracted to Dandy Jim, a signatory to the 1910 Declaration of the Tahltan. Dandy Jim, known as Tu ū·tzE (Strong Rocks) in his own language, was fluent in English, Tahltan, and Tlingit. He was married to a woman known as "One-eyed Susie," who accompanied him in the recording of several love songs and dance songs (fig. 6).

Teit published a number of Dandy Jim's texts in English in the *Journal of American Folklore* (Teit 1919). These texts, which included "The Blind Man and the Loon," were collected at Telegraph Creek. In 1915 Teit returned and recorded more of Dandy Jim's songs and tales. He also took numerous photographs of Dandy Jim and his other Tahltan sources. More about Dandy Jim and his relationship with Teit appears in Judy Thompson's excellent tribute to Teit, *Recording Their Story* (2007).[2] Dandy Jim died in 1918.

Knud Rasmussen's Sources

It is impossible to present portraits of all the storytellers Knud Rasmussen worked with because, as with Boas, they often remain unnamed, or, if named, undescribed. In the previous chapter I wrote about some of Hinrich Rink's sources for "The Blind Man and the Loon," though it still

Fig. 6. Dandy Jim and wife Susie, ca. 1902. Accession no. 193501-001; call no. E-01160. Courtesy of the Royal BC Museum, British Columbia Provincial Archives, Victoria.

remains unclear whether those sources were storytellers, collectors, or students, or represented a combination of such identities.

However, from the perspective of contemporary folkloristics, Knud Rasmussen was one of the best collectors because he often provides biographical sketches and photo portraits of his sources, talks about storytelling performance situations and field methods, interprets texts as narrative poems, and records them in the Native language from both men and women. This cross-gendered humanistic approach, as exemplified in Danish scholarship, helps to set Rasmussen apart from most of his contemporaries, predecessors, and many modern-day scholars.

All of this is true only of Rasmussen's five Canadian storytellers from the Fifth Thule Expedition (1921–24). His ten Greenlandic sources for the tale of the Blind Boy and the Loon are generally credited by name, but little other information is given.[3] We know very little, for instance, about Jonasine Nielsen, Sofie Jørgensen, Cecilie Olsen (Sísê/Sissili), Arnâluk, Gert Lyberth, Gaba Olsen (Gâba, Gaaba, Gabriel), or Kuania.

According to Kirsten Thisted (1998, 217) Gert Lyberth was "a writing storyteller," novelist, and illustrator who lived from 1867 to 1929. In 1924 Lyberth, who worked as a trading station manager, wrote a manuscript for Knud Rasmussen that contained "a number of stories from the oral tradition." Presumably, this collection included the variant SB 1895.

Due to the scant information available about Rasmussen's Greenlandic storytellers, we will look primarily at the five Canadian storytellers Rasmussen worked with during the Fifth Thule Expedition. One variant collected by Rasmussen from the Iglulik Eskimo in 1921 comes from the storyteller Ivaluardjuk at Repulse Bay, on Hudson's Bay; it was published in 1929. Ivaluardjuk (the little caribou sinew-thread, fig. 7) was married to Aligiaq and had an adopted daughter named Amaaq. When Rasmussen met him, Ivaluardjuk was living with his family at Naujân on Repulse Bay. Ivaluardjuk's photo appears in *Intellectual Culture of the Iglulik Eskimos* (Rasmussen 1929, 16); he is shown as an old man with a long white beard. Ivaluardjuk also served as Rasmussen's expert ethnogeographer, drawing him two detailed maps of the region, which led to the elicitation of about one hundred place names.

Ivaluardjuk was a recognized shaman and the brother to Aua, another shaman who supplied Rasmussen with stories and information. Rasmussen dubbed him "a duly qualified wizard, but rarely practised his art, his specialty being folk tales, of which over fifty were written down from his dictation" (1927, 124). Reserved at first, Ivaluardjuk softened up after Rasmussen recited for him some old Greenlandic tales, which Ivaluardjuk recognized in his own repertoire. Ivaluardjuk was a noted singer and his version of the Blind Man and the Loon tale, called "How the Moon Spirit First Came," embodies several songs.

The Copper Inuit version was collected from Rasmussen's sled dog traveling companion and guide, a young man named Netsit (fig. 8), the son of Ilatsiaq, a powerful shaman. The fact that Rasmussen was able to collect stories from such a young man is in itself remarkable, given that most young Natives defer to their elders, usually declining to perform stories for outsiders, even when they know them well.

In December 1921, Rasmussen wrote about his first day of traveling with Netsit by dog team, headed for Bathurst Inlet:

> At the end of the first day's run, we found a comfortable snowdrift, and proceeded to build ourselves a hut for the night.
>
> I had with me a few cigarettes, which I kept for special occasions, and this evening, after a meal and a cup of coffee, felt inclined to indulge. I therefore lit a cigarette and gave one to my companion. To my surprise, he did not light up himself, but packed the cigarette carefully away in a piece of rag. Our snow hut would not perhaps have been considered specially warm and cosy by any save those who had like ourselves been thrashing for ten hours against a bitter wind. But as it was the tiny blubber lamp seemed to shed a cheerful golden glow all about us; we felt in the mood for a little entertainment.
>
> We made an extra cup of coffee, and I suggested that Netsit should tell a story or so. To make ourselves thoroughly comfortable before starting, we gave the hut a good coating of loose snow to caulk any possible leaks, sealed up the entrance so that not a breath of air could get in, and then settled down in our sleeping bags, entertainer and audience ready to drop off as soon as either wished. . . .
>
> I listened with interest to one story after another, and Netsit, encouraged by my appreciation, went on untiringly. He told a host of stories that evening. Of the Boy who lived with a Bear, The Bear that turned into a Cloud, The Eagle that carried off a Woman; The Woman that would not Marry and Turned into Stone; Navarana, the Eskimo Girl Who Betrayed her People to the Indians; The Man who made Salmon out of Splinters of Wood; and The Inland-dweller with a Dog as Big as a Mountain and so on and so on. Many of them were but different versions of stories current in Greenland, and one little

fable I remembered distinctly having heard almost word for word years ago at my own place in Thule. This uniformity is the more remarkable when we reflect that there has been no sort of intercourse between the two peoples for at least a thousand years. (Rasmussen 1927, 251–53)

We cannot tell from these notes whether "The Blind Man and the Loon" was one of the stories Netsit actually told on this occasion, but even if it was not, we can appreciate the context and ambience in which it was performed, if not on that evening, then presumably on another similar occasion. Netsit's story "The blind one and the loon" appeared in Rasmussen's *The Intellectual Culture of the Copper Eskimos* in 1932. Rasmussen presents it in free English translation and then in Inuktitut with an interlinear literal translation. The English itself is derivative, the original translation having been written first in Danish. Rasmussen tags it as a "Fragment of the tale of the sun and the moon," even though the Sun and the Moon tale usually appears independently or as a sequel to the Blind Man and the Loon story. It is only in central and eastern Canada (Regional Group B) that the Sun and the Moon story is conjoined to the Blind Man and the Loon. This is not the case in either Greenland or Alaska.

Rasmussen recorded two versions of the Blind Man and the Loon from the Netsilik Eskimo under the title "The tale of the sun and moon," an extension or sequel to the standard tale (see appendix A, Trait L2). When visited by Rasmussen in 1923, the Netsilingmiut were scattered between Committee Bay, Victoria Strait, and Somerset Island. Most Netsilingmiut now live in or near the modern government-built settlements of Taloyoak and Pelly Bay on Boothia Peninsula and in Gjoa Haven on King William Island.

Rasmussen tells us that he had spent nearly six months with the first narrator, a woman of about forty-five years of age named Nâlungiaq (the infant), a mother of two boys who was married to Inûtuk, her third husband. After months of questioning her and getting only partial answers, Rasmussen says that one night she simply sat down and started telling him everything he wanted to know. However, instead of grabbing pen and paper he was afraid of making her self-conscious and simply listened carefully, asking occasional questions and trusting his memory to write it all down later. What he wrote filled up six and a half pages. Cornelius Remie (1988) maintains that Rasmussen began to use this method to avoid paying his storytellers. Among the Netsilik especially, Rasmussen discovered that if he took notes in the presence of his sources, they would demand payment (generally ammunition, gunpowder, and shot), but if he just carried on a conversation and gathered information that way, there were no such demands (Remie 1988, 107–8).

Nâlungiaq (fig. 9) said that she learned all of her stories from her uncle, a shaman named Unarâluk. As we shall see later, part of the power of the Blind Man and the Loon story lies in its close association with shamans and shamanistic beliefs. While Nâlungiaq was extremely knowledgeable about Netsilik traditions, Rasmussen did not think of her as an especially outstanding performer of them. At the same time, Nâlungiaq persuaded him that "in many respects their religion is entirely based upon the tales" and "these tales are both their real history and the source of all their religious ideas" (Rasmussen 1931, 207). Nâlung-iaq interpreted the story by saying, "The sun and the moon murdered their mother, and though they were brother and sister, they loved each other. For that reason they ceased to be humans" (Rasmussen 1931, 210). Matricide was followed by incest. In fact, Nâlungiaq believed that all of the heavenly bodies, including the stars, were formerly humans who had ascended into the sky.

The second Netsilik storyteller, an old man named Ikinilik (fig. 10), who resided in a different area from Nâlungiaq, and belonged to the Utkuhikjalingmiut, is portrayed by Rasmussen as "the best singer." Rasmussen gives us this fetching little portrait: "Ikinilik settled himself comfortably among the soft caribou skins, and lighting his pipe—the bowl of which was about the size of a small thimble—started off with a laughing allusion" (1931, 524). In contrast to Nâlungiaq, Ikinilik gave him straightforward dictation. Rasmussen recorded Ikinilik's story at Itivnârjuk on the Back River near Franklin Lake in the spring of 1923. The Back River flows from Aylmer Lake northeast through Garry Lakes and Franklin Lake to the Arctic Ocean at Chantrey Inlet. It is a long river, 1,077 kilometers (673 miles), very remote and difficult to access even today.

One of the most intriguing and heroic persons to ever perform the story of the Blind Man and the Loon was the woman Kibkârjuk (fig. 11), the oldest wife of Igjugârjuk, a powerful shaman and chieftain among the Caribou Eskimos or Pâdlermiut. Igjugârjuk's youngest and prettiest wife was named Atqâralâq and lived in a separate tent from her rival. Despite her secondary, almost servant status, Rasmussen characterizes Kibkârjuk (the little gnawed-off bone) as "one of my best story-tellers" (1930, 65). In 1921–22 the whole family was living at Qamanerjuaq, near Hikoligjuak Lake.

Two stories about Kibkârjuk are worth repeating here. First, she managed to accept her husband Igjugârjuk even though many years before, he killed her parents and two brothers and their wives, suspecting that they were planning to spite him and give her away to another man. Rasmussen says, "I could not help being astonished at the really faithful love his woman had for her husband. He had murdered all her family, all her nearest and dearest, it made no difference" (1930, 35). Despite this history of violent bloodletting, Rasmussen found that Igjugârjuk was "wise, independent, intelligent, and exercised great authority over his fellow-villagers" (1930, 33). Rasmussen also learned much from him.

The second story is that Kibkârjuk had saved her whole community from starvation just a month or so before Rasmussen arrived. After her husband was unsuccessful in hunting game for many days, Kibkârjuk and her adopted son set off in the middle of a snow storm, dragging a little sled behind her and only some salmon fishing gear to forage with. They got lost in the blizzard and were attempting to reach a small lake several days' journey away. Lacking food or sleeping robes, they were forced to stop and build snow houses along the way and had no lamp to warm themselves with. When at last they reached the lake, Kibkârjuk found that it was full of fat salmon trout. She caught many of them and then returned to feed all the others in the village.

Regitze Søby, who has inventoried Rasmussen's folklore collections, reports that Rasmussen did not write down all of the texts that ended up in his collections. "It can be seen from the numerous notes in his archive that various people helped him in collecting these tales, e.g. catechist students, catechists, etc. The storytellers too, or their families, occasionally sent written versions" (Søby 1988, 194). Among these would be the Greenlanders we have already mentioned above, such as Gert Lyberth.

Fig. 7. Ivaluardjuk. From Knud
Rasmussen, *Across Arctic
America* (1927).

Fig. 8. Netsit. From Knud
Rasmussen, *Across Arctic
America* (1927).

Fig. 9. Nâlungiaq. From Knud Rasmussen, *Across Arctic America* (1927).

Fig. 10. Ikinilik. From Knud
Rasmussen, *Across Arctic
America* (1927).

Fig. 11. Kibkârjuk (*left*) and Huwakzuk (*right*). From Knud Rasmussen, *Across Arctic America* (1927).

And as Tiger Burch has observed, Rasmussen published his collection of Alaskan legends without any analysis or comparison with those of other Inuit groups. Part of the problem was that he had too many of them. Because he used a form of shorthand to record the texts, Rasmussen's versions of the tales are often "significantly reduced," resembling "basic outlines" (Burch 1988, 155). Still, he must be duly credited with being one of the first to recognize Inuit storytelling as an art form. Because of his diligence, we may still enjoy the authentic faces of Blind Man and the Loon tradition bearers such as Ivaluardjuk, Netsit, Nâlungiaq, Ikinilik, and Kibkârjuk.

Eric Holtved's Source: Amaunalik

One of the most colorful narrators of "The Blind Man and the Loon" is a Polar Eskimo woman named Amaunalik, interviewed by Eric Holtved in Thule, west Greenland, during the late 1930s and mid-1940s. Holtved's upbeat photo of her wearing her splendid polar bear skin pants and a white-collared sweater is a classic among ethnographic images (fig.

12). It is telling that she wears polar bear fur pants, since in the story the Blind Man shoots a polar bear with his bow and arrow. We could almost say she is wearing the story on her legs.

When she was interviewed, Amaunalik brought several of her young children along: "The children withdrew," Holtved writes, "but Amaunalik herself kept it up for three to four hours or more" (Holtved 1951, 15). He adds: "Her manner of telling is very vivid, when she narrates freely, and at the same time that the narrative is in a measured style and is delivered in a recitating tone, she herself actually 'lives' in it" (15). Blessed with a "joyous and equable temperament," Amaunalik said that she had learned her legends from her grandmother. Presumably this was her mother's mother, Itugssarssuat, recognized as "the ancestress of about one fifth of the whole population" at the time of her death in 1939.

The setting for Amaunalik's Greenlandic stories is also made vivid by Holtved. He describes the location as the Thule wireless Station, which had generator noise going constantly in the background. At first Holtved took dictation from her, but after receiving a Telefunken disc recorder in the spring of 1937, he began to record her. He then confirmed and revised his transcriptions of the original texts during a return visit in 1946–47. They are published both in Kalaallisut with literal interlinear English translations and also freely in English. On his return visit in 1946, Holtved says, "I read what had been written down to the person in question, who then corrected me. In this manner the original records were reconstructed and written down in intelligible language, though at the same time keeping the whole character of the original" (Holtved 1951, 10–12).

Jean Malaurie's Source: Pualuna

Shortly after Holtved's fieldwork was completed, the Polar Eskimos were visited by the French ethnographer Jean Malaurie (1985) in 1950. Malaurie worked with the elder storyteller, Pualuna, who was living outside of Thule in the small settlement of Siorapaluk. Despite repeated questioning, Pualuna could not recall his birth year, which Malaurie estimated at about 1874. Malaurie investigated Pualuna's family history and found that he was a former shaman with four wives, six children, fifteen grandchildren, and thirteen great grandchildren (Malaurie 1955, 205).

Fig. 12. Amaunalik, ca. 1937–38, by Erik Holtved. Photo no. 42660. Courtesy of the Arktisk Institut, Copenhagen.

Ironically, despite this huge family, Malaurie found Pualuna living alone in a tattered tent, recently separated from his latest wife. Like many of the other performers of the Blind Man and the Loon story (under the local title of "Pigtail and Narwhal Tusk") Pualuna led a very rich and interesting life. He had once been a companion of the arctic explorers Robert Peary and Frederick Cook and was also a carver. Malaurie (2003, 67) says he would get regular visits from Pualuna, who always carried a "spitting box" into which he frequently coughed blood.

Togiak Source: Annie Blue

Annie Blue, whose Yup'ik name is Cung'auyar, was born in Qisaayaaq, a small settlement on the Togiak River, Alaska, on February 21, 1916. She was raised in a family of nine children and spent most of her childhood in another former village called Cauyarnaq. She had a sickly childhood and half of her body was paralyzed to the point that her mother would have to hand-feed her. Like the blind man in the story, she too had to overcome a debilitating physical handicap. As noted earlier, the lives of the storytellers also become texts if they are carefully documented. In her early teens Annie married a man named Cingarkaq and together they had seven children, only four of whom survived to become adults. Sadly, she has now outlived all but one of them.

She moved to Togiak, a coastal fishing community on Bristol Bay, in 1942, where she continues to live. In 1999 she was honored as the Alaska Federation of Natives Elder of the Year, and in 2000 she was named the AFN Culture Bearer of the Year. She received these awards not only for her great storytelling expertise, but because she is also a distinguished Yup'ik grass basket maker.

Annie once visited the Museum of the American Indian when it was located in New York, and through her friendship with the renowned Alaskan anthropologist Ann Fienup-Riordan, she has traveled to the Museum fur Volkerkunde in Berlin as an Expert in Traditional Yup'ik Knowledge to study artifacts from the Yup'ik region. In recent years she collaborated on "Math in a Cultural Context," a series of elementary school math modules based on traditional Yup'ik knowledge funded by the National Science Foundation. In 2008 she received an Honoring Alaska's Indigenous Literature (HAIL) award, and in 2009 she was given an honorary doctorate in humane letters by the University of Alaska Fairbanks (fig. 16).

Despite all of her family heartache, Annie is well known for her lively sense of humor, and many of her stories are comical. She often mimics and parodies the voices of the characters in her stories. She attributes many of her stories to a woman storyteller named Saveskar and insists that all of her tales are "true." Her variant of "Blind Boy and the Arctic Loons" ("Cikmiumalria Tan'gaurluq Yaqulegpiik-llu") appears in a bilingual printed edition and on a compact disc included in her own book (Blue 2007).

Conclusion

The diversity of these various personalities is stunning, even though it is important to acknowledge that not all traditional storytellers are gifted and spellbinding. In the words of Linda Dégh, "research has to focus on the outstanding storytelling personalities of a given community in order to gain through them an insight into the community's tale tradition . . . but we must also consider the lesser talents" (1969, 165).

Collectively, however, we can say that the photographic portraits of the storytellers shown here and in chapters 4 and 7 constitute an important iconography of the tale of the Blind Man and the Loon. Their weathered faces represent it well. Robert Bringhurst has lamented the fact that "rarely do we encounter an actual oral text," and even more rarely do we encounter an actual speaker or performer of that text. "The result is that the real human beings who inhabit oral cultures disappear and stereotypes replace them. Native American oral poets have so often been mistreated in this way that their namelessness has come to seem routine" (Bringhurst 1999, 16).

It must also be recognized that a few traditional storytellers doubled as scholarly collectors. To accomplish this they had to be both literate and fluent in their own Native languages. The first of these were several Greenlanders, whose early nineteenth-century writings found their way into manuscript if not into print. In the previous chapter, for example, I mentioned the amazing Frederick Steenholdt, Jakob Lund, Amos Daniel, and Jens Kreutzmann, who all wrote tales in Greenlandic and sent their work to Peder Kragh and Hinrich Rink.

Fig. 13. Peter Kalifornsky. Courtesy of the Alaska Native Language Center, Fairbanks. © 1986 by Roy Shapley, *Peninsula Clarion*.

We now also recognize the remarkable accomplishments of Franz Boas's bilingual literate collaborators, Henry Tate and George Hunt, in British Columbia, despite their limitations. Modern day writer-storytellers include Arnaitok Ipellie (in Inuktitut) of Iqaliut, Nunavut (1997) and Peter Kalifornsky (in Dena'ina) of Kenai, Alaska (1991; fig. 13). I once had the good fortune to work for a few days with Peter and was struck by his soft-spoken genius. Each of these individuals must be credited as exceptionally gifted, straddling two worlds, with the talent and motivation to document traditions in their own Native tongues. We must remember that every one of them has a voice, a name, a face, and a life.

66

CHAPTER FOUR

The Telling of the Tale

A Biographical Sketch of Maggie Gilbert

Maggie Gilbert (Maggie Jyah) was a Gwich'in Athabaskan woman born at Shuman House on the Porcupine River in northeastern Alaska in 1895 or 1896. Her father's English name was William and her mother was Laura, but after her mother died in 1909 she was raised by her uncle, Chief Christian, in the upper Chandalar River country.

Maggie's first husband was Titus Peter, and her children from Titus include Naomi (Tritt) and Kias Peter. An early photograph of her with husband Titus was taken in Arctic Village in 1927 (fig. 14). In 1931, sometime after Titus died, she married James Gilbert, who was fourteen years younger than herself and a Native minister in the Episcopal Church (fig. 17). He was also a noted Ch'aadzaa K'eech'iigilik, or square dance caller. With James she had three children: Mary, Trimble, and Florence (Newman). Mary died as an infant.

In 1940, James was elected chief of Arctic Village. James and Maggie and their family moved around and lived in many different places. She had a Native Allotment at K'aii dzuu zhit gwitsik (the mouth of little willow creek), a family fish camp located on the East Fork of the upper Chandalar River, inside the Arctic National Wildlife Refuge. Around 1956, however, Maggie gradually went blind from cataracts. Consequently, she and James eventually settled down in a small one-room log cabin in Arctic Village; this is where I met her in April 1973. Despite her handicap, she still continued to cut fish and process ducks. As her son Trimble recalls, "She's talk all the time, but my father . . . he never did tell me very much, unless I asked him. . . . And my mother,

67

Fig. 14. Maggie Gilbert with her first husband's family (detail). *Left to right*: Martha Peter, Jo Ann Peter, Maggie Peter (Gilbert), possibly Linus Peter, and husband Titus Peter. Arctic Village, 1927. John Mertie Jr., Mertie Collection, U.S. Geological Survey archives, Denver.

any time you ask, you come to the house, and then she start telling you this story." (Gilbert, 1991 1986)

Arctic Village is a remote Gwich'in community located in Alaska's central Brooks Range, approximately one hundred miles north of Fort Yukon, well above the Arctic Circle. According to the federal census, the population of Arctic Village in 1970 was eighty-five. By 2010, it had grown to one hundred fifty-two. The community depends largely on caribou, moose, and freshwater fish for subsistence.

Maggie Gilbert and James Gilbert's Memorial Potlatch

When Maggie Gilbert's children held a memorial potlatch for her and her second husband, James Gilbert, in Arctic Village in July 2003, one of the social activities was for the family to hand out small gifts to the many visitors who were invited to attend. I was lucky to be one of them. Among the items given away were pouches of Red Man chewing tobacco, a favorite of Maggie's, a brand produced in the United States since 1904. Villagers and guests all had a chew in her remembrance. At that time I gave a copy of Maggie's 1973 tape recording to her daughter Florence. Neither Florence nor Trimble recalled ever hearing their mother tell the Blind Man and the Loon story, but both of them gave their consent to my having it published here, as another way of honoring their mother's memory.

The Performance Context

When I recorded her, Maggie was dressed in red corduroy skirt with three narrow bands of trim above the hem, wore a yellow and white cotton blouse under a black cardigan sweater, unbuttoned, and had a gold chain around her neck and a brown and red shawl over her gray hair. She sat on the corner of her bed with her shoes off, propped up by a pillow. As with many who are blind, she wore sunglasses. It is ironic, but especially intriguing, that the story of the Blind Man and the Loon was first told to me by a blind woman.

Maggie's husband James Gilbert sat in on some of the stories, but went in and out of the cabin as the stories unfolded, putting wood in the stove and heating a kettle of water. The cabin was a clean, well-lighted place, punctuated every quarter hour by chiming clock bells. We had two recording sessions, one on April 21, 1973, and a second two days later on April 23. The first session was held at Maggie's house with Ernest Erick present as an interpreter. Ernest did not translate the stories for me but facilitated the interview and discussion.

One of the major topics on that day was a story about her uncle, Chief Christian (Christian Choh). She also sang a New Year's song and a song she made for her grandson. For the second session, held at 9:30 a.m. in the same place, her husband James assumed the role of interpreter and facilitator. Maggie was essentially monolingual in Gwich'in and heard many of her stories from her maternal grandmother, Ellen Tr'eenaatsyaa, Chief Christian's mother.

On April 23, Maggie led off with a song for her grandson, Albert Gilbert, and then told "The Blind Man and the Loon." This was a tale

I already knew about from printed sources and which I specifically elicited. Next I asked for a brown bear story, and she surprised me by producing three, all of them about Brown Bear and Crow. The third one of these was her variant of "Raven Brings Daylight," another tale known all over the continent. She then finished the session with the story of how Crow and Loon decorated each other. The original cassette tape, recorded on a Sony TCM-500 deck with an external microphone, is still in my personal collection.

These stories were all recorded during the 1973 Arctic Village Spring Carnival, an annual multiday event featuring dog sled races, various outdoor games and contests, and nightly fiddle music dances. Maggie's son Trimble was one of the featured fiddlers, and husband James was the K'eechigilik, or square dance caller. I never saw her after that. Maggie died in March 1983, and James died on December 15, 1998. They are both buried in the cemetery at Arctic Village.

Maggie's version of "The Blind Man and the Loon" was later translated for me by Nena Russell, also of Arctic Village, around 1975. In 2007, I contracted with Fannie Gemmill to transcribe it in the new Gwich'in orthography and retranslate it. Then Maggie's grandson, Lincoln Tritt, proofread the transcription and made several corrections and clarifications. Finally, Maggie's granddaughter Caroline Tritt-Frank and her husband Kenneth Frank also proofread it and retranscribed it in greater detail. Maggie's recorded performance of the tale lasts just a little over eleven minutes (fig. 18).

I subsequently edited and arranged the text in verse format, using pauses of various lengths, clause endings, conjunctions (such as the ubiquitous initial particle pair, Aii ts'à'), and reporting speech to identify and define lines, allowing for enjambment. One thing that is quite distinctive about Gwich'in prosody is that lines sometimes end with a conjunction, such as gàa or ts'à', followed by a pause, while in English we are more accustomed to putting conjunctions at the beginnings of lines after a pause.

The Blind Man and the Loon (Gwich'in Text)
Maggie Gilbert, Arctic Village

Recorded by Craig Mishler at Arctic Village, April 23, 1973
Preliminary transcription by Fannie Gemmill
Edited by Kenneth and Caroline Frank and Lincoln Tritt

Line numbers and understood words are shown in brackets [ ].
For orthography and pronunciation assistance see www.omniglot.com/writing/
gwichin.php. English translation begins on p. 77.

Dinjii Vaagweech'in kwaa ts'à' Ts'aɬvit hàa Googwandak

Aii dinjii t'iiyàhnyàa aii, *family* leii [di'ii] vàràhnyàa, t'aihnyàa,
Aii ts'à' va'at gòolii ts'à' aii [dinjii],[1]
Vaagweech'in kwàa.
Googàa than hee neegihiinjìk gooràhnyàa,
T'ahnyàa gooràhnyàa.[2] [05]
Nats'ahts'à' gwihk'iighai' vaagweech'in kwaa goodlit vàràhnyàa,
Aii vanaldaii kwàa.
Googàa aii dinjii aii vaagweech'in kwaa ts'à' aii,
Vigii aii va'at naii khaihɬee ts'à' nijùk geedàa.
Neegihiidal kwaii datthak neegiihan'ee gooràhnyàa. [10]
Akhai' aii va'at aii, dinjik nigiiɬ'in gooràhnyàa.
"Aah, dinjik nitsii vijì' nitsii reh."[3]
Khaiits'à' gòonɬii dee'.
Aii gwik'it'ôonch'yàa aii gwiizhìt reh.
"Aii ts'à' dinjik choo viji' choo gòonɬii," vaihnyàa aii, [15]
Neeɬ'in ts'à' t'ee.
Aii dakai' aii hàa gwaandak, vàràhnyàa.
Aii ts'à' aii veeghaii,
"Niighit kwaa gwa'àn gwats'à' shihiin'ee ts'à'" aii,
Jyàa yàhnyàa vàràhnyàa. [20]
Aii ts'à' t'ee gwik'it'iiyàh'in ts'à',
Łyâa niinghit kwaa, tr'aɬ gòonlii ts'à' niinghit kwaa yeeniinzhii ts'à'
    t'ee,
"Zhit k'ii'àn vats'à' k'į' niinchii ts'à' aii, oohaɬdak," yàhnyàa,
    vàràhnyàa.
Aii vaagweech'in kwaa aii.

Aii ts'à' gwik'it'iiyiinlik. [25]

Ts'à' yikk̠'į' k'ii'àn yats'à' łyaa niintin gwiizhìt k'iinji' jyàa niint'aii
   yełtsaii,

K'iinji' jyàa t'iiyàhthan gwiizhìt.

Yik̠'į' yats'à' k'igwaa'ee łaa niintin ts'à' hee yuunahdak, vàràhnyàa.

Aii dinjii.

Akhai' yiłdàii, yaandàii vàràhnyàa. [30]

Yiłdàii vàràhnyàa.

K'į' zhyaa vats'à' k'igwaa'naii k'it'iizhik vàràhnyàa.

Gwiizhìk hee adan aii yaandàii vàràhnyàa.

Dinjii aii.

"Łyâa gwinzii vadhaalch'ii tth'ak," vàràhnyàa. [35]

Yàhnyàa vàràhnyàa.

Gaa niighit kwaa ts'à' yaandàii reh.

Aii ts'à' zhyaa,

"Dhahdai' kwaa t'inch'yàa," yàhnyàa,

Ts'à' yee'at dakneet'ii yeełnąįį, vàràhnyàa. [40]

Aii dakai' t'ah'ìn.

Aii ts'à' it'ee reh,

Digii naii ts'ee hoozhii ts'à' ree.

Aii naii teeneegwiłjik ts'à' reh.

Aii dinjik aii ts'à', haazhii gooyaaghàt t'aihnyàa aii akhoonyaa,
   vàràhnyàa. [45]

Dinjii aii.

Akhai' yuunyaa ts'à' digii naii ee'vàn reh.

Aii dinjik aii ts'à' haazhii aii ts'à' reh.

Datthak łàa khadiiyiint'ùu, vàràhnyàa.[4]

Aii ts'à' geh'àt van ch'ii'ee jeiinch'yàa gwinyàa. [50]

Nijùk gahaajil goovaandaii kwaa ts'à' t'ee zhyaa reh.

Nangwinjir gwa'ànhee zhyaa neech'idzaha'àk gaa reh.

Digii naii chan nehdeedan'àn vàràhnyàa.

Aii ts'à' t'ee, nijin yek'eehaandal kwaa gòo'aii,

Izhit gwits'à' hee aii dinjik datthak niinlii łee vàràhnyàa. [55]

Aii tr'ìnjàa.

Aii vigii naii gwintłò'o tee gwintsii kwaa vàràhnyàa.

Aii ts'à' aii dinjik *datthak* nijin vanvee hee,

Naahchii izhik hee.

Ch'agaihk'it gwachoô hee yeenjit gwiłtsaii ts'à' deeyaat'ùu,
   vàràhnyàa. [60]
Akwats'à aii dinjii t'aihnyàa aii zhyaa reh,
Nangwinjir gwà'àn heezhyaa neech'a dzaha'àk hàa jyàa dii'in hàa
   gohch'it daajii li'?
Jyàa diinch'yàa reh.
Akwat nideedaan'ii vàràhnyàa,
Gwiizhik chan, [65]
Ya'ghà' ch'aghwaa chan atthat vàràhnyàa.
Niikhyuk yaah'ìn kwàa,
Ts'à' tii'in t'iràhnyàa dahłii?
Aii ts'à' aii, ch'aghwaa kwaii atthat ts'à' reh,
Yeendaa dee'àn. [70]
Aah, ch'agaihk'it gwachoo gwiłtsaii aii datthak ts'à' reh.
Dinjik t'ahtsii datthak deedhit'uu ch'ik'eh kwaii gàa reh.
Gwinzii ch'aga'àa gooràhnyàa.
Gwiizhìk reh, ch'aghwaa dinjik ghwaa datthak atthat ts'à' reh.
Akhai' reh, gwizhik aii dinjii t'aihnyàa reh. [75]
Zhyaa ch'ii'àn neech'adzeeha'àk akhai' reh.
Dzaa zhat, chųų zhit zhyaa taanjìk reh, vàràhnyàa.
Aii ts'à' kwat zhyaa van k'it'iinch'yàa vee k'it t'oônch'yàa izhìk ree,
Ch'iindaa ch'idzee'aa akhai' taanjik ts'à' ree,
Zhìk gwa'àn neehaandak akhai' zhree łyâa van k'it vaat'iiyinch'yàa,
   vàràhnyàa. [80]
Aii dinjii aii gineenlyàa vàràhnyàa.
Mèdicìne màn niłii vàràhnyàa.
Aii dinjii.
Aii ts'à' tee, akhai' reh, gweenyaa zhyaa reh.
Ts'ałvit reh, [85]
Yahts'à' teedhivii łee vàràhnyàa.
Aii ts'à' t'ee yahts'à' teedheevii ts'à' t'ee.
Ch'iindaa jyàa diizhìk ts'à' reh.
"Shakat deedhiinkhaii," yàhnyàa, vàràhnyàa.
Gwik'it t'ee yiinlik ts'à' ree ch'iindaa yàa. [90]
Nehts'eenvii vàràhnyàa.
Nehts'eenvii ts'à' reh.
Gehdaa niighit kwaa jeench'yàa ts'à' yaachiinzhii, vàràhnyàa.

Aii ts'à' ge'hndâa hee yaahaaneevii akhai' reh.

"Gwintsal reh, vaagweech'in," vàràhnyàa. [95]

Yu'aakat akhai' hee,

"Jyàa dôonch'yàa?" yàhnyàa, vàràhnyàa.[5]

Aii ts'à' chan hee yaa chineezhii vàràhnyàa.

Gehndâa hee yaa kheekiitthaii, vàràhnyàa.

"Juk izhik yu'?" yàhnyàa khai'. [100]

Zhit datthak kwat zhyaa *gwintł'òo* vahgweech'in naanaiin vàràhnyàa.

Vindee gohłii t'inch'yàa tsal gaa kwaa vàràhnyàa.

It'ee datthak gwaah'in o'.

Aii ts'à' t'ee reh, yeendak teeghai' yahtr'ineevii ts'à' t'ee.

Yakat diineezhii ts'à' reh, [105]

Ya'ghà' nankat reh.

Neehidik gwizhik ts'ałvit yeendaa tr'ineevii gwinyàa.

Vagweech'in ts'à' reh.

Aii ts'à' t'ee,

It'ee goovankantii, vàràhnyàa. [110]

'An jyàa dii'in, *roll* ahtsii k'it t'ii'in ts'à',

'An łeehaa ts'à' jyàa dii'in, akhai' reh.

Aii vàn choh vee dii'in, t'igiinjil łee vàràhnyàa.[6]

Aii vàn zhyaa jeiinch'yàa oondit vanvee,

Oondit ch'ahgaii k'it gwachoo gwił'ą̀į̀ łee yik'yaanjik vàràhnyàa. [115]

Aii ts'à' t'ee, it'ee gwats'à' hàazhii aii yik'į' chan oonjik, vàràhnyàa,
    t'aihnyàa.[7]

Aii va'at aii.

Yik'į' chan tee gwiłjik oo'at akhaiiyuunyaa aii zhit hee,

Dik'ì' keehaandak hàa kantii gàa,

Hiłjii yàandàii. [120]

Akhai' aii yik'į' aii ts'à' teegwiłjik łee vàràhnyàa.

Aii ts'à' t'ee, yeegooveegoh'ik neezhii ts'à' ree.

Ch'adan ch'ii'ee ts'aii hee goots'à'.

Niikhyuk kwaa niinzhii ts'à' oo'àn goovaa'in ts'à' t'ee,

Neetł'eedeedii ts'à' t'ee. [125]

Oo'àt gwa'àn gwats'à' vagweech'in kwaa adaa'ii ts'à' chidzee'aa,
    vàràhnyàa.

Akhai' reh,

Vaagweech'in kwaa gwinjik ch'idzee'aa,

Vaagweech'in kwaa ideeltsàii reh.

Yits'à' ch'idzee'aa, vàràhnyàa. [130]

Akhai', ch'aghwaa atthat reh yagha' chii'ee nich'idziin'aii vàràhnyàa.

Aii zhik daii 'ee.

"Sha'at" ginyaadài'ee,

"Tr'ìnjàa" ginyàa gooràhnyàa.

Neeghit daii gwich'in naii. [135]

"Tr'ìnjàa łyâa chǫǫ eenjit shidaiingaii," yàhnyàa, vàràhnyàa.

Ya'ghà' aii jidii dachanch'ik vàràhnyàa aii.

Chǫǫ giizhìt dinii giiyaa'ii reh.

Aii ahtsit ts'à' yeetthan van ts'à' k'igwaa' naii, vàràhnyàa.

[Aii] tr'ìnjàa. [140]

Va'at reh.

Gwiizhìk reh, zhat jyànch'yàa, vàràhnyàa.

Vagweech'in kwaa ts'à' zhyaa zhat dhidii vàràhnyàa.

It'ee, chan łyâa niighyuk hiłjii vàràhnyàa.

Niinzhuk hiłjii, vàràhnyàa. [145]

Aii dachan k'ik vàràhnyàa aii,

Chehtsi' yizhilii.[8]

Chǫǫ vizhìt tah'ìn.

Aii ts'à' chehtsi' yizhilii aii ts'à' t'ee,

Chehtsi' t'at yiłtsaii vàràhnyàa. [150]

Aii gohch'it dee ch'iikyaa chǫǫ neekàa vàràhnyàa.

Chǫǫ hàa needyaa vàràhnyà'a.

Aii zhyaa yantł'iintrat vàràhnyàa.

Akhai' yaah'ìn,

Akhai' reh, yantł'iintrat ts'à' zhyaa gii chǫǫ zhyaa chehtsi' t'at iłtsaii
      t'ah'ìn łee ts'à' reh. [155]

Ya'ghà' tth'àn atthat gwats'à' teenahozhraa vàràhnyàa.

Chehtsi' heenjyàa yuunyàa dahłee.

Akhai' aii izhit jyànch'yàa ts'à' tth'àn atthat gwiizhìt hee reh.

Ya'ghà' reh, aii dinjik ghwaa atthat reh.[9]

Akhai' aii ch'ihlak ahtsi' hàa reh, yihchiitth'àn iłkhàa vàràhnyàa. [160]

Zhat dee'àn zhat nat'aa'naii,

Akwat t'ee reh, łyâa yiiłkhwaii reh.

Aii ch'aghwaa hàa yihchiitth'àn gwintł'òo iłkhàa ts'à' reh,

Oo'àn t'eeheelnaii vàràhnyàa.

Aii tr'iinin naii jyàa dahahyàa kwaa gàa, [165]
Dagahan jyàa gĭinlii.
Izhik geh'àn dik'į' zhrih tee neegwiłjik ts'à' t'ee.[10]
Nijin gwa'àn dinjii t'inch'yàa reh.
Gwats'à' haazhii vàràhnyàa.
Aah! Łyâa gohłii t'iinch'yàa tsal gàa kwaa ts'à' reh.[11] [170]
Jyàa diinch'yàa ts'à' zhyaa goołeehaashii ąįį, vàràhnyàa.
Tr'iinin naii.
Gwiizhìt dinjik datthak giin'àl ts'à' t'ee.
Deegaa jii łi'?
Angadlit dahłii? [175]
Aii akodagoovahah'yàa kwaa gaa ya'ghà',
Digiti' aii eenjit dagahan naii jyàa giinlii aii geh'àn jyàadagooviinlik
      gooràhnyàa.
Dàgahàn jyàa giinlii kwaa ji' jyàa goveeheelyàa kwàa.[12]
Nijin gwa'àn dinjii t'inch'yàa hee, gwats'à' tr'iinzhii ts'à' t'ee reh.
Izhit gwa'àn dinjii naii hàa t'inch'yàa dhidlit. [180]
Aii juu akhàiiyuunyaa vaihnyaa aii,
Goovankee neegwàraa'ya' googàa kwaa gooràhnyàa.
Dalàk naii tee neezhii aii tthak ts'à' giiyeenjit shoo dhidlit kwaa ts'à'
      zhyaa.
Neegoogą̀ąyà', googàa kwaa gooràhnyàa.
Aii t'ahnyàa. [185]
Aii ts'à' tee, it'ee reh.
Ako' t'ee zhreh chat vagwandak daanaa'ài'.
James Gilbert: *Nothing more.*

Blind Man and the Loon (English Translation)

Maggie Gilbert, Arctic Village

Recorded by Craig Mishler at Arctic Village, April 23, 1973
Translated by Caroline Tritt-Frank and Kenneth Frank
Edited by Craig Mishler
Gwich'in text begins on p. 71.

Story of the Blind Man and the Loon

That man you're referring to had a family, they say, I'm saying.
And that man had a wife,
But he was blind.
Even so, they were a nomadic family, they say.
That's what they say about them. [05]
Just exactly how they say he became blind,
I don't recollect.
But wherever that blind man went,
His kids and his wife went with him.
They all traveled around together, and they led him, they say about
    them. [10]
And then, his wife and all of them saw a moose, they say.
"Aah, there's a big moose with big antlers" [his wife told him].
It was during the hunting months of autumn.
It seems as though it was like that, during that time.
"So take me closer to the big moose with the big antlers," he told her. [15]
They spotted that moose.
So she told her husband about it, they say.
Right close there beside him,
"Lead me to it over there."
That's what he said to her, they say. [20]
So she did what he wanted her to do.
It wasn't far, but there was lots of brush, so she brought him closer to it.
"Take this arrow and point it straight at the moose," he said, they say.
That blind man.
So she did it. [25]
She pointed the arrow right straight at it
While he was drawing back the bow.

And he shot the moose, they say.
That man.
So then he knows he shot it with his arrow, they say. [30]
He shot it with his arrow, they say.
It's just like the arrow disappeared into it, they say.
Meanwhile he knows that he shot it with his arrow, they say.
That man.
"I really heard it hit," they say. [35]
That's what he said to her, they say.
He knows it's not very far.
But then right there,
"You did not shoot it over there," she said to him.
She threw him upside down real hard, they say. [40]
She did that to her husband.
And so that's it.
She went back to her kids.
She gathered them up.
So then she took her kids and walked over to that moose, they say. [45]
That man—
She left him and went over there with her children,
And so they walked over to that moose.
And then she cut it all up, they say.
There was a lake right by this man, so they say. [50]
He didn't know where they went.
There was nothing else to do,
And so he just crawled around, they say.
She was keeping her children quiet, they say.
Then she took all the moose meat to a place where he wouldn't hear
    her, they say. [55]
That woman.
Her children were very small, they say.
Then she carried *all* that moose meat down by the lake shore,
And put it there.
Then she made a big drying rack and cut it all up, they say. [60]
That man I am talking about
Was crawling all over the wilderness, wondering where he was.
That's the way it was.

She was trying to keep quiet, they say.
Also meanwhile, [65]
They say she was crushing the moose bones.
She did not see him for quite some time,
So maybe that is why she was doing it?
So she was crushing those meat bones
Over that way. [70]
Ah, she built a very large drying rack,
And she put all the moose meat and fat on it, to dry.
They were sure eating good, they say.
She was crushing all the meat bones.
Meanwhile, as that man I am talking about [75]
Was crawling around all over the wilderness,
His hand went into the water, they say.
It was on the shore of a lake.
And then while he was crawling around, his hand went into the water.
And it really seemed like it was a lake to him, they say. [80]
That man was a dreamer, they say.
He was a *medicine man*, they say.
That man.
And then, meanwhile, swimming straight toward him,
An arctic loon, [85]
Came right up to him, they say.
And then it swam right up to him.
And then the loon turned around and faced the lake.
"Get up on top of me," it said to him, they say.
He did that, and the loon turned and swam out. [90]
So the loon turned and swam out there, they say.
It swam out with him.
And then it dove under the water, they say.
Then he came up out of the water not far from where he first dove in.
"I can see a little bit," they say. [95]
So the loon asked him,
"How about now?" it asked him, they say.
And then he dove in the water with him once again, they say.
He came back up a little farther away, they say.
"How is it now?" it asked him. [100]

He could see everything *very* clearly, they say.
And nothing at all was wrong with his eyes, they say.
Because now he saw everything.
So then he went by the shore and got off the loon,
Right on the land. [105]
While he was looking around,
That loon started to swim away, they say.
And so then he could see.
And so,
Now he started to look around for his family, they say. [110]
He was going forward, little by little, rolling over and over.
So he was going further along, tracking them down.
They were by the shore of a big lake, they say.
And across the lake by the shore line,
He saw that his wife had a huge drying rack, they say. [115]
But she had already taken his arrows from where she had left him,
    they say, I'm saying.
That wife of his.
She took his arrows from the place where she left him.
He was groping around for his arrows, but
He knew they were gone. [120]
But she took all his arrows, they say.
Then he hid himself from them.
He came back around to a different place.
And then he pretended he still couldn't see.
So he got back down on the ground. [125]
That blind man started crawling toward her, they say.
And then,
He was crawling back.
He pretended he was still blind.
He was crawling toward her, they say. [130]
Back up to where she was crushing the femur bones, they say.
Back in those days,
When they wanted to say "my wife,"
They would just say "woman," they say.
Those old-time Gwich'in. [135]
"Woman, I'm really thirsty for water," he said to her, they say.

Right there was a wooden dish, they say,

That they used for drinking water.

She quickly grabbed that dish and hurried off toward the lake shore,
    they say.

That woman. [140]

That wife of his.

Meanwhile, he just stayed put, they say.

They say he just sat there pretending that he couldn't see.

O.K. now, she was really gone for quite some time,

Gone for a *long, long* time, they say. [145]

That wooden dish, they say,

She filled it with water bugs.

She also put water in it.

And so she filled it up with those water bugs.

Making the water thick with them, they say. [150]

She was finally coming back with the water, they say,

She was bringing the water, they say.

And she quickly gave it to him, they say.

And then he saw her.

And he was looking in that bowl and saw that it was thick with water
    bugs. [155]

And then she quickly went back over to where she was crushing the
    meat bones, they say.

She just assumed he would drink those water bugs.

While she was there pounding those bones.

Then right over there he grabbed one of the moose's leg bones, the
    femur.[13]

And he hit her over the head with it, they say, [160]

She fell down right there and was killed,

While she was pounding those leg bones for grease.

He hit her head so hard

That she fell over quickly, they say.

He wasn't going to do that to the children, but [165]

They were helping their mother [work against him].

So that's why he took his bow and arrows.

And went to where some other people were living.

He went over there, they say.

81

Aah! There was really nothing wrong with him. [170]

He left them like that, they say.

His children, that is.

So they ate up all the moose meat.

But where are those children now?

Maybe they're all dead? [175]

He wouldn't have done this to them [i.e., left them to starve to death],

But they say he did it because they went against their father and helped their mother.

If they were not partners with her, he wouldn't have done this to them.

He came to a place where there were some other people.

He was now with these people. [180]

Yet they never even looked for those children

Whom he left behind, they say.

He returned back to his own relatives, but they were not at all happy with him.

And they never did see any of his children again.

That's what is said about it. [185]

And so that's it.

That's the end of his story.

JG: *Nothing more.*

Analysis and Commentary

Robin Ridington has observed that the best Americanist writing is that which is "multi-vocal, reportorial, and reflexive" (1996, 487). Maggie Gilbert's twelve-minute oral performance of the story of the Blind Man and the Loon includes all of the above, but it is especially multivocal. It becomes simultaneously traditional and personal. Its artistic and stylistic complexity as representative of Regional Group G (the moose group) may be at least partly understood and appreciated by reflecting on the three following elements: the voices of the characters, the voice of tradition, and Maggie's own voice. As Maggie's virtual audience, we must make the attempt, in the words of Paul Zolbrod (1995), of "reading the voice."

The Voices of the Characters

First, we hear the voices of characters or actors in the story: the blind man, his wife, and the loon. Their words may be called spoken dialogue or reported speech, transcribed with quotation marks. For example, in line 12 we read: "'Aah, dinjik nitsii viji' nitsii reh. / Aah, there's a big moose with large antlers,' [his wife told him]." Such dialogue seems to have been carefully memorized, and it is restricted to brief statements. The only characters without voices are the blind man's children and the blind man's relatives. Presumably they have voices, but we never hear them.

The ability of the loon to talk to the blind man [lines 89, 97] tells us that this is a distant time when the world was quite different than it is now. The great Gwich'in storyteller Johnny Frank, who knew Maggie quite well, reminds us of this world view in his story "Denaa Dài' Dinjii Zhuu / The Early Days Indians":

Nobody knows how long there have been men on this earth.
Even the small animals that were alive back then were people, they say.
The wolverines, the wolves, and the brown bears were all people.
Even the foxes were people.
The fish in the water were people, they say . . .
A human could talk back and forth to the fishes and to the birds.
And they in turn could talk to humans.
In the beginning, they say, there was really only one language.
(Mishler 2001, 18–21)

The romantic and comforting idea that loons are closely bonded friends with humans prevails across cultures. The loons in the Blind Man and the Loon tale are quite anthropomorphic across the spectrum. "Shakat deedhinkhaii / Get up on top of me," the loon says to him in Gwich'in [line 89]. "Alingnaqvaa-il' elpeni! / Alingnaqvaa, my goodness, look at you!" it declares in Central Yup'ik (Blue 2007, 10–11). "Aqunnut uvunga ikilaurit / Get on my back," it says while extending a friendly invitation in Inuktitut (Kublu 1999, 165). "Ch'a t'ent'an dit? / What are you doing?" it says to him in Dena'ina (Kalifornsky 1991, 147). From variant to variant, the loon speaks to the blind man in Gwich'in, Yup'ik, Inuktitut, Dena'ina, English, and numerous other tongues.

The dialogue and turn-taking between these characters help generate much of the tale's dramatic tension. This understanding is reinforced when we recognize that the Canadian Gwich'in have turned several of their traditional tales into bilingual radio readings, with different elders performing the speech of characters within those tales. The resulting collaboration has been broadcast in a series of hour-long programs on CBC Radio One.[14]

The Voice of Tradition

But the voices of the human and animal characters are not the only voices we hear in Maggie's story. Others are heard speaking in the background — her own ancestors. The story is loaded with formal ethnopoetic devices, especially with respect to reporting speech. Reporting speech is speech about speech, and in Maggie's narrative, reporting speech is central. It not only highlights the reported speech spoken by characters in the story but also signifies to the listener that the story, or gwandak, is very traditional, a genre defined by continuous retelling. Reporting speech figures prominently in the design and architecture of the story.

"The Blind Man and the Loon" is not Maggie's own personal story, as she reminds us over and over with the line-endings translated in the third person as "they say." But just who are "they"? "They" represents what I call the social voice, the collective voice of the ancestors who passed the story down to her. We could also call it the voice of antiquity. Because Maggie herself was not a witness to the events described, her continuous use of "they say" validates the authenticity and authority of the story. We also hear this voice in many of Johnny Frank's stories. "They say" is an indirect way of reporting events or speech acts. It traditionalizes and tells the listener, "This is not something I made up or saw or heard myself."

This cue, "they say," is a reporting speech idiom that has approximately the same function rhetorically and semantically in a wide corpus of tale texts recorded in Native American languages. It is an idiom found not only in Gwich'in, but also Dogrib, Chipewyan, Koyukon, Beaver, Tanaina, Ingalik, Navajo, Chiricahua, Mescalero, and Jicarilla Apache (virtually the entire Athabaskan family) as well as in Ojibwa, Maidu, Yuchi, Haida, Nootka, Kwakiutl, Crow, Aleut, and Iñupiaq, among others (see Mishler 1981).

As Dell Hymes has noticed, "When a tradition uses a quotative element ('they say'), its presence marks a verse" (2003, 98). In Gwich'in this reporting speech is indicated by the quotative, -*nyàa*, which manifests itself in the following forms: *nyàa* (he or she said), *ginyàa* (so they say), *gwinyàa* (that's what they say), *yàhnyàa* (he or she says to him or her; he or she is talking about him or her), *vaihnyàa* (he or she said to him or her), *vàràhnyàa* (that's what they say about him or her), *gavaihnyàa* (somebody said that's the way it was), *t'igwinyàa* (so they say), *gooràhnyàa* (so they say about them), and *t'aihnyàa* (I'm talking about).

These quotative forms substitute for the quotation marks writers depend on to create dialogue. The anthropological linguists Silver and Miller (1997, 38) insist, "If there is a single obligatory evidential in a language, it is almost always the quotative, which discriminates hearsay from eye-witness reports and is a very common feature of American Indian languages."

For Maggie, these forms are often doubled up, as in lines 1 and 116: *vàràhnyàa t'aihnyaa*; or lines 20, 23, 36, 97, and 136: *yàhnyàa vàràhnyàa*. Such forms have a marked rhythmic and distinctly poetic effect, since *vàràhnyàa* appears at the end of nearly every line, or every other line (a total of fifty-seven times). As I have argued elsewhere (Mishler 1981), "they say" figures as a steady rhythmic element that sustains two contrapuntal melodic lines (i.e., the sequence of narrated action and the reported speech of the characters). On this point I have to disagree with Karl Kroeber when he generalizes that "myths never depend on the rhythmic patternings which for us distinguish poetry" (1998, 147). Reporting speech provides many of those patternings.

Lines 29–34 are especially striking, in that the abrupt "Aii dinjii" is framed symmetrically with its inverse, "Dinjii aii," and all four of the lines in between them end with *vàràhnyàa*. Then too there are any number of lines (2, 19, 24, 117, 146, 181) that symmetrically begin and end with "Aii/aii".

Another rhythmic and stylistic device is the interjection *reh*. Maggie often pairs *reh* with *t'ee* or *ts'à'*, as in *t'ee reh* or *ts'à' reh*. These words have no referential meaning, but they do contribute rhythmically, and they help to mark line endings. Vàràhnyàa is pronounced by Maggie and most Gwich'in storytellers with the first syllable silent, so that the line endings t'ee reh or ts'à' reh alternating with -*ràhnyàa* produce a pleasing echo-like vocal pattern. This pattern is highlighted by low-high and low-low vowel tones, as in these lines (163–64):

Aii ch'aghwaa khàa yehkiitth'àn gwintł'òo ełkhàa ts'à' reh.
Oo'àn t'eehee ilnaii vàràhnyàa.

The transitional phrase *Aii ts'à'* (And then or So then), which marks the beginning of so many lines, appears twenty-six times and is doubled up twice, in lines 48 and 149. Since Gwich'in is a tonal language, the redundancy of such line beginnings, line endings, and tonal patterns draws us into their poetics, even though they are not as regular or predictable in their pairings as rhymed couplets or iambs. My own aesthetic appreciation of these forms derives much more from listening to the recording than from reading the transcription. Indeed, I encourage listening to the story on my companion web page, http://www.uaf.edu/loon/audio/.

Finally, Maggie documents the ethnography of speaking Gwich'in in the section where the blind man coldly addresses his wife as "woman" (tr'ìnjàa) instead of "my wife" (sha'at) (lines 133–34). This may indeed have been a traditional form of address, but in the context of the story, it is also a clue that the blind man's marriage has soured. Any terms of endearment are vacated when he realizes what his wife has done to him. Once again, there is a doubling up of reporting speech: *ginyàa gooràhnyàa*. It is repetition controlled with variation.

Maggie's Own Voice

Maggie's own contribution and imprint on the tale is distinguished by her interstitial reflexive asides, questions, and explanations, where she directly interacts with the listener and reveals her own inner thoughts. There are six instances of these:

1. LINE 1: "Aii dinjii t'iiyàhnyàa aii, *family* leii [di'ii] vàràhnyàa, t'aihnyàa, / That man you're referring to had a family, they say, I'm saying." In this line we hear both the voice of tradition (vàràhnyàa) and Maggie's own voice (t'aihnyàa), beautifully juxtaposed at the end of the line. This same juxtaposition emerges again in line 116: "Aii ts'à' t'ee, it'ee gwats'à' hàazhii aii yik'i̱' chan oonjik, vàràhnyàa, t'aihnyàa. / But she had already taken his arrows from where she had left him, they say, I'm saying."

2. LINES 6–7: "Nats'ahts'à' gwihk'iighai' vaagweech'in kwaa goodlit vàràhnyàa, /Aii vanaldaii kwàa." "Just exactly how they say he became blind, / I don't recollect." This shows Maggie's own honesty and humility as a storyteller—admitting she doesn't remember the story perfectly. There are some missing details and motives, as we find out in her other asides.

3. LINE 12: "'Aah, dinjik nitsii vijì' nitsii reh.' / 'Aah, there's a big moose with big antlers.'" With this quotation from the blind man's wife or possibly one of his children, Maggie is discreetly elaborating and expanding on the traditional story line. We know this immediately because of the conspicuous absence of vàràhnyàa, the reporting speech we would expect to hear at the end of the line. This deft stylistic touch is only evident to Gwich'in-speaking listeners. See endnote 3.

4. LINE 61: "Akwats'à aii dinjii t'aihnyàa aii zhyaa reh, / That man I am talking about." Here Maggie breaks the frame of the story and briefly reminds us of her role as narrator. Her self-reference injects an informal, conversational tone. The same thing happens again in line 75.

5. LINES 67–68: "Niikhyuk yaah'ìn kwaa, / Ts'à' tii'in t'iràhnyàa dahłii?" "She did not see him for quite some time, / So maybe that is why she was doing it?" This question directly engages the listener. Although the wife wants to conceal her location from her husband by moving the meat away from him and keeping her children quiet [lines 54–55, 64], she carelessly gives herself away by pounding loudly on the moose femur bones to extract the grease. According to Kenneth Frank there was a traditional tool used by the Gwich'in just for this purpose. It was a stone mallet, made by lashing a stone with babiche to a wooden handle. The leg joints of moose and caribou were pounded for bone grease. All of this is reminiscent of another Gwich'in tale, the story of Wolf and Wolverine, in which Wolverine overhears Wolf and Wolf's mother breaking up caribou leg bones (McKennan 1965, 126–27).

In Walter Titus's Lower Tanana telling of the story (Titus 1972), the sounds that give the wife away come from her pounding on dry meat to soften it. During the performance Titus even pounds dramatically on the table with his hand to imitate what she was doing. But here in these lines Maggie attempts to understand the motivation and thoughts of the wicked wife. She points up the inconsistency of her noisy pounding and her earlier attempts to remain quiet to avoid sharing the moose meat with her husband. The result is a bit of dry humor.

This sharp ambient noise from the wife's pounding parallels the soft thud of the blind man's arrow hitting the moose in lines 31–35. From his past experience he knows the sound of an arrow hitting a game animal. This alerts him to the fact that his wife is misleading him. The sound of bone crushing in turn alerts him to where she is.

Such acoustic, auditory elements add an important dimension to the story, somewhat reminiscent of *Sir Gawain and the Green Knight* when the Green Knight is whetting his axe on a grindstone: "What! It made a rushing, ringing din, rueful to hear." In the wilderness, the Gwich'in are trained to listen for such sounds as arrows hitting their targets or the distant crushing of bones. These sounds speak truth and identity. The story is as much about hearing as it is about eyesight.

6. LINES 174–75: "Deegaa jii łi'? / Angadlit dahłii?" "But where are those children now? / Maybe they're all dead?" Here Maggie injects her own curiosity into the story, perhaps a curiosity that has lingered since the first time the story was told to her. She seems to acknowledge a loose end in the narrative—the blind man's children are left to fend for themselves even though they are small and young (line 57). She raises the ethical question of whether the children should pay for the crimes of their mother, apparently by starving to death.

Considering their tender age, Maggie may be suggesting, with a touch of ambiguity, that the blind man was too harsh toward them. He spares them from violent revenge but then abandons them to their own fates because "they were helping their mother" (line 166). The relatives he goes to seem despondent or angry: "but they were not at all happy with him" (line 183). Perhaps the wicked wife is not the only one who contributes to the destruction of the family.

English Words

Maggie's own voice is also visible and audible in her use of a few pro-vocative English words. These words season the text, like a sprinkling of salt or pepper. She rarely spoke English during my visits, but clearly, she had some grasp of it. There are just a few English words in the story, and most of these are situated "in the moment" for emphasis. In Kenny

Thomas Sr.'s Tanacross version, told primarily in English, it is the Tanacross words that are contrastive (Thomas 2005, 203–5).

In line 1 of Maggie's story, for example, the word *family* is stressed. The strength of family ties through kinship rights and obligations is a central theme of the story. The wife's multiple betrayals are not only harmful to her husband; they eventually destroy the entire family.

Then in line 82, Maggie tells us the blind man is a "*medicine man*." This identifier is critical in that it tells us he has a special relationship to the loon, his spiritual protector or helper, to whom he dreams (see McKennan 1965, 78–83; Teit 1921, 227n2). In Gwich'in spirit helpers are called *yits'oochii*. The species identified in Maggie's version is *ts'ałvit* (*Gavia arctica*), the arctic loon, but in Kenny Thomas's Tanacross version, the species is *ah'aala*, the common loon. I discuss the significance of shamanism in the tale in chapter 7.

Then, in line 111, *roll* is used to describe the man's body language and behavior after his eyesight is restored. He rolls onto the shore before he can stand up and walk back to his wife's camp. It is not readily apparent why Maggie chose to use this English word.

Finally, in line 188, James Gilbert uses the English words *Nothing more* to announce to me that the story is finished. Following only nonverbal clues and not knowing very much Gwich'in at the time (1973), I was not fully aware of Maggie's formulaic closing, "Aii ts'à' tee, it'ee reh" (line 186), marking the boundary of the performance frame, so James spoke English as a quick prompt for me to turn off the tape recorder.

Besides using English, Maggie emphasizes a few other words by enunciating them forcefully and loudly in Gwich'in. These are also shown in italics. For example, the word *datthak* in line 58 and *gwintł'oo* in line 101 receive this treatment, as do *It'ee* in line 144 and *Niighyuk* in line 145.

Structures

Maggie's tale may be seen as having a seven-part dramatic structure. We can think of these in terms of scenes. Part 1 (lines 1–10) establishes the principal characters, the blind man's status, and their nomadic way of life. Part 2 (lines 11–37) describes their subsistence moose hunt. Part 3 (lines 38–74) delineates the wife's first betrayal and abandonment. Part 4 (lines 75–108) portrays the loon's diving down and healing, restoring the blind man's eyesight. It also alerts us to the blind man's special status as a medicine man. Part 5 (lines 109–31) consists of the blind man's return and reunion with his family. Part 6 (lines 132–58) is the wife's second betrayal with the polluted drinking water. And Part 7, the conclusion and denouement (lines 159–87), depicts the blind man's violent revenge and abandonment of his children.

Parts 3 and 6 are in a sense symmetrical, in that we see the wife's disloyalty twice. The first time she lies to her husband and starves him, and the second time she tries to persecute him and make him suffer. Despite the insistence of Dell Hymes (2003, 96) that many Native American oral narratives should be understood as structured by relations of twos and fours or threes and fives, I was not able to discern these relations consistently in Maggie's variant, at least within the present transcription. As we have just seen, however, that does not mean there is any dearth of other ethnopoetic features.

There are two other archival sound recordings of the story in Gwich'in, one from Old Crow told by Ellen Bruce (1980), and one from Tsigehtchic told by Eliza Andre (1974). Both variants have been translated and published (Vuntut Gwitchin First Nation and Smith 2009, 19–20; Heine et al., 2007, 324). It is deeply disappointing, nevertheless, that neither one has been transcribed in Gwich'in to allow a direct comparison with Maggie's version. One major difference in the endings of these tales is that the Andre and Bruce variants have the blind man clubbing and killing his children instead of abandoning them to starve to death, as in the Gilbert variant. At the same time, all three of them, as well as Petitot's nineteenth century variant, solidly belong to Group G: Moose—the Interior Alaska Indian Subtype, as shown in chapter 1 (map 1).[15]

Retrospective

Robert Bringhurst, who has studied Haida storytellers, concludes that "blind mythtellers are figures of myth themselves, of course. They are figures of history too. They are frequent in the record of oral poetry all around the world and of Native North American oral poetry in particular" (1999, 390). Bringhurst draws special attention to the Haida poet Ghandl, recorded by John Swanton, as well as the sightless Chipewyan poet Ekunélyel, interviewed by Émile Petitot, and numerous others, noting that many of them were victims of measles and smallpox, conditions that enabled them to become true "visionaries." Maggie Gilbert certainly belongs to this select group.

In Maggie's verbal art, "voice" has to be recognized as a major organizing principle. The tension and excitement in the story is largely due to its multivocality. Mikhail Bakhtin ([1934] 1981) once reflected on this same phenomenon in his essay "Discourse in the Novel," coining the term *heteroglossia,* the diversity and stratification of languages or voices found within an artistic work. The dialogic voices of the characters, the social voice of tradition, the performer's own first-person voice, and the spice of occasional English words all work in concert to articulate the dramatic structure of Maggie's tale. Ultimately, of course, all of the voices and personas are hers.

CHAPTER FIVE

The Art of the Tale

As noted earlier, the story of the Blind Man and the Loon is widely distributed across Greenland, Canada, and Alaska. Although the tale is just as well known among northern Indians as it is among Eskimos, it is primarily the Inuit or Eskimo subtype that has inspired a remarkable wealth of folk art, including sculptures, prints, sketches, and wall hangings. In chapter 4 I talked about the artistry of the language used to tell the tale through one of its many authentic oral performances, but here I want to explore the great wealth of other art forms inspired by the tale.

Most of the folk art associated with the tale springs from eastern Canadian communities in the territory of Nunavut and the Nunavik region of northern Québec. This is the region associated with Regional Group B oral variants, the Canadian Eskimo oicotype (see chapter 1, map 1). Franz Boas (1888) identified them as the Central Eskimo, but today they are better known as the eastern Inuit, and their language is made up of several dialects of Inuktitut spread over a vast geographic area.

The Visual Arts: Some History

With a set of images, I want to look at how artists have dynamically interpreted specific scenes and themes in the narrative. The panoply of art coming out of the tale stands in a secondary, derivative position to the tale itself (i.e., the tale as oral performance and text) but offers additional ways of reading, hearing, or "seeing" it. In this respect the folk art is reminiscent of illuminated manuscripts from the Middle Ages and the Renaissance. The oldest written variants of the tale hearken back to Greenland in the 1820s, with many internal suggestions that it was developed in antiquity, but as far as art history is concerned, the oldest representations of the tale only go back to northern Canada in the late 1950s and early 1960s.

A conspicuous exception to this pattern is the ink drawing included in Hinrich Rink's redaction of the tale, published in Danish in 1866. Rink does not say who did the drawing but notes that some of his illustrations were designed and engraved on wood "by natives of Greenland." Chief among these woodcut artists was Aron of Kangek (1822–1869), who contributed heavily to Rink's first collection of tales, *Kaladlit okalluktualliait: Kalâdlisut kablunâtudlo* (1859), and to his ethnographic opus, *Danish Greenland: Its People and Its Products* (1877).

The single sketch or woodcut associated with "The Blind Man Who Regained His Sight," included in Rink's *Eskimoiske Eventyr og Sagn* (1866) and its subsequent translation, *Tales and Traditions of the Eskimo* (1875), shows a small boy crawling out of a sod or stone house tunnel to see a ghostly figure standing above him (fig. 15). Presumably this faceless person, who appears to be standing on a polar bear hide, is his abusive mother, stepmother, or grandmother. The sketch artist, who might be Aron of Kangek, is not identified.

Then too, we must mention the commercial art the story inspired in the William Toye and Elizabeth Cleaver (1977) volume, discussed briefly in chapter 2. A full-length essay about Cleaver's fifteen illustrations recognizes *The Loon's Necklace* as one of "the first full-colour picturebooks with identifiable Canadian themes and images" (Saltman and Edwards 2004). Even more insightful is Cleaver's own autobiographical essay, "Idea to Image: The Journey of a Picture Book" (1984), where she traces the development of her book with Toye in considerable detail, from first drawings to the finished work. Excerpts from Cleaver's diary (1984, 163) are instructive and show considerable thought and preparation:

April 15, 1977: I start my research by going to the National Museum of Canada Library in Ottawa, where I discovered variants of the legend. Even though William Toye has done the retelling I will illustrate, I

Fig. 15. Woodcut from Hinrich Rink's *Tales and Traditions of the Eskimo* (1875).

am interested in understanding how the characters are portrayed, and what incidents are important, in other versions. I collect visual material relating to Tsimshian artifacts that I may use in my pictures: totem poles, huts, articles of clothing. During my two-hour bus drive each way between Montreal and Ottawa, I work on an outline for the twenty-four-page picture book.

April 19: I continue my picture research at McCord Museum and its library in Montreal. I consult anthropological journals and books by Diamond Jenness, Franz Boas, Marius Barbeau, and Viola Garfield. I think about my travels in 1969 through the mountains of British

Columbia, by air and by bus and try to recapture the spectacular environment, especially the mountains and the trees.

April 22: I make my first linocut of the loon and try to visualize a cover design.

Artistic Samples

There are many, many examples of folk art inspired by the tale (see listings by artist at the end of this chapter). As noted earlier, most of this art is of Canadian Eskimo/Inuit origin, but there are also some examples from non-Native commercial and fine artists who have been inspired by it, notably Rie Muñoz, Jacques and Mary Regat, and Stefano Vitale, in addition to Elizabeth Cleaver. Dene artists such as Carla Rae Gilday and Robert Sebastian have also contributed significantly to the corpus.

Altogether I have discovered eighty-six artistic works based on the Blind Man and the Loon story, created by no less than fifty-four different artists. Of all the communities where this art has been created, more artists (nine altogether) hail from Cape Dorset, Nunavut, than any other place, making it something of an artistic epicenter. The second-most number, eight, are from Puvirnituq, Nunavik, Québec, only a few hundred miles to the south, and the thirdmost, five, were produced in nearby Inukjuak, Québec.

It is telling that there are at least ten Inuit communities in Canada where artistic works interpreting the story of the Blind Man and the Loon have been created but where no oral or written texts have yet been recorded and published. My hypothesis is that these artistic works reveal the existence of many "invisible variants" still circulating in these communities.

Just as astronomers infer that certain distant stars have unseen exoplanets orbiting them based on the stars' orbital "warp" or "wobble" (a result of gravitational pull), so too must we infer that the following communities which have produced artists and artistic pieces about the Blind Man and the Loon also have the tale circulating in oral tradition: Akulivik, Aujuittuq, Cape Dorset, Hall Beach, Happy Valley, Holman, Kangiqsualujjuaq, Kimmirut, Kuujjuaraapik, and Paulatuk (map 2). Although it is conceivable that Inuit artists in these eleven polar communities learned the story of the Blind Man and the Loon from reading it or from films, it seems more likely that the artistic works coming out of these villages mirror living oral narratives. In short, the research opportunity to document these invisible variants awaits. We now know where to look.

Artistic Categories

To make sense of this diverse collection of art works, I have classified them into ten categories. The first eight categories illustrate actual scenes that occur in oral and written variants. In this sense they are akin to a series of conventional tale traits (see appendix A). That is, the scenes in the art are created and viewed individually, but collectively, they stand for the narrative structure or syntax of the tale. It occurs to me that such a structure could be assembled in an art gallery by bringing together at least one print from each category and hanging them sequentially on a wall, or arranging a linear series of sculptures in a glass case.

However, the ninth category illustrates scenes not actually found in the documented texts but still attributed to them, and the tenth and final category consists of stylized symbolic images which, like those in the ninth category, lie outside of or on the periphery of oral tradition. The works in these latter two categories have their own nonliteral aesthetic sensibilities. In chapter 3, I made the case that the portraits of the storytellers constitute one iconography of the tale. Taken collectively, the artistic works discussed here constitute a second iconography of the tale. Examples are identified according to their numerical listing (or #) as itemized at the end of this chapter.

Category 1

This first group illustrates the blind man shooting the polar bear. Interestingly here, two paintings, those by Rie Muñoz (#16) and one by Kananginak Pootoogook (#14a), show that the bear is not killed by the blind man through the window of the house or igloo but rather outside of it. I know of no narrative variants that describe the killing of the bear from outside of the house, so this art in a sense distorts the narrative. However, in Pootoogook's later depiction of the very same scene (#14d, fig. 20), the blind man is clearly inside the house, and the polar bear is outside climbing up on the roof, closely following the oral and

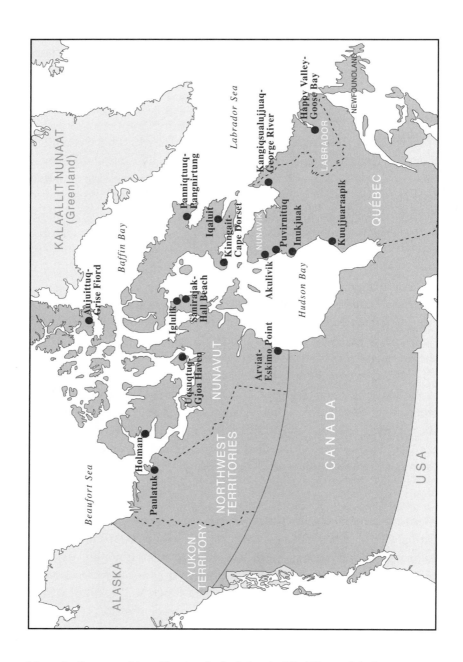

Map 2. Inuit communities with artworks depicting the Blind Man and the Loon.

Fig. 16. Annie Blue, 2009. Photo courtesy of Todd Paris, University of Alaska Fairbanks.

Fig. 17. James and Maggie Gilbert at Arctic Village, April 1973. Photo by Craig Mishler.

Fig. 18. Kenneth and Caroline Frank, editing Maggie Gilbert's Gwich'in text. Anchorage, May 2008. Photo by Craig Mishler.

Fig. 19. Kenny Thomas Sr. in Tanacross, October 30, 2000. Rendering of a video freeze frame taken in performance of "The Blind Man and the Loon." Photo by Craig Mishler.

Fig. 20. *Aulajijakka: Things I Remember #5,* by Kananginak Pootoogook, Cape Dorset. Reproduced with the permission of Dorset Fine Arts.

Fig. 21. *Blind Man and the Loon,* by Jacques and Mary Regat. Bronze, 1992. Photo by Craig Mishler. Reproduced with the permission of the artists.

Fig. 22. *The Loon Gives Lumaq His Sight*, by Germaine Arnaktauyok, Igloolik and Yellow-knife. Etching aquatint, 2003. Reproduced with the permission of the artist.

Fig. 23. *Blindman Sees Loon*, by Robert E. Sebastian, ca. 1970s. Unframed serigraph. Accession #U990.14.836. University of Victoria Art Museum, Victoria BC. Reproduced with permission of the artist and the University of Victoria Art Museum.

Fig. 24. *The Old Man and the Loon*, by Carla Rae Gilday, Yellowknife and Victoria. Acrylic, 2008. Deline Land Corporation. Photo and permission courtesy of the artist.

Fig. 25. *Lumak*, by Davidialuk Alasua Amittuq, Povungnituk/Puvirnituq. Stonecut, 1962. Canadian Museum of Civilization, POV 1962-134. Reproduced with the permission of the Inuit Art Foundation.

Fig. 26. *The Legend of the Blind Boy*, by Toonoo Sharky, Cape Dorset. Green stone, brown stone, ivory and baleen inlay, 1998. National Gallery of Canada. Reproduced with the permission of the artist and Dorset Fine Arts.

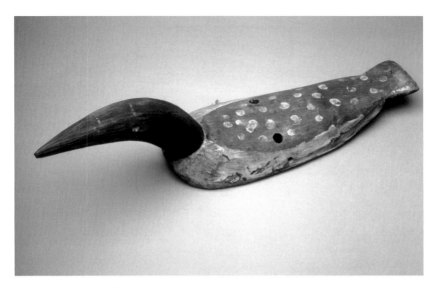

Fig. 27. Old Hamilton loon mask, artist unknown. Collected in 1934. University of Alaska Museum of the North, Fairbanks. Catalogue Number UA 64-7-22. Photo by Barry J. McWayne, courtesy of the Alaska Museum of the North.

Fig. 28. *Blind Man and the Loon*, by Jacques and Mary Regat, Anchorage. Wood bas-relief, n.d. Fairbanks North Star Borough Noel Wien Library. Photo by Clark James Mishler. Reproduced with the permission of the artists.

The
Loon's Necklace
—an Indian Legend

★ *A Film Sponsored by*
THE CANADIAN EDUCATION ASSOCIATION
through the courtesy of
IMPERIAL OIL LIMITED

Fig. 29. *The Loon's Necklace* film pamphlet cover, 1949. Reproduced courtesy of Michal Anne Crawley.

written texts. Pootoogook's early stencil (#14a) represents the oldest (1957–59) print by an Inuit artist of any I have found directly tied to the story. Some other examples of Category 1 include Agnes Nanogak Goose's print (#11a), Stefano Vitale's print (#36), George Aden Ahgupuk's drawing (#51), Davidialuk Alasua Amittuq's ink sketch (#6g), and Aisa Qupiqrualuk's carving (#29a).

Category 2

There is only one instance of this category, which portrays the wicked mother deceiving her blind son while butchering the polar bear. The key work here is a piece by Kananginak Pootoogook called *Aulajijakka (Things I Remember) #4* (#14c), which shows the blind man wandering behind the house with aid of two walking sticks. The artist's caption is: "When the bear died, the mother butchered it, making sure her son wasn't aware. She told her daughter not to tell her brother."

Category 3

This group depicts the blind man being fed secretly by his sister. It is represented only by two carvings made by Aisa Qupiqrualuk of Povungnituk/Puvirnituq, Nunavik, Québec. One is entitled *She brought him food inside her parka,* and the other is titled with a quote from the carver's own text: *"My brother, good dog meat"* (#29b and c). This caption illustrates the sister's deception, hiding from her mother the fact that she is feeding her brother bear meat. Photos of both sculptures have been published in Nungak and Arima (1969, 48–51).

Category 4

This group, interpreted by many artists, shows the blind man diving under water with a loon or loons to restore his eyesight. These images are centrally important because they reveal the all-important healing ritual embodied in the tale, something I want to explore in depth in chapter 7.

Examples of Category 4 are represented by Agnes Nanogak Goose's prints (#11b and c); Germaine Arnaktauyok's stunning dream-like aqua etching (#4, fig. 22); Jacques and Mary Regat's bronze sculpture (#18b, fig. 21); Lukassie Tukalak's print (#20b); Billy Gauthier's sculpture (#28); Simiunie Sivuarapik's sculpture (#47); Patrick Thompson's dramatic outdoor wall mural in Iqaluit (#42); Laszlo Gal's sketch (#52); Silas

Kayakjuak's ivory and antler miniatures (#40a, b, and c); and Nin-geokuluk Teevee's print (#31). Aisa Qupiqrualuk's sculpture (#29d) and Robert E. Sebastian's serigraph *Blindman Sees Loon* (#46, fig. 23) also belong to this group, although they depict the blind man meeting the loon just before or after the dive.

Sebastian, of Hazelton, British Columbia, says he heard the story told in English while he was growing up. He says it is an ancient story that took place at Fraser Lake, during a distant time when it extended all the way to the present townsite of Smithers. As he heard it from a storyteller named Ketlo, the loon talked to the blind man and told him to duck his head under water four times to restore his eyesight. When he did this and could see again, he cried tears of joy. Those tears, shown streaming down his face, fell on the loon's back and became its white markings.

Robert Sebastian is a member of the Wolf Clan of the House of Spookx of the Hagwilget Village First Nation on the Skeena River in northern British Columbia. Although he is Athabaskan, Sebastian studied at the Gitanmaax School of Northwest Coast Indian Art in Hazelton and paints in the Northwest Coast style. This style employs geometric designs such as ovoids, black formlines, and distinctive ink combinations such as red, blue, and black.

The Lukassie Tukalak print *Legend of the Loon that helps the Blind Man See* (see Hessel 2006, 223) is notable in that it illustrates part of the story and tells it simultaneously, via the Inuit syllabic orthography used in Canada. This is also a characteristic present in many of Davidialuk's prints. In translation, this is what Tukalak's syllabics say: "The story of a man: when he heard the loon calling, the man wished that his sight would return. Then the loon came to the man and led him to a lake and told him, 'I will take you diving under the water several times. Let me know when you can breathe no longer and need to return to the surface.' Then the loon asked the man if he could see anything by the huge mountain. The man was able to see a lemming on the mountain, at a great distance from the lake" (Hessel 2006, 223, translator not identified).

Davidialuk Alasua Amittuq's print (#6b, see Finley 1998, 31) shows the blind man upside down in the water with just his feet sticking up.

According to the way Davidialuk tells the tale, which is an anomaly, the loons cure the blind man by holding his legs and dunking him upside down in the water. In nearly all other variants, the blind man holds onto the loon's neck or back while it dives underwater with him.

In the Germaine Arnaktauyok etching (fig. 22), the artist has given us a new perspective on the tale. Although the blind man and the loon are swimming deep underwater, they are also soaring upward, as if flying high through the sky overhead. Their ascent toward the light inspires hope. Arnaktauyok also helps interpret the story by magnifying the size of the loon as compared to the man, thereby giving it supernatural powers. This trait is also present in the Billy Gauthier sculpture and in Jacques and Mary Regat's bronze.

Carla Rae Gilday's acrylic painting *The Old Man and the Loon* (#30, fig. 24), one of the most recently produced artworks to be reviewed as of this writing, shows the blind man diving with the loon in a sequence of seven images. The images are arranged in a clockwise motion to complete a full circle. The painting depicts only one specific scene from the story, but it does so with a sequence of related images, almost like a film strip, with lots of movement. We see the blind man and the loon above and below water at the same time. In the *Northwest Territories Artists' Newsline* the artist says the painting was "inspired by Dene legends told to me by my mother Cindy Kenny-Gilday . . . Although I live far from home on Vancouver Island, painting the legends helps keep me connected to my roots, to the north" (2009, 8). It was purchased by the Deline Land Corporation on Great Bear Lake, Northwest Territories, and is now on display in their building lobby.

Category 5

There is only one known artistic example of this category, so it should not at present be considered part of a group. In many texts we are told that the healed blind man returned to his mother's igloo to find an outstretched bear skin (Malaurie 1985, 101), but only a very few mention that he cut it up in anger (e.g., Boas [1888] 1964, 625). Lypa Pitsiulak and Hanna Akulukjuk's wool tapestry (#17b) illustrates this scene in a way that no other artist has attempted. It is one of a kind.

Category 6

This group visualizes the healed blind man harpooning a beluga or a narwhal with his mother or grandmother attached to the line. Examples of Category 6 include Ekidluak Komoartuk's stencil (#10); Johnnieapik's sculptures (#22a,b); Kiakshuk's prints (#1a,b); Davidialuk Alasua Amittuq's ink sketch (#6i); and Lukassie Tukalak's print (#20a).

The powerful colored stencil by Komoartuk reveals the crux of the story, a betrayal of trust between close kin. The artist has hauntingly titled it *My Mother Lies to Me*. Johnnieapik's sculpture is very naturalistic, a realistic miniaturization. The Kiakshuk prints, *The Legend of Lumiuk* and *Lumiuk and the Whales*, were two of the very first to appear in the modern era, in 1960 and 1961.

Category 7

This group depicts the wicked mother or grandmother being towed into the sea by a beluga or narwhal or walrus right after it is harpooned, hollering for her ulu knife. It follows immediately from the scene depicted in Category 6. From an artistic point of view, this is the most popular and vivid scene in the entire story. Category 7 is richly exemplified by several prints. See for example, the prints by Daniel Inukpuk (#13), and Peter Boy Ituukala (#34). Other significant works in this category are Davidialuk Alasua Amittuq's, Napachie Pootoogook's, and Kalluak's respective ink sketches (#6i, #15, and #38); and sculptures by Lucassie Echalook (#39), Jobie Uqaituk (#23), Judas Ullulaq (#27), and Aisa Qupiqrualuk (#29e).

Judas Ullulaq's carving (#27, see Hessel 2006, 222) is unusual in that it depicts two separate scenes—the shooting of the polar bear through the igloo window (Category 1) and the evil mother being towed into the sea by a whale (Category 7). Ullulaq (1937–1999) of Gjoa Haven/Taloyoak is one of the Inuit artists whose work has become highly collectable and whose pieces now sell for as much as $16,000 CDN.

Category 8

In this group there are illustrations of the wicked mother or grandmother being transformed into a narwhal or beluga. In Pitseolak Ashoona's print (#5a) the wicked mother's braided hair becomes the twisted tusk of a narwhal, with the divine assistance of two birds. This print echoes the words of the storyteller George Kappianaq, who says: "She surfaced once more still twisting her hair which had now become long. Her hair then transformed into a spiraled tusk. And so from the old woman did the narwhals come into being" (MacDonald 1998, 216). As other marine mammals look on, the scene seems to suggest a happy rather than a tragic ending to the story. Transformational imagery is an important theme in Inuit art and Inuit belief. People turn into animals and vice-versa, and it is commonly believed that in ancient time people and animals could speak to one another.

One of the most interesting manifestations of Category 8 is the snow sculpture produced by Kimmirut village sculptors at the annual Ottawa Winterlude snow sculpture competition in February 2002. Representing Team Nunavut, a group of three artists, including Donny Pitsiulak, Ooloopie Killiktee, and Eyesiak Pudloo, created a huge snow sculpture based on the legend of the Luumajuq. "I chose this story because it will look good down there, and it's a long-time story and it really happened too," said Pitsiulak. "We're going to make a woman with an amauti [hooded parka] dragged by a whale, and whole story will be written on the side, too" (Hill 2002). It took the team thirty-eight hours over three days to finish the sculpture.[1] Other Category 8 examples include Peter Morgan's stonecut print (#25) and Pitaloosie Saila's stonecut stencil (#32).

Category 9

This category contains scenes not generally found in recorded oral variants of the narrative but clearly attributed to it. Again, courtesy of Lypa Pitsiulak, there is only one work that fits into this category. I know of no oral or semi-literary variants in which the blind man dances with the loon (#17a).

One might think at first that Pitsiulak is adding new variants or motifs of the story through his art. But he has said he sometimes sees spirits, so he may well have produced his works as a result of visions or dreams about the story. It is also possible that his print depicts a scene from oral variants of the tale not previously recorded, although this seems unlikely.

Pitsiulak says, "I do drawings that may not seem to make any sense at all to some people because they are about the really old, old way of life. My drawings seem to come from up in the air and they don't seem to be going anywhere until I put them on paper or carve them. The images might not make sense to someone who doesn't know the Inuit way of life" (in Latocki 1983, 19). Pitsiulak's linocut print is listed online as one of the best-selling available prints over the last ten years at the Uqqurmiut Centre in Pangnirtung.

Category 10

This final category contains stylized symbolic images that do not attempt to replicate specific scenes in the story. In other words, they embody the story without resembling it in a literal way. They do so by being boldly imaginative and invoking a multitude of moods, themes, and ideas. And yet they still take an important place in the tale's iconography.

There is a wealth of examples from this final category: Toonoo Sharky's elegant mask sculpture (#19, fig. 26); the Old Hamilton loon mask (#48, fig. 27); John Hoover's cedar carving (#12); Jacques and Mary Regat's wall-mounted bas-relief (#18a, fig. 28); Pitseolak Ashoona's print (#5a); Paulusi Iqiqu Amarualik's stone sculpture (#3); Alec Lawson Tuckatuck's sculpture (#33); and Aisa Amittu's sculpture (#37).

The Sharky sculpture is described online at the National Gallery of Canada as "an imaginative visual summary of the entire story. On the front, for example, the missing eye on the face symbolizes the boy's blindness, while the normal eye represents his sight regained. The large webbed feet on which the piece balances and the face on the back, framed by wings, refer to the loon, both as living creature and as spirit-helper."[2] To this we might add that the extended tail flukes behind the face remind us of the beluga whale or narwhal that drags away the wicked mother. Sharky's piece is striking for its simplicity and its complexity. It is simple in its color and complex in its form.

The Old Hamilton loon mask from the mouth of the Yukon River does not depict a specific scene from the story but is closely associated closely with a partial text of the tale, suggesting that the story was once dramatized in a Yup'ik Eskimo motion dance and that the two small eyeholes in the mask symbolize the blind man's poor eyesight (fig. 27).

During an interview I conducted with Jacques and Mary Regat (August 31, 2009) at their home in Anchorage, I was struck by several things. *The Blind Man and the Loon* wood bas-relief was conceived by Jacques

Regat after he heard the story performed orally in English by an Upper Tanana Athabaskan man many years ago in Fairbanks. Unfortunately, that storyteller's name is now forgotten. The bas relief (fig. 28) shows three figures: the blind man (on the left), his long-haired son (in the middle), and his wife (on the right). His wife is pouring out the dish of water that she brings to him full of insects. Next to her on the lower right is a food bowl imprinted with moose tracks. In the center next to the loon is the mask of blindness, shown with its eyes closed.

This mask helps connect the bas-relief to the other Regat depiction of the story, a bronze sculpture of the Blind Man riding on the back of the diving loon (fig. 21), which belongs to Category 4. *The Blind Man and the Loon* bronze was inspired by Tlingit culture, in contrast to the bas-relief, which was inspired by Athabaskans.

Tlingit hats are emblems of clans. That's why the blind man on the loon's back in the bronze is wearing a hat. The object in his hand is the dentalium necklace he is about to bestow on the loon for restoring his eyesight. The mask of blindness on the tail of the loon, like that seen on the bas-relief, has its eyes closed. This mask of blindness is not actually a tale trait found in oral tradition but a new symbol introduced by the artists.

According to Jacques Regat, "Art calls people to the artist. That's why you are here talking to us today. Legends signify not just a story but a whole way of life. I like them because they show me a different world" (pers. comm., 2009). "They make you think."

In another stylized work, Aisa Amittu, Davidialuk's son, and his wife Tilly have completed a three-piece sculpture from soapstone, serpentine, aluminum foil, and caribou antler that is semi-abstract and took eight years to complete (#37). It includes a loon figure but also a pipe, a sphere intended to resemble a bubble, the Katjutajuut (big-headed monsters), and the wicked mother being dragged away by the whale. In the artist's own words, "the sculpture tells the story of Lumaaq . . . This story is significant because it teaches us that we need special help if we are to see the truth. This sculpture also has many unrelated thoughts" (Amittu 1998, 109).

It should be noted that there is one scene in the story of the Blind Man and the Loon which is not depicted by folk art, at least not yet. This scene is of the son being blinded by his wicked mother or grandmother.

In some variants he is blinded by accident or born blind, but usually he is the victim of his mother or grandmother's cruelty or evil shamanism. Also, no artist to my knowledge has depicted any of the sequels to the main story: the people without anuses, the clawed people, the sun sister and moon brother, and so forth. There certainly are depictions of the sun sister and moon brother story, but only when it is considered as a separate tale type, not as it is linked to "The Blind Man and the Loon."

Analysis

In retrospect, what can we say about the relationship of all this art to the tale that inspired it? The first purveyors of Inuit art were nineteenth-century commercial whalers, who collected carved amulets, masks, harpoons, kayaks, and clothing, so Inuit graphic art is clearly new, all coming from the late twentieth and early twenty-first centuries. The Canadian government encouraged Native arts beginning in the 1950s, seeing it as a strategic way for arctic communities to adapt their economy from a nomadic to a sedentary lifestyle.

More than a handful of the carvers and graphic artists whose work I discuss here have earned reputations as famous storytellers and tradition-bearers. Davidialuk Alasua Amittuq, for one, created at least nine different works illustrating the story, revisiting the scenes in it over and over. In *Lumak* (#6d, fig. 25) he uses a combination of realism and abstraction to show two human faces and a beluga whale as well as one person (the mother) dressed in a traditional Inuit parka. The print also contains a few syllabics, a Davidialuk trademark. The aquamarine color suggests the ocean. The prolific Davidialuk also contributed drawings to the animated short film, *Lumaaq, an Eskimo Legend*, directed by Co Hoedeman (1975). Along with the art, we are indeed very fortunate to have a translated text of Davidialuk's own telling of the Lumak story (Seidelman and Turner 1994, 126–28).

A second storyteller-artist is Aisa Qupiqrualuk of Puvirnituq, Québec, who produced five soapstone sculptures depicting scenes in the story. And a third is Robert Mayokok, of Wales, Alaska, who did an ink sketch to illustrate his own text (#50; 1960, 14) and then a few years later added a series of three additional sketches for the "The First Narwhal" text of Helen Caswell's book *Shadows from the Singing House* (1968, 42–47).

One way to understand the modern-day panoply of prints, wall hangings, murals, and sculptures is to see them as a collection of synechdoches and metonymies. For a Native audience at least, one part of the story represents the whole. If you know the story, the visualization of one powerful scene or image invokes the entire narrative sequence.

However, the non-Native spectator must know the principal characters and the syntagmatic narrative axis of the tale well ahead of viewing the artworks representing it, or the art that interprets them becomes referentially empty and pointless. That is, even if visual examples from Categories 1–8 were hung together on a wall to demonstrate the correct syntax of the tale, in a real or virtual gallery, it would still be nearly impossible to reconstruct the narrative verbally. There may still be genuine aesthetic pleasure in beholding the formal lines, colors, textures, and shapes, but the substance and meaning of the forms will escape into thin air.

At the same time, the inverse is also true. For those of us who know the story, works of art inspired by it can quickly be associated with it, even when the title of the piece is rhetorically disconnected. This is demonstrated by Pitaloosie Saila's print, *Out of the Sea* (#32), from Cape Dorset. The title is misleading and appears to be unrelated to the motifs of the story. But Saila's print shows us a woman who is transformed into a whale, or at least has a whale's tail, and she is waving an ulu in her right hand. Because we know from numerous oral texts that the terrified mother was waving or hollering for her ulu when she was pulled into the sea by a harpooned beluga or narwhal and that oftentimes her final words were, "My ulu! My ulu! My ulu!" (Malaurie 1985, 101) or "Throw me my *ulu*!" (e.g., Millman 1987, 37), we can view Saila's piece with considerable certainty as a depiction of the final scene of the tale, another instance of Category 7.

The carver Aisa Qupiqrualuk comes the closest to telling the full tale in his series of five carvings, each depicting a separate scene (#29a–e, see Nungak and Arima 1969, 48–51). Still, folk art cannot teach folktales in the same way as a storyteller can teach them, enabling its beholders to internalize all of the characters and actions. At the same time it can do much to evoke or recall the tales and interpret them. Or, to pursue an idea suggested by Ruth Finnegan (2004, 2011), it is also plausible to see folk art as a visual means of quoting folklore. Finnegan astutely observes that proverbs have a history of being embedded in art, both in Europe and in Africa.

Conclusion

So what do all these pieces of folk art taken together say collectively about the tale? Folk art provides its creators with self-employment and a ready cash income that traditional storytellers can only dream about. This helps explain why some of the greatest artists, such as Davidialuk, Kiakshuk, and Agnes Nanogak Goose, were storytellers well before they became artists, and why many collections of Inuit folktales have been illustrated by Inuit artists. Davidialuk, among others, realized that folktales were the raw materials of his Native culture and drew upon them as a resource for making a living. Perhaps this was the incentive that kept leading him back to new interpretations and revisualizations of the same tale.

While there is surely a market for collections of folktales, especially when they are sanitized and tailored to children, there is a much, much bigger and more lucrative market for folk art. The market for Inuit folk art exploded in the 1970s and 1980s and has not looked back since. At auction and in private galleries prices continue to climb steadily for the most collectable work. Many pieces sell for thousands of dollars.

Why this demand? As one critic has observed, most Inuit art really preserves an ideal world that hasn't existed for over one hundred years, and southern buyers of this art are essentially "buying fictions of a pristine northern world" that is primordial and unspoiled (Berlo 1993, 9–10). Folk tales may not be the same thing as fictions, but they do substantially document and preserve the drama of this ancient way of life.

Inuit art has fostered innumerable books, hundreds of web pages, and its own artist-controlled journal, the *Inuit Art Quarterly*, started in Ottawa in 1986. Inuit art is still the rage with dealers, galleries, and museums all across North America, but especially in Ottawa, Toronto, Winnipeg, and Vancouver. Art derived from "The Blind Man and the Loon" is now created in the villages, marketed on the web, and sold to a worldwide clientele. Of course it is only one example of many Inuit tale types, but it is among the most well-known.

These various art works were never intended to be seen collectively in the way I have assembled them here, as a kind of virtual gallery. They have only come together here because I was able to search for and find photo reproductions of them. At the same time, Inuit artists, long isolated by geography in remote villages, are today more and more aware of each other's expressive work through the *Inuit Art Quarterly*, which is distributed free of charge to practicing artists across Canada.

For the artist Agnes Goose, paintings were simply a way of helping other people remember the stories passed on to them in oral tradition. But the remarkable wealth of works by multiple artists about the Blind Man and the Loon attests to the tale's enduring power, and to its template of social and cultural values passed down from antiquity. These embedded values may be expressed as the importance of sharing food to bond families through kinship; the importance of maintaining subsistence hunting as a sacred way of life in the arctic; the importance of respecting disabled or handicapped persons; and the importance of commemorating the beauty and transformative power of animals as spirit helpers.

The folk art and fine art of "The Blind Man and the Loon," seen as a collection of vivid visual metonymies or icons, provide a new way of translating, preserving, mediating, and animating many of those values, while also helping the Inuit and Dene join the global cash economy. It is an idealized and nostalgic cultural resource that keeps renewing itself, and it can lead us to the discovery of new oral texts. Amazingly, there are now almost as many artistic works portraying the story as there are oral and printed variants of it.

Artworks Depicting the Tale of the Blind Man and the Loon

Images of many of the artworks listed here are available for viewing on the Internet. These are indicated with an asterisk (*) at the beginning of the entry. Since the URLs for specific images change frequently, they will be updated online at this book's companion website, http://www.uaf.edu/loon, where they are more easily kept current. Here, too, new artworks will continue to be added as they emerge.

1. Kiakshuk (1886–1966), Cape Dorset, Nunavut
* a. *The Legend of Lumiuk*. 1960. Stonecut print, 37.5 x 60 cm. Collection of the West Baffin Eskimo Co-Operative Ltd., on loan to the McMichael Canadian Art Collection, Kleinburg, Ontario.
* b. *Lumiuk and the Whales*. 1961. Stonecut print, 27.9 x 35.6 cm. Mac-Kenzie Art Gallery, University of Regina Collection, Saskatchewan.

2. Johnny Aculiak (1951–), Inukjuak, Québec
Blind Boy and Loon Legend. 1976. Soapstone (Steatite) sculpture, 7 in. H x 10.5 in. W x 2.5 in. D. Inuit Images, Sandwich, Massachusetts.

3. Paulusi Iqiqu Amarualik (1917–1986), Cape Dorset, Nunavut
* *The Lumaaq Story*. 1965. Grey-black stone sculpture, 10.9 x 31.4 x 14.2 cm. National Gallery of Canada (no. 30071), Ottawa.

4. Germaine Arnaktauyok (1946–), Igloolik, Nunavut, and Yellowknife, NWT
* *The Loon Gives Lumaq His Sight*. 2003. Etching aquatint, 21 x 16.875 in. Webster Galleries, Calgary, Alberta.

5. Pitseolak Ashoona (1904–1983), Cape Dorset, Nunavut
* a. *Legend of the Narwhal*. 1968. Stonecut print, 62 x 56 cm. National Museum of the American Indian, Washington DC.
* b. *The Legend of the Blind Boy and the Loon*. c. 1970. Drawing with syllabics, 14 x 10.75 in. Sold by Galerie Elca London, Montreal.
 c. *The Blind Man Depicted Before and After Killing the Bear*. c. 1980. Drawing, 45 x 62 cm. Published 1984 in *The Beaver* 64 (1).

6. Davidialuk Alasua Amittuq (a.k.a. Davidialuk Alaasuaq Amittuk and Davidialuk Alasua Amittu) (1910–1976), Puvirnituq, Québec
* a. *Légende de Lumaaq*. 1975. Stonecut print, 48.5 x 56 cm. Avataq Cultural Institute. Acc. No. DAV.2004.4. Fédération des coopératives du Nouveau-Québec.
* b. *Legend of Two Loons Opening a Blind Man's Eyes*. 1973. Stonecut print, 25 x 29 in. Published in Carol Finley, *Art of the Far North* (Minneapolis: Lerner Publications, 1998), 31. On the print, "Davidi's story" is written in syllabics. Courtesy of La Fédération des Coopératives du Nouveau Québec. Offered for auction by Waddington's Toronto, in April 2011.

* c. *Legend of Lumak*. 1964. Stonecut print, 19 x 24 in. Galerie Elca London Ltée, Montreal.
* d. *Lumak*. 1964. Stonecut print, 75.9 x 63.1 cm. Canadian Museum of Civilization, Ottawa. Published in Ernst Roch, ed., *Arts of the Eskimo: Prints* (Barre MA: Barre Publishers, 1975), 127.
* e. *Lumak*. 1965. Stonecut print, 54 x 43.2 cm. Canadian Museum of Civilization, Ottawa.
* f. *The Blind Boy Dreaming of the Loons While He Is under Water*. 1976. Stonecut print, 13.75 x 19.75 in. Offered for auction by Waddington's, Toronto, in April 2011.

g. Untitled ink sketch. 1971. Published in Bernard Saladin d'Anglure, *Être et renaître Inuit: Homme, femme ou chamane* (Paris: Gallimard, 2006), 110. Shows the blind man shooting the polar bear as it attempts to break into the igloo.

h. Untitled stonecut print. n.d. Fédération des coopératives du Nouveau-Québec. Published in Saladin d'Anglure (2006, 114). Shows the blind man calling for help from the red-throated loons.

i. Untitled ink sketch. 1971. Published in Saladin d'Anglure (2006, 114). Shows the blind man harpooning a beluga whale with his mother attached to the line.

7. Angie Eetak (1956–), Arviat, Nunavut
Blind boy and the Loons. n.d. Caribou hide applique, wall hanging. 47 x 156 cm (18.5 x 61.5 in.). Arctic Trading Company, Churchill.

8. Thomasie Etuangat (1959–), Iqaluit (Frobisher Bay), Nunavut
Lumaaju with Whales Necklace. n.d. Sterling silver pendant, 3 x 1.75 in. From an exhibition in 2000 at Spirit Wrestler Gallery, Vancouver.

9. Daniel Komoartuk (1976–), Iqaluit (Frobisher Bay), Nunavut
* *Takunnangittuq Aksuruqtuq (The Blind Guy Is Having a Hard Time)*. n.d. Sterling silver and soapstone sculpture, 2.75 x 2 in. diameter. Sold following an exhibition in 2000 by Spirit Wrestler Gallery, Vancouver.

10. Ekidluak Komoartuk (1923–1993), Pangnirtung, Nunavut
* *My Mother Lies to Me*. 1986. Stencil print, 24 x 17 in. Inuit.net Aborigin-art, Vancouver.

11. Agnes Nanogak Goose (1925–2001), Holman, NWT
a. Untitled color print. 1972. Published in Maurice Metayer, ed. and
trans., *Tales from the Igloo* (Edmonton: Hurtig Publishers, 1972), 94.
b. Untitled color print. 1972. Published in Metayer (1972, 97).
* c. *Blind Boy*. 1975. Stonecut print, 45.7 x 61.1 cm. Print by Harry Egotak,
b. 1925. Published in National Museum of Man (Canada), *The Inuit Print*
(Ottawa: National Museums of Canada, 1977), 188. Collection of The
Winnipeg Art Gallery, Gift of Holman Eskimo Co-operative G-90-264.

12. John Hoover (1919–2011), Cordova, Alaska, and Washington State
The Blind Man and the Loon. 1980. Cedar wood carving. Published in
Julie Decker, *John Hoover: Art and Life* (Anchorage: Museum Associa-
tion and the University of Washington Press, 2002), 98.

13. Daniel Inukpuk (a.k.a. Upatitsiak) (1942–), Inukjuak, Quebec
* *Legend of Lumaaq*. 1975. Stonecut print, 15 x 24 in. The name of Sarah
Elijassiapik, the printmaker, is carved in syllabics on the stone block.
Published in National Museum of Man (1977, 169). "Legend of Lumaaq"
was also published in Chip Colwell-Chanthaphonh, Stephen E. Nash,
and Steven R. Holen, *Crossroads of Culture* (Boulder: University of
Colorado Press, 2010), 69, plate 25.

14. Kananginak Pootoogook (1935–2010), Cape Dorset, Nunavut
* a. *Legend of the Blind Man and the Bear*. 1957–59. Stencil in blue on
wove paper, 38.1 x 61cm. West Baffin Eskimo. Used in the 2012 Inuit Art
calendar. Co-operative Ltd., National Gallery of Canada (no. 36594).
b. *Aulajijakka (Things I Remember) #3*. Caption: "There is a legend
regarding a blind boy. His mother asked him to harpoon a small whale,
as the boy had tied a rope around her waist." Linocut, late 1970s.
c. *Aulajijakka (Things I Remember) #4*. Caption: "When the bear died,
the mother butchered it, making sure her son wasn't aware. She told
her daughter not to tell her brother." Linocut, late 1970s.
d. *Aulajijakka (Things I Remember) #5*. Caption: "They were the only
ones at the camp when a bear approached so the mother asked the
blind boy to shoot at the bear through the air hole." Linocut, late 1970s.
e. *Aulajijakka (Things I Remember) #11*. Caption: "The son harpooned the
large whale and he was using his mother as a float. The whale started

dragging her down and every time she came up for air she cried, 'lu, lu!' Therefore she was named Lumaajuuq." Linocut, late 1970s.

Note: The Spirit Wrestler Gallery is offering for sale and displaying items 14b, c, d, and e.

15. Napachie Pootoogook (1938–2002), Cape Dorset, Nunavut
Legend of Lumaaq. 1988–1989. Ink and pencil sketch, 20 x 26 in. Formerly at Feheley Fine Arts, Toronto.

16. Rie Muñoz (1921–), Juneau, Alaska
* *Polar Bear Legend*. 2001. Silkscreen print, 20 x 8.5 in. Rie Muñoz Gallery, Juneau.

17. Lypa Pitsiulak (1943–2010), Pangnirtung, Nunavut
* a. *Blind Man Meets the Loon*. n.d. Linocut/Relief print. Printmaker: Geela Sowdluapik. Kozuke Natural, 56.5 x 74 cm. Uqqurmiut Centre for Arts and Crafts, Pangnirtung.
* b. *Blind Man's Anger*. 1990–91. Wool tapestry designed by Lypa Pitsiulak and woven by Hanna Akulukjuk. 44 x 57 in. Uqqurmiut Centre for Arts and Crafts, Pangnirtung.
* c. *Trusting the Loon*. 1986. Etching, 16 x 11 in.

18. Jacques and Mary Regat (1945–), Anchorage, Alaska
a. *Blind Man and the Loon*. n.d. Wood bas-relief, 5 x 7 ft. North Star Borough Library, Fairbanks, Alaska.
b. *Blind Man and the Loon*. 1992. Bronze sculpture, 19.5 x 33 x 10 in. Artists' private collection.

19. Toonoo Sharky (1970), Cape Dorset, Nunavut
* *The Legend of the Blind Boy*. 1998. Green stone, brown stone, ivory and baleen inlay sculpture, 47 x 57 x 15cm. © West Baffin Eskimo Cooperative Ltd. National Gallery of Canada, Ottawa.

20. Lukassie Kuuniluusi Tukalak (1917–2003), Puvirnituq, Québec
* a. *Legend: Lumak Has Been Carried Away by a White Whale*. 1977. Stonecut print, 15 x 25 in. (38.1 x 63.5 cm). Offered for auction by Waddington's Gallery, Toronto.

* b. *Legend of the Loon That Helps the Blind Man See.* 1990. Stonecut print, 15 x 14.5 in. Published in Hessel (2006, 223) A second print is in the Avataq Cultural Institute, Montreal, under the title *Blind Man Who Recovered His Eyesight from the Loons.*

21. Ashevak Tunnillie (1956–), Cape Dorset, Nunavut
* *Lumaajuuq.* Serpentine and string sculpture, 18 x 6.5 x 7 in. Inuit Gallery of Vancouver.

22. Juaniapi Angutigulu Uqaitu (a.k.a. Johnnieapik)
(1935–), Puvirnituq, Québec
* a. *Inuit Whale Hunt Lumaaq Legend.* Sculpture, apparently serpentine or soapstone (four figures), 5.25 x 4.25 in. H. 5 x 7.5 in. W; Human Figures 4.5 x 3.75 in. x 1.25 in. H. Sold in 2005 by Seahawk Auctions, Burnaby BC.
* b. *Inuit Whale Hunt Lumaaq Legend.* Sculpture, apparently serpentine or soapstone(three figures), 6 1/2 x 5 1/4 in. H. x 6 1/2 in. W. Human Figures 9 1/2 in. L. x 2 3/4 in. H. Sold in 2005 by Seahawk Auctions, Burnaby, BC. Sold in 2005 by Seahawk Auctions, Burnaby BC.

23. Jobie Uqaituk (a.k.a. Ohaituk) (1946–), Inukjuak, Québec
* *Lumaaq Legend.* 1990. Serpentine sculpture. Art Nunavik.

24. Tumasi Illuta Quissa (1948–), Akulivik, Québec
* *Lumaaq: The Legend of the Blind Boy.* Soapstone sculpture, 3 x 15 x 10 in. Spirit Wrestler Gallery, Vancouver.

25. Peter Morgan (1951–), Kangiqsualujjuaq, Québec
The Legend of the Woman Who Became a Narwhal. 1975. Stonecut print. Carleton University Art Gallery, Ottawa.

26. Joshua Sivuarapik (1949–), Puvirnituq, Québec
The Woman Who Became Narwhal. Sculpture, apparently soapstone or serpentine, 8 x 14.75 x 5.75 in. Formerly in Kulik Art Inuit, Québec City.

27. Judas Ullulaq (1937–1999), Gjoa Haven, Nunavut
Legend of the Blind Boy and the Loon. 1975. Stone, caribou antler, ivory, and sinew sculpture, 4 x 10.75 x 9 in. Heard Museum, Phoenix. Published in Hessel (2006, 222).

28. Billy Gauthier (1978–), Happy Valley, Labrador

* *Blind Boy and the Loon*. n.d. Serpentine, labradorite sculpture, 10 x 5 x 4.5 in.

29. Aisa Qupiqrualuk (a.k.a. Aisa Qupirualu Alasua) (1917–2003), Povungnituk/Puvirnituq, Québec

A set of five sculptures. Published in Zebedee Nungak and Eugene Arima, eds. *Eskimo Stories: Unikkaatuat*. National Museum of Canada Bulletin No. 235. A.S. 90. (Ottawa: 1969), 48–51.

a. *The bear peeping in the window hole* a.k.a. *The Legend of Lumak and the Bear*. 1957.

b. *She brought him food inside her parka*. n.d.

c. *"My brother, good dog meat."* n.d.

d. *The loon leading the blind boy to the water* a.k.a. *The Blind Boy and the Loon*. 1957.

e. *The mother being towed under by the white whale* a.k.a. *Lumak's Revenge* and *Lumiak and the Whale*, 1958. Stone, 33 cm. Collection of the Art Gallery of Ontario, Toronto. Published in Emily E. Auger, *The Way of Inuit Art: Aesthetics and History in and Beyond the Arctic*. (Jefferson NC: McFarland, 2005), 112.

30. Carla Rae Gilday (1980–), Yellowknife NWT

* *The Old Man and the Loon*. c. 2008. Acrylic color painting on self-constructed canvas. Thumbnail published in the newsletter *Northwest Territories Artists' Newsline* (Summer 2009), 8.

31. Ningeokuluk Teevee (1963–), Cape Dorset, Nunavut

* a. *Lumaaq (Legend of the Blind Boy)*. 2009. Etching and aquatint, 14.75 x 14.75 in. Galerie Elca London and Ninavik Art Gallery.

* b. *Untitled (from the story of Lumaaq)*. 2005/2006. Ink and colored pencil on paper, 20 x 23 in. Marion Scott Gallery, Vancouver.

32. Pitaloosie Saila (1942–), Cape Dorset, Nunavut

* *Out of the Sea*. 1986. Stonecut Stencil, 55 x 71 cm. Dorset Fine Arts, Toronto. Offered for auction by Waddington's, Toronto.

33. Alec Lawson Tuckatuck (1976–), Kuujjuaraapik, Québec
* a. *Lumack (Legend of Lumack)*. n.d. Wonderstone, Musk Ox horn sculpture.
b. *Legend of Lumaaq*. c. 2012. Soapstone and alabaster sculpture, 9.75 x 16.75 x 6.25 in.

34. Peter Qumalak Ituukala (1954–), Puvirnituq, Québec
Luumaq. 1989. Stonecut print with syllabics, 15 x 14 in. Sold by Inuit Art Zone, Québec City.

35. Elizabeth Cleaver (1939–1985), Montreal, Québec
Untitled linocut prints. n.d. Published in William Toye, *The Loon's Necklace* (New York: Oxford University Press, 1977), 1–24.

36. Stefano Vitale (1958–), Venice, Italy
Untitled print. n.d. Published in James Bruchac and Joseph Bruchac, *The Girl Who Helped Thunder and Other Native American Folktales* (New York: Sterling Publishing, 2008), 87.

37. Aisa Amittu (1951–), Akulivik/Povungnituk
Untitled sculpture of soapstone, serpentine, aluminum, and caribou antler. n.d. Published in *American Indian Art Magazine*, 23, no. 3 (Summer 1998): 109.

38. Mark Kalluak (c. 1941–), Arviat/Eskimo Point, Nunavut
Untitled ink sketch. n.d. Published in Mark Kalluak, *How Kabloonat Came and Other Inuit Legends* (Yellowknife: Department of Education, Govt. of the Northwest Territories, 1974), 47.

39. Lucassie Echalook (1942–), Inukjuak, Québec
The Legend of Lumaaq. 2009. Serpentine sculpture, 12.75 x 9.25 x 5 in. Sold by the Ontario Crafts Council via The Guild Shop, Toronto.

40. Silas Kayakjuak (a.k.a. Qayakjuak) (1956–), Hall Beach, Nunavut
a. *Boy Riding Loon*. n.d. Miniature ivory sculpture. Sold by the Snow Goose Gallery, Ottawa.
* b. *Legend of Blind Boy Riding Loon*. n.d. Ivory sculpture, 1.5 x 2.25 x 1 in. Spirit Wrestler Gallery, Vancouver BC.

* c. *Blind Boy on Loon.* n.d. Antler and serpentine sculpture, 2 x 4 x 2 in. Spirit Wrestler Gallery, Vancouver BC.

* d. *Cry of the Red Throated Loon (Legend of the Blind Boy and the Loon).* n.d. Antler, inlay, sculpture signed in syllabics. 9.5 x 2 x 1.5 in. Sold at auction by Waddington's, Toronto, Ontario.

41. Looty Pijamini (1953–) Aujuittuq/Grise Fiord, Nunavut

* a. *Lumaaq Story.* 1992. Sculpture from the exhibition *Arctic Art Masterworks: Selections from the Balshine Collection of Sculpture by Inuit.* Vancouver: Arctic Art Museum Ltd., 1998.

b. *Lumak Legend.* 1991. Ivory and antler, 20 x 55 x 37.5 cm. From the Exhibition of Inuit Sculpture at the Winnipeg Art Gallery, July 18, 2009, to November 15, 2009.

42. Patrick Thompson (1978–), Ottawa
The Blind Boy and the Loon Jam. 2009. Wall mural in Nunavut.

43. Larry Vienneau Jr. (1955–), Lake Mary, Florida
Untitled sketch. n.d. Published in John Smelcer, *A Cycle of Myths: Indian Myths from Southeast Alaska.* (Anchorage: Salmon Run Books, 1993), 59.

44. David Ruben Piqtoukun (1950–), Paulatuk NWT and Toronto
Lumak Legend. c. 1990s. Stone and marble sculpture. 12 x 24 in. Formerly offered for sale on eBay.

45. Johnny Kakutuk (1946–), Akulivik, Québec
* *Lumaq Legend.* n.d. Gray stone sculpture, stained darker, 15.7 x 31.8 cm. Art Gallery of Ontario, Toronto.

46. Robert E. Sebastian (1952–), Hazelton, British Columbia
Blindman Sees Loon. c. 1970s. Unframed red and black ink serigraph, Northwest Coast style. University of Victoria Art Collections, Maltwood Art Museum and Gallery, Victoria BC.

47. Simiunie Sivuaq Sivuarapik (1946–2000), Puvirnituq, Québec
* Untitled stone sculpture. n.d. Steatite, 7 x 17 x 8 cm. Avataq Cultural Institute. Westmount and Inukjuak, Québec.

48. Artist unknown, Old Hamilton, Alaska
Untitled loon mask. n.d. Wood carving, painted, in two pieces, Yup'ik Eskimo. Catalog number UA64-7-22. Collected by Otto Geist in 1934, accompanied by tale text collected in 1935. University of Alaska Museum of the North, Fairbanks, Alaska.

49. Stanley Nachosak, Nain, Labrador
Untitled color print. 2001. Apparently commissioned for illustrating a reprinted text and published in Dale Blake's *Inuit Life Writings and Oral Traditions: Inuit Myths* (St. Johns NF: Educational Resource Development Co-operative, 2001), 11.

50. Robert Mayokok (1903–1983), Wales, Alaska
Untitled ink sketch. n.d. Published in Robert Mayokok, *Eskimo Stories* (Nome AK: Nome Nugget, 1960) cover, 14. Three additional ink sketches of the tale appear in Helen Caswell, *Shadows From the Singing House: Eskimo Folktales* (Rutland VT: C. E. Tuttle, 1968), 42–47.

51. George Aden Ahgupuk (1911–2001), Shishmaref, Alaska
Untitled pencil sketch. n.d. Published in Edward Keithahn, *Alaskan Igloo Tales* (Anchorage: Alaska Northwest Publishing Company, 1974), 77. Illustrates the story of the "Wicked Mother."

52. Laszlo Gal (1933–2005), Hungarian-Canadian
Untitled black and blue sketch for "The Origin of the Narwhal." 1997. Published in Ronald Melzack's *Why the Man in the Moon Is Happy and Other Eskimo Creation Stories* (Toronto: McClelland and Stewart, 1977), 30.

53. Frank C. Terry (n.d.)
Untitled ink sketch for "The Ant Lady and the Blind Man." 1979. Published in John Billum, *Atna' Yanida'a: Ahtna Stories*, transcribed in Ahtna by Molly Billum with English translation by Millie Buck. (Anchorage: National Bilingual Materials Development Center, 1979), 48.

54. Mary Elijassiapik, Inukjuak, Québec
Story Tapestry #11: The Legend of Lumaaq. 2009. Felt tapestry, embroidery thread, 45 x 29.5 in. Formerly for sale at Inuit Artists' Shop, Ottawa.

CHAPTER SIX

The Mediated and Theatrical Tale

Art and song everywhere begins in folk culture:
celebration, dance, music, story, song, poem.
—GARY SNYDER, *BACK ON THE FIRE*

In her ground-breaking book, *American Folklore and the Mass Media* (1994), Linda Dégh discusses what happens to folklore when it is enters the electronic world. While purists might think this is a bad thing, a corruption, Dégh argues that mass media actually liberates folklore and makes it more accessible to all. "The time is ripe," she writes in anticipation, "for folklorists to think about a new type of fieldwork for a more systematic, scientific study of folklore transmission in the age of the electronic explosion" (1994, 13). For Dégh and other folk narrative scholars, media continues to be a hot topic at the annual meetings of The International Society for Contemporary Legend Research.

Starting in the nineteenth century, oral tradition has become more and more entwined in mass media, and the process of that entwining, called mediation, consists of various forms of communication. The mediated world consists largely of books, newspapers and magazines, radio and television, records, tapes, and compact discs, the telephone and smartphone, and the Internet. Except for telephones, smartphones, and the Internet, these are essentially impersonal, one-way means of communication. And, compared to oral tradition, they are oftentimes commodified. That is, you usually have to pay money to access them.

In addition to its many published texts and its artistic representation in the graphic arts, the tale of the Blind Man and the Loon has now been interpreted in the form of three short films, several audio compact discs, a ballet, a piece of classical chamber music, at least two radio broadcasts, and untold theatrical performances by professional

119

storytellers and actors. Through these multiple delivery systems, as well as its dissemination on the Internet, the tale has rocketed from terrestrial folk culture (affectionately known in Alaska as "the mukluk telegraph") into the orbit of mainstream popular culture.

Films

1. *The Loon's Necklace* (1949)

Since its release when it won the first-ever Canadian Film of the Year Award, *The Loon's Necklace* has had wide distribution across the United States and has become a staple in Alaskan and Canadian elementary school film libraries. The film was initially released in English and French (as *Le Collier Magique*). The credits for this eleven-minute film are: produced and directed by F.R. "Budge" Crawley (1949), scripting by Douglas Leechman, cinematography by Grant Crabtree, editing by Judith Crawley, and narration by George Gorman (English) and François Bertrand (French). It was a product of Crawley Films and was distributed by Encyclopedia Britannica Films.[1]

One can openly speculate that this film has influenced oral performances of the tale outside of southern British Columbia, where Douglas Leechman first found it. The trait by which the blind man rewards the loon with a dentalium shell necklace appears to be a symbolic extension of Dene culture from Alaska, the Yukon, and northern British Columbia, where chiefs are distinguished by such necklaces at potlatch ceremonies and other formal occasions (see map 1, Group F). However, the film is not at all representative of the many Eskimo variants or the Eskimo subtype.

The film script for *The Loon's Necklace* was written by the ethnographer, archaeologist, and folklorist Douglas Leechman, who was affiliated with the National Museum of Canada. He presents it to viewers as a morality tale, prefaced with the scrolled text: "This story is based on a Canadian west coast Indian legend. It is a tale about the spirits of good and evil which these people believed were all around them."

The first words of the film are "In the Indian village of Shulus, on the banks of the Nicola River, there lived an old blind medicine man named Kelora." The Nicola River is a tributary of the Thompson River in southern British Columbia and is the homeland of the Nlaka'pamux (Thompson) and Okanagan First Nations, who both speak Interior Salishan languages, and of the now-vanished Nicola Athabaskans or Stuwix.[2] Today Shulus is occupied by the Lower Nicola Indian Band.

To my knowledge, the story of the Loon's Necklace has never been recorded among these people or in any of these languages, unless Leechman himself did it, and there is at least some evidence that he did. In terms of geography, the closest documented oral variants to Shulus come from the Carrier and the Chilcotin of north central British Columbia, who speak Athabaskan languages (see Morice 1892; Farrand 1900, 35–36). Of his collaboration with the Crawleys, Leechman writes:

> It didn't take me long to convince them of the possibilities concealed in the West Coast Indian masks. All that was need was a suitable theme for a scenario. I suggested using an Indian story which had been told to me by a native girl in the far west some years ago, the story of how the loon received the white necklace he still wears, as a reward for restoring the sight of an old blind medicine man. I had already published the story in two slightly variant versions [see Leechman 1931, 1942] and now I re-wrote it for the film. (Leechman n.d.)

Who was this "native girl in the far west"? We know that as a young man of twenty-one Leechman found time to visit the area to collect and photograph Nicola Valley string records. He writes in a monograph that he collected string records and other artifacts tucked inside a deerskin case in 1911, which were "hanging on a corner-post of a fence surrounding an Indian grave in a cemetery near the Indian village of Tsulus, in Nicola valley, about four miles north of Merritt, British Columbia" (Leechman and Harrington 1921). This "Tsulus" is surely one and the same place as the village of "Shulus" in the film's script. However, he never identifies the "native girl" who told him the Loon's Necklace story on this early trip, if that is when he met her.

At any rate, Leechman's filmic story, a semi-literary rendering of a British Columbia Indian legend, seems to come directly or indirectly from an article he wrote which first appeared in the January 1931 issue of *Forest and Outdoors*, a magazine published by the Canadian Forestry Association (see Leechman 1931). This text seems like a fairly complete telling of the Indian subtype except that it omits the blind man's revenge against his wife at the end. It also contains some suspect aberrant material in that the villagers are threatened by starving wolves.

Leechman's second text, which is quite similar to the first, was published in a most curious place, *The Civil Service Review*, a labor union publication, just a year after he received his doctorate from the University of Ottawa (Leechman 1942). A third text, which condenses the 1942 version and nearly mimics the film script, appeared in his textbook, *Native Tribes of Canada* (Leechman 1956) with the subtitle "A Legend of the Interior Salish," and a fourth, identical with the third, was included in a later anthology (Leechman 1964). None of these texts is attributed to a named Indian storyteller.

The 1931 and 1942 versions make use of several local place names, including Tulameen, Coyote Valley, Mamette Lake and the Nicola River, which are near the present-day community of Kamloops, British Columbia, not far from Spences Bridge, the home of the famed folklorist James A. Teit. At first I wondered if Leechman had picked up on one of Teit's texts, but a review of Teit's many publications has not yielded any Loon's Necklace variants besides the Tahltan one he collected from Dandy Jim. Leechman's two earliest renderings contain the motif of the blind man shooting a deer and his wife's subsequent lie, betrayal, and abandonment. These important episodes are omitted from both the 1956 and 1964 text versions and by the film. In the film the blind man's wife is simply a scolding old hag. She is not a true villain.

The Loon's Necklace film, released six years after *The Civil Service Review* edition, has probably familiarized more people with the story of the Blind Man and the Loon than all the printed variants and oral texts combined. At the same time, it is antiseptically purged of the cruel betrayal and violent revenge motifs that are integral to nearly all of the oral variants. The semi-literary variants, most of which are redactions written for children, also censor these motifs.

The Loon's Necklace film has been strongly criticized by the Canadian film historian George Melnyk, who notes, "The story and its fable-like presentation ossified Aboriginal culture in a mythological universe that deprived the viewer of any historical context that might show the cultural onslaught that the dominant society had been waging against the very culture that the film claimed to glorify" (2004, 93). It strikes me that this criticism is not entirely fair since the film's full historical context still remains somewhat elusive, but the editing and censorship does render it into more of a fantasy. Leechman's motivation for making the film, nevertheless, remains a mystery. Is it an honest extension of oral tradition, and does it actually honor indigenous culture?

Melnyk discovered that *The Loon's Necklace* went on to rack up sales of $1.5 million over thirty years. That revenue did not accrue to the filmmakers, however, since Imperial Oil of Canada (Esso) bought the film from Crawley for $5,000 and then gave it to the Canadian Educational Association. It is now estimated that the film has been seen by a combined audience of 33 million people.

One reason it has been seen by so many people, especially in Canada, is that it was once used as a filler on the Canadian Broadcasting Corporation whenever there was a technical malfunction with a taped program. Larry MacDonald, a retired CBC veteran, remembers that back when television was black and white and full of technical problems, a "stand-by film" was always kept loaded and ready to air in case the system broke down. It was always the same short film, *The Loon's Necklace* (Brown 1985). Of course, the film's audience was substantially extended when a French language version was distributed in 1950; later, versions were also produced in German, Italian, Portuguese, and Spanish.

The film is illustrated by ceremonial masks from collections in the National Museum of Canada in Ottawa, but sad to say, there is no logical connection between the carved masks and the Loon's Necklace story, except in their both being from the Northwest Coast (fig. 29). The decision to bring the masks to life was at the prompting of Leechman, who was employed by the Museum as an anthropologist, and Leechman secured access to the masks for the filmmakers. The masks had been collected long before on the Northwest Coast by Marius Barbeau, but their ceremonial context and significance remains a complete mystery. In Leechman's papers at the British Columbia Provincial Archives, there is a detailed list of exactly which masks from the Museum were used in the film.

Michal Anne Crawley, the daughter of the film's producers, "Budge" and Judith Crawley, says that the *Loon's Necklace* story actually came to them from Marius Barbeau, who was a close friend of her parents (Crawley, pers. comm. 2012). While Leechman seems to have been the guiding hand in writing the script, Barbeau commissioned the Nisga chief William Beynon to record and translate Tsimshian texts as early as 1915 and may very well have learned the story from Beynon. Franz Boas also hired Beynon to collect stories, and Beynon's unpublished papers are now divided between the Canadian Museum of Civilization and at the American Philosophical Society archives in Philadelphia. Beynon, the son of a Welsh father and a Nisga mother, was an active scholar from 1915 until his death in 1958. He spoke both the Nass and Gitskan dialects, and worked in the same part of northern British Columbia as the contemporary Northwest Coast artist Robert E. Sebastian (see fig. 23).

This film was reviewed by Hans Guggenheim (1971) and by Susan Dwyer-Shick (1974). Guggenheim's commentary is especially perceptive. He evaluates *The Loon's Necklace* with several other films based on Indian oral narratives and concludes that together they form a genre because they are "infused with a romantic view of the primitive world" and "create a reassuring view of primitive peoples," adding that "the simple beauty of the film is hampered by occasional slips into didacticism and ethnographic mysteries." Guggenheim concludes that one of the dangers of the film is that it "singles out one version of the myth over others and popularizes it, thus restricting the range of mythic experiences open to audiences." Another danger is that the film links the story to one set of visual images and thereby restricts the experience of the audience to that single set of images.

Crawley Films went out of business in 1989. However, as a testament to its lasting popularity, *The Loon's Necklace* film was selected in 2001 as a classic Masterwork by the Audio-Visual Preservation Trust of Canada, a charitable nonprofit organization dedicated to promoting the preservation of Canada's audiovisual heritage. Along with hundreds of other Crawley films, it has been donated to the National Archives, where it is being preserved in a state-of-the-art facility in Gatineau, Québec.

2. Lumaaq, an Eskimo Legend (1975)

This animated version is directed by Co Hoedeman with black and white drawings by the celebrated artist Davidialuk Alasua Amittuq (see chapter 5 earlier). It is produced by Pierre Moretti, edited by Richard Robesco, contains background music (an annoying Jew's harp) by Aikimie Novalinga, and voices by Akinisie Novalinga and Mina Mathews. It is distributed by the National Film Board of Canada, Department of Indian Affairs and Northern Development. The film is just seven and a half minutes long, and the dialogue is in Inuktitut, but there is also a French version.

Lumaaq tells the legend as it was known to Davidialuk and the community of Povungnituk/Puvirnituq, Québec. The result is a series of graphic prints in motion. The dialogue, music, and artwork make this film a direct visual translation of the oral tradition. The plot is neatly and tightly summarized in English at the very beginning: "A snowblind boy is cruelly rejected by his own mother. For the wrong she does him, he takes revenge." The film is produced without any other commentary.

Hoedeman is a Dutch-Canadian filmmaker who made a series of animated films based on Inuit legends: *The Man and the Giant, The Owl and the Lemming, The Owl and the Raven,* and *Lumaaq.* During the early 1970s he collaborated closely with artists in the Arctic communities of Iqaluit and Povungnituk/Puvirnituq to illustrate these legends using sealskin puppets, soapstone carvings, and drawings.

3. *Nunavut Animation Lab: Lumaajuuq* (2010)

In the same spirit as *Lumaaq, an Eskimo Legend* comes another animated short, just under eight minutes in length, but produced in color instead of black and white. It is written and directed by Alethea-Ann Aggiuq Arnaquq-Baril, an Inuit woman from Iqaluit, Nunavut, who owns a small production company called Unikkaat Studios. The film has been released in both English and French by the National Film Board (NFB) of Canada and has already won two awards. It won the Golden Sheaf Award at the Yorkton Film Festival, 2011, in the Best Aboriginal category. And it won an award at The imagineNATIVE Film + Media Arts Festival in Toronto for Best Canadian Short Drama in 2010.

On the NFB web site, the story of the film is described: "*Lumaajuuq* is a tragic and twisted story about the dangers of revenge. A cruel mother mistreats her son, feeding him dog meat and forcing him to sleep in the cold. A loon, who tells the boy that his mother blinded him, helps the child regain his eyesight. Then the boy seeks revenge, releasing his mother's lifeline as she harpoons a whale and watching her drown. As the boy's sister cries over the fate of their mother, the boy realizes the futility of seeking vengeance." In the soft-spoken female voice-narrated script, Arnaquq-Baril says that the son "was blinded by revenge" and adds the explicit moral that "Just like his mother, the boy's act of revenge solved nothing and led to a life of cruelty and suffering. And today the narwhal will forever be a reminder that every act of revenge is a link in a chain that can only be broken by forgiveness." This interpretation is consistent with that of the traditional Yup'ik storyteller Andy Charlie (1997, 25)—see the discussion in chapter 7.

Arnaquq-Baril concludes that eight minutes is not enough time to tell the full tale, perhaps thinking that she needs to expand it to include some of the common sequels. At least it is not redacted or sugarcoated. In an October 25, 2010 post in the news section of her web page (http://www.unikkaat.com), she writes: "I look forward to someday doing a full animated series on the same story. It's a huge epic legend, and although I was able to squeeze a small section of it into my short animation, it really needs to be done on a full scale to give it the treatment it deserves. Someday. . .when we have more trained Inuit animators and production crew to be able to make it happen."

4. The Blind Boy and the Loon (2011)

Yet another animated variant of the story has appeared at the online site of the East of England Broadband Network (e2bn), which developed a full series of sixty stories called "Myths and Legends" for the benefit of elementary age school children and their teachers. In the category of Digital Storytelling, the Myths and Legends website was voted one of the Top 25 Websites for Teaching and Learning 2011 by the American Association of School Librarians. This media variant, narrated by a male with a decided British accent and spiced up with exaggerated dramatic voices from the wicked stepmother and the loon, is more like a cartoon strip than a true film, although there is some animation within the approximately thirty-six frames. The provenance of the story is given only as "Canada." The sound track is optional in that it can be muted, and students are encouraged to read the story as they watch and listen to it.

Theatrical and Performing Arts

"The Blind Man and the Loon" has also been transformed for popular consumption through theatrical performances in front of both small and large live audiences. A rather surprising spin-off of *The Loon's Necklace* film is a Canadian ballet. During the early 1950s, *The Loon's Necklace* was performed as a ballet with music composed by pianist Calvin Jackson and choreography by Willy Blok Hanson ("Calvin Jackson, Pianist"

1985).[3] Jackson, an African American jazz pianist and composer, once received an Academy Award nomination for the score of the movie *The Unsinkable Molly Brown*. *The Loon's Necklace* is included in a repertoire list of the Willy Blok Hansen dance group found in Douglas Leechman's papers at the BC Archives in Victoria.

In the November 1953 premiere of the ballet in Toronto, all the dancers except the loon wore Northwest Coast–style masks. Those dancers mentioned in a performance review were the old blind man Kelora, played by Hanson, and the Loon, danced by Charlotte de Neve, who wore a leotard with the distinctive markings of the loon. Jackson's score was played as a piano duet featuring Leo Barkin and Margaret Clemens. According to Herbert Whittaker, the *Toronto Globe and Mail* drama critic, the work "was most favorably received" (quoted in Chambers 2008, 40). The ballet was performed several more times in 1954 and 1955, usually on the same bill with another Jackson-Hanson ballet called *Maria Chapdelaine*. In 1955 the ballet dancers were accompanied by a full orchestra. Unfortunately both of Jackson's ballet scores have disappeared.

A twenty-minute piece of chamber music, composed by Keith Bissell in 1971 and titled *How the Loon Got Its Necklace*, was released on an LP vinyl record in 1974. Bissell, a composer, lecturer, and educator strongly influenced by folklore and folk song, conceived the piece largely in terms of the 1949 film and Douglas Leechman's script. Like the film itself, this music was designed for children. Children's concerts, supplemented by program notes and comments from the conductor or an assistant, have gradually become a Canadian institution.

The Bissell piece, performed by a string quintet, features two violins, a viola, a violoncello, a double bass, percussion, and a voice narrator. It is divided into ten sections: I. Prelude; II. Kelora dreams; III. The scolding wife; IV. Kelora talks with the loon; V. The wolves; VI. Kelora's mystical song; VII. Killing the wolf; VIII. The city of the loon; IX. Kelora tosses the shells; X. Postlude. Bissell's score has been preserved at the Centre for Canadian Music in Toronto,[4] and a newly recorded version of it appears on track 3 of the *Storyteller's Bag* audio compact disc (Hills 2006). It was performed again by the Musaeus String Quartet for a children's concert at the University of Lethbridge, Alberta, in 2011.

In 1981 a play called *The Loon's Necklace* was staged by the Great Canadian Theatre Company of Ottawa. As stated on their web site (http://

www.gctc.com), the company was founded in 1975 with a nationalist, leftist, and populist agenda and with a vision "to place Canadian stories and Canadian history front and centre in our country's universities and theatres." With a script written by Robin Mathews and music by Robert Rapley, a small cast of three went on tour in Canada from October 1 through December 31, 1975. Mathews, a university professor and poet, is a militant Canadian nationalist and political activist, and *The Loon's Necklace* play was an expression of that nationalism and of Canadian identity.

The cast consisted of Robert Bockstael as the Boy and the Deer, François Delisle as the Old Man, and Peggy Sample as the Old Woman, the Loon, and the Owl. The drama was directed by J. D. Campbell and featured several masks. A publicity photo of the three actors show them all lined up together aiming imaginary bows and arrows, apparently imitating the blind man (Rubin 1982, 145).

Then in 2001 the National Arts Centre Orchestra in Ottawa presented *The Loon's Necklace* under conductor Boris Brott. Parts of this program featured a narration by Tara-Louise Montour, a member of the Mohawk First Nations, who has been praised as "North America's foremost classical Aboriginal violinist." In 2005 the National Arts Centre Orchestra went on tour and performed the concert for a number of communities in Alberta and Saskatchewan. This time the First Nations narrator was Jean Naytowhow.

And I would be remiss to overlook the efforts of professional storytellers who use the Blind Man and the Loon or the Blind Boy and the Loon story in live public appearances. One such storyteller, a non-Native by the name of Elinor Benjamin, includes the Blind Boy and the Loon in a program of stories of "birds and feathers." Benjamin, who tours and performs at storytelling festivals in eastern Canada, performed the story of the Blind Boy and the Loon at the Feather and Folk Festival, Traditional Newfoundland Dinner, held at Port Aux Basques, Newfoundland on May 27, 2009. A former librarian born in Nova Scotia, Benjamin specializes in Norse and Mi'Kmaq tales.[5]

Benjamin (pers. comm. 2011) says that her performances derive from three sources: the semi-literary redaction written by Ramona Maher (1969), the Maurice Metayer version (1972) now posted on the Internet, and the audio CD of *Inuit Legends, Volume 2* produced by the CBC

(Worthy 2003; discussed later). Benjamin uses no props but does give the wicked grandmother a raspy voice. Since she did not learn the story on her mother's knee, she sees herself as a "revival" storyteller.

On Tuesday, August 26, 2008, I was fortunate to be present at a performance of "The Ant Lady," a variant of the Blind Man and the Loon, told indoors at the Alaska State Fair in a session called Ahtna Legends. It was a multimedia slide show presentation, using illustrations similar to cartoons, projected from a laptop computer using PowerPoint or a similar program. The storyteller was Patricia Wade, an Ahtna Athabaskan from Palmer, Alaska, and a member of the Chickaloon Village Traditional Council. Wade had little illustrated booklets for sale for several of her stories, but "The Ant Lady" was not one of them.[6] The illustrations used in the slide show were drawn by Wade's son, Dimi Macheras. Wade now tours Alaska, giving similar oral and visual performances at museums and other venues.

When Wade performed the story she narrated it in a small room without notes and included it in a sequence with three other tales. All four of them were learned from her mother, Katherine Wade. In attendance were several Ahtna relatives and a young couple with a baby, as well as a few others. In Wade's version, the blind man is married to the ant lady from the beginning of the story. And when his sight is restored, it is due to help from swan rather than a loon. At the end, the blind man hits his wife with his axe, and that leaves her back parts connected by a little thread such as we see in ants today. According to Wade, this story shows that if you mistreat the handicapped, you will have a fate that is worse than the person you mistreated. She indicated to me that this was a traditional belief of the Ahtna.

Audio Recordings and Radio Broadcasts

The tale of the Blind Man and the Loon has also led to some dramatic readings available on audio compact discs. *The Storyteller's Bag*, a compact disc with "How the Loon Got Its Necklace," is apparently a reprise of a long-playing record by the same name that was released by Radio Canada International in 1974. Keith Bissell's chamber music is used as a prelude and as background for the dialogue. Designed for children, this newer production (Hills 2006) uses Ojibway actors and is purportedly based on Ojibway oral tradition, but the actual source of the story is never given.

The Storyteller's Bag production is loosely based on the Douglas Leechman script for *The Loon's Necklace* film. Wolves are made out to be a threat to the people, and the blind man has to shoot one to save the village. Lasting 12 minutes and 34 seconds, the performance consists of an overacted, hyped-up dialogue between the blind man and his shrewish wife, followed by a dialogue between the blind man and father loon. The loon is rewarded with a shell necklace for having restored the blind man's sight, but the shrewish wife never gets her comeuppance.

Barbara Worthy's double CD, entitled *Inuit Legends, Volume 2*, was released by the Canadian Broadcasting Corporation (CBC) in a bilingual Inuktitut and English format (Worthy 2004). It contains a dramatic reading of "Lumaajuuq the Blind Boy." The Inuktitut version is on track 4 of the Inuktitut CD and lasts for 20 minutes, 19 seconds. The English version is on track 2 of the English CD and lasts only 14 minutes, 23 seconds. It would be a fair assessment to say that the English version is a summary translation of the Inuktitut original. While Barbara Worthy (2003) is the producer and editor, the discs contain original music, sound effects, and reading voices by Celina Kalluk, Madeleine Allakariallak, Elisha Kilabuk, and Orla Osbourne.

Even the English version contains many Inuktitut words, giving it a sense of authenticity. The mother is made to seem extra cruel when she strangles their dog and hangs its skin up to dry. With a literary touch, the narrator pronounces judgment on the mother, saying she doesn't treat her son fairly or well. This is always implied in oral versions but is never made explicit by traditional storytellers. This production claims that the unusual sound heard today in a pod of swimming belugas is "the sound of a mother calling to her son." She not only calls out but sings a kind of sad lullaby. All in all, this dramatization follows Inuit oral tradition fairly closely and seems fairly well suited to radio broadcast.

Another audio recording of "The Loon's Necklace" with strong connections to oral tradition is the interactive *Anishinaabemdaa* compact disc (Pheasant n.d.). This recording contains an Anishinaabemowin Native language version ("Maang Donaabkowaaginim") from the Little River Band of Ottawa Indians in Manistee, Michigan. Anishinaabemowin belongs to the Algonquian language family. The producer, Kenny Neganigwane

Pheasant, grew up on the Wikwemikong Reservation in South Bay, Ontario, and his CD is the product of a grant from the Administration for Native Americans to help perpetuate his Native language and culture. In addition to story texts, the CD contains games, puzzles, video clips, and language lessons.[7]

Yet another phenomenon worth mentioning here is the 1972 audio-tape recording of Walter Titus, a Lower Tanana Athabaskan from Minto, Alaska, who was born in nearby Nenana. His tape, made by Karen McPherson, was recorded in both English and Lower Tanana and is now archived as part of the Oral History Collection at the Rasmuson Library, University of Alaska, Fairbanks. Originally on cassette, it is now available on compact disc through many Alaska libraries as part of the *Songs and Legends* series, volume 93, track 2. Titus's English version of the tale of the Blind Man and the Loon is about seven minutes, but his Lower Tanana language version lasts only about three minutes. This compression may have entirely to do with his audience, a non-Native woman. Both tracks may be listened to at http://www.uaf.edu/loon/audio/.

A rather surprising and interesting use of the tale is a musical composition called "The Loon's Necklace," featured on the self-published compact disc called *The Catamount Is Back: Banjo Dan's Songs of Vermont, Vol. II* (1992). This piece was arranged by Dan Lindner and his group Banjo Dan and the Mid-Nite Plowboys, a Montpelier, Vermont-based bluegrass band. It features the dubbing of a loon's cry and a female vocalist, Jaye Lindner, apparently Dan's wife. The instruments used are a bass, guitar, and flute. The ballad-like piece, which is not a bluegrass arrangement, attempts to romanticize how the loon got its distinctive markings and makes no mention at all of the mother's betrayal or the blind boy's revenge.

The lyrics of this song are highly fanciful and reflect precious little of the story that circulates in oral tradition. In fact, after the blind boy's eyesight is restored, it is ironic that he *and* his mother both rejoice: "The young boy and his mother [were] filled with gratitude and joy." Another distortion of oral tradition on this recording has the blind boy weeping by the shore of the lake, feeling sorry for himself and his people.

A letter I sent to Lindner resulted in a brief reply saying that he was not sure where he heard or read the story the song is based on. Indeed his song seems to be a hybrid mixture of the Eskimo and Indian subtypes.

That is, it concerns a blind boy and his mother (Eskimo subtype), but he rewards the loon with a shell necklace (Indian subtype).

Of great interest to students of oral tradition is that in 1971 the anthropologist David Smith collected a Chipewyan variant of the Blind Man and the Loon from Ellen Unka at Fort Resolution, which Unka learned directly from a CBC radio broadcast in Yellowknife.[8] Another variant, told by Gwich'in elder Eliza Andre of Tsiigehtchic, was recorded by Louie Goose and broadcast on CHAK-AM radio, a CBC affiliate in Inuvik NWT, in 1974 (see appendix B).

Since CBC North affiliates in Canada are highly supportive of First Nations languages and the art of storytelling, it seems unlikely that these are isolated cases. Storytelling in Native languages is a daily or weekly feature for many stations in the rural North, and radio allows Native voices to be heard by other Natives. In Canada the CBC sponsors an active series called The Legends Project, and in Alaska there are many public radio stations in rural communities which feature elders speaking live or in recorded Native language broadcasts.

Internet Variants

Through the Internet, the story of the Blind Man and the Loon has rapidly become globalized, reaching across time and space to connect dozens of languages and cultures. At this juncture I have identified fifteen Internet versions of the Blind Man and the Loon. Some of the online electronic texts are taken directly from limited edition books. That is, the hosting Internet site essentially digitizes a text that first appeared in a paper edition and then went out of print. Others are "stolen" directly from books without any attribution. Still others look authentic but come from unknown sources. Many variants are here today and gone tomorrow, as web sites are reorganized, renamed, or discontinued altogether. For this reason it would be rather futile to list these variants using specific web addresses. To find them, it is easy enough to Google such keywords such as "Blind Man and the Loon," "Blind Boy and the Loon," "Lumaaq," or "Narwhal legend."

On the Internet there is a short syndicated program called *Nature-Watch*, produced by Finger Lakes Productions International of Ithaca, New York, and sponsored in part by the National Science Foundation.

NatureWatch is estimated to reach 650,000 listeners daily on more than 140 public radio stations across the United States and is broadcast internationally to more than 120 countries and territories via Armed Forces Radio. Its purpose is to teach natural history.

On June 9, 2006, *NatureWatch* released a ninety-second podcast called "The Loon's Necklace" (NW060609), narrated by David Kinder, in which a truncated semi-literary variant of the story is presented, but without the betrayal and revenge motifs.[9] The loon leads the blind man back home, but surprisingly there is no mention of their diving down into the lake or of the loon restoring his sight.

There is a distinct danger in accepting such Internet texts as equivalent to authentic oral tradition texts simply because they appear neatly in print or sound bites. This is because many of those who create web pages often do so in a casual, careless way that leaves us wondering about provenance. Storytellers' names, even when known by the person posting the text, are often not acknowledged. The time and place of the recordings also slip by unnoticed. Such postings have been described in some places as "digital storytelling" or "e-texts." So far, local tradition bearers themselves are not using the Internet to tell "The Blind Man and the Loon," but many collectors and popularizers are.

Conclusion

In contrast to the graphic arts and carvings created by indigenous peoples, most of the film, audio, and other media works generated by the tale of the Blind Man and the Loon are rather apocryphal and truncated, with loose, tenuous connections to oral tradition and strong links to semi-literary adaptations.

In contrast to oral tradition, these multimedia works have been largely produced by non-Natives for non-Natives. Because of this, they are not as subject to the social constraints and community norms that guide traditional oral performances. Still, as metaculture, they have greatly fostered the story's popularity, wrapping it in distinctly different packages.[10] Reflexively and semiotically, the book I am writing here is one additional sign of this mass mediation. For all of these reasons the tale of the Blind Man and the Loon remains powerful not only in spite of its mediated and theatrical reformulations but also because of them.

CHAPTER SEVEN

The Power of the Tale

A story can bring the past to the present, open people up for the experience of being healed, and prepare them to do the work of healing themselves.
—EDITH TURNER, *AMONG THE HEALERS*

The Quest

As mentioned in chapter 1, "The Blind Man and the Loon" has traveled for thousands of miles and has been performed for hundreds and perhaps thousands of years for thousands of people over a very large part of northern and western Canada, Alaska, Greenland, and the western United States. Most exciting of all is the fact that it is still very much a living tradition.

My exercise on the morphology of the tale in chapter 1 demonstrates the tale's great popularity and its ability to bend and transcend many cultural and linguistic boundaries, but it offers little or no insights into *why* it has traveled so widely and *why* it has persisted so strongly in oral traditions right up to the present day. Why has it become part of virtually every Native storyteller's repertoire throughout the North American Arctic and Subarctic?

To answer these questions I have turned my eye toward the tale's underlying semiotic. The significance of the story is arguably somewhat opaque, at least to a non-Native audience, but it becomes increasingly transparent as we study its performers and its cultural milieus. Diving down under the formal surface of the story, its shape and texture, I am interested in its significance to myself as a reader and listener and to the people who continue to perform the story and listen to it. In the words of my friend Kenneth Frank, we have to "go under the ice."

I am also attempting to gain a better understanding of the cultural and performance contexts of the tale, even though such contexts are sadly absent from nearly all published oral texts. I really have only my

135

own unpublished collection of texts and field notes to draw upon, an extremely small fraction of the total listed in appendix B. But they offer at least a small keyhole to peer through.

As Terry Thompson and Steven Egesdal declare in the introduction to their book *Salish Myths and Legends*:

> One of the problems with a Western audience understanding, let alone appreciating Salishan narratives is that often they are decontextualized to the point of being incomprehensible. The narratives seem terse, laconic, and spare, because much if not most presupposed cultural knowledge is missing. That leaves outsiders with a problem grasping the actual themes of the narratives. (2008, xxxiv)

I would argue that this problem extends today to almost any Native American oral tradition, including those which have maintained the Blind Man and the Loon in their repertoires.

In Tanacross, Alaska, it is crucially important to know that Kenny Thomas Sr. (2005: 203–6) performs "The Blind Man and the Loon" as the opening episode in a much larger story cycle about the man Yamaagh Telcheegh. The full Yamaagh Telcheegh story, which reportedly takes seven nights to tell, can only be performed in the fall during the month of October, suggesting that it is closely associated with the seasonal round, particularly with moose hunting. And indeed in Tanacross tradition (Group G) the game animal the blind man shoots with his arrow is always a moose. The name Yamaagh Telcheegh glosses as "He went all around the world in anger," a name given for his response to the way his wife treated him when he was blind.[1]

Another feature of the tale that deserves more attention is the repertoire of hand gestures that travels with it. In Kenny's performance, one notable gesture is the arching and flick of his wrist each time the loon dives under water with the blind man (fig. 19). The repeated gesture may be seen in the video companion to this volume at http://www.uaf.edu/loon/video. This simple gesture would seem to be an integral part of the performance, but we will need to have visual documentation of other narrators and other performances in order to confirm this.

Yamaagh Telcheegh starts out as the blind man we are familiar with in other variants, but in subsequent episodes he quickly takes on the identity of the Traveler. The Traveler is a familiar figure in Northern Dene folklore who goes around the country fixing all the animals who are hostile to humans. In Gwich'in he is known as Vasaagìhdzak or Ch'iteehàwąįį. Among the Utes, the blind man is identified as Coyote, joining him with yet another famous cycle of tales (Mason 1910, 301).

So to understand the Blind Man and the Loon as an independent stand-alone oral narrative misses a major point, which is that in many areas the story behaves like a free morpheme. It takes on a wealth of additional local or parochial meanings depending on the many sequels, songs, beliefs, and rituals attached to it. At Barrow, Alaska, collectors Robert F. Spencer and W. K. Carter noticed that some dynamic and marked differences between the texts of narrators there "suggest that the story reaches the group in two different versions at varying points in time or that it has been recast to fit the changed patterning vested in a younger generation" (Spencer and Carter 1954, 65).

In some of the Eskimo variants, as I noted earlier, the blind boy and his sister leave their dead or narwhal-transformed mother and go on to other adventures. Sometimes they themselves are transformed into the Sun and the Moon, becoming part of another widely-known Eskimo tale of incest and shame. In another sequel they visit a strange land of people who have claws and in another sequel they meet up with a group of people who lack anuses. Sometimes they meet up with shadow people who turn out to be cannibals. So the story is often linked to a much larger repertoire, and that repertoire is part of its context. It is embedded. It is connected.

Values and Themes

I am convinced that the tale of the Blind Man and the Loon is told by Natives everywhere in the North because it weaves together several basic themes or tenets of indigenous Native American and First Nations life. It articulates the fundamental importance of the subsistence way of life no matter whether the animal being hunted by the blind man is a bear, a caribou, a moose, or a buffalo, and it is centrally concerned with the importance of sharing food through kinship in the nuclear family.

The narrative of "The Blind Man and the Loon" also has universal appeal because it reveals deep-seated conflicts within the nuclear family unit. Females pitted against males in the same household are like protons pulling against electrons, and the conflict is dangerous enough to explode the most fundamental of all social atoms. At the same time, the Eskimo subtype contains a different kind of kinship atom than the Indian subtype: a blind man squares off against his mother or grandmother (sometimes with the aid of his sister). The key relationships are consanguineal. In the Indian subtype, a blind man squares off against his wife (and sometimes their children). The key relationship is affinal.

What more essential kin relations are there than those between a mother and her child, between a grandmother and her grandson, or between a man and his wife? When these kinship obligations begin to disintegrate, as the story illustrates so vividly, the result is isolation, starvation, and tragic death. Along with the development of language and small monogamous families, argues the archaeologist Lewis Binford (1983, 27), the sharing of food among adults is one of the most basic things that makes us human. It is this behavior that separates us from our nonhuman ancestors and other animals.

To both Native and non-Native audiences the story of the Blind Man and the Loon elicits sympathy and respect for the handicapped, not just out of pity for their undeserved suffering but by demonstrating that the handicapped and the elderly can and often do contribute importantly to group survival. This is the obvious subtext of Velma Wallis's best seller *Two Old Women* (1993), based on her mother's Gwich'in folk tale. A few years ago I collected a Tanacross legend about a crippled boy who hopped on his knuckles for over a mile to warn a neighboring village that enemy warriors had surrounded them and were about to attack. In doing this he overcame his handicap and saved the village (see Thomas 2005, 223–36).

There is still more in the ethnographic record regarding the disabled. Dr. John Simpson, one of the very first ethnographers to visit the Inuit in northern Alaska during the mid-nineteenth century, observed at Barrow that:

> For the tender solicitude with which their own infancy and childhood have been tended, in the treatment of their aged and infirm parents they make a return which redounds to their credit, for they not only give them food and clothing, sharing with them every comfort they

possess, but on their longest and most fatiguing journeys make provision for their easy conveyance. In this way we witnessed among the people of fourteen summer tents and as many boats, one crippled old man, a blind and helpless old woman, two grown-up women with sprained ankles, and one other old invalid, besides children of many ages, carried by their respective families, who had done the same for the two first during many successive summers. Here, again, the tie of kindred dictates the duty. (Simpson [1855] 1988, 520)

And back in 1911 Vilhjalmur Stefansson (2001, 263) observed that "One [Inuit] man of about forty-five, Avranna, is totally blind and has been for a long time. He seems tenderly cared for and goes walking about outside with his cane, guided by the shouts of grown people or children warning him of obstacles and telling him where to go."

There is an abundance of evidence that during the nineteenth century, Inuit children, along with the handicapped and elderly, were very highly respected and well cared for. Writing of the Ammassalik Eskimo in East Greenland, William Thalbitzer found that each person usually has been given several names and thus has several ancestral souls: "The Eskimo does not punish his child. At its baptism the child gets the name of some deceased person, and, with this, inherits the soul of the deceased (or, more correctly, one of the souls). To scold the child, or to punish it, would in most cases be equivalent to provoking the deceased, the child's namesake. It would be an act of profanity, and might cause one of the souls to leave the child in anger, and so bring sickness to the child" (Thalbitzer 1941, 600; see also Holtved 1967, 150).

Harold Seidelman and James Turner, in their provocative book *The Inuit Imagination*, note, "In every area of the Arctic a story is told of a mistreated orphan boy who gains revenge against his tormentors. This legend deals with the universal themes of abandonment and powerlessness, some of the central concerns of Inuit life" (1994, 124). Although the blind boy in our story is not strictly an orphan, he is mistreated as if he were an orphan.[2] He is all but abandoned, yet he acquires power and metes out revenge. In addition to the Lumaaq story, other Inuit tales that employ these same themes and values are those told about Qaudjaqdjuq and Kiviung (Kiviuq, Qiviuq).

Another major theme is that of transformation, as people or creatures magically change their identity. Our tale contains several transformations: the transformation of a blind man into one that sees, the transformation of a wicked woman into a narwhal, beluga or ant, and in some variants of the tale known as "the loon's necklace," the transformation of an undistinguished black bird into a bird brightly decorated with dentalium shells.

On an even deeper level, the appeal of the story itself seems to lie in its emotional transformation of the listener or reader. It begs for what Samuel Taylor Coleridge once called "the willing suspension of disbelief." These various transformations carry overtones of shamanistic practice and ritual healing. It is noteworthy that at least one traditional performer of the story, Della Keats of Kotzebue (see appendix B and Creed 1984), was a widely celebrated and honored Iñupiat Eskimo healer.

Ethnographic Dimensions: Bear Lore, Rites, and Taboos

The Eskimo subtype of the Blind Boy and the Loon story also carries an important subtext about the rules for respecting the spirit of the polar bear. Knud Rasmussen pointed out several Netsilik taboos that had to be observed to prevent the killed bear's spirit from becoming an evil spirit causing sickness and distress (1931, 183–84). Still other protocols were in effect for the distribution of a killed polar bear, especially in East Greenland. Other rites and taboos have been outlined by Helge Larsen in his essay on the Eskimo Bear Cult (1969). As William Thalbitzer (1941, 643–44) once observed among the Ammassalik Eskimo:

> With bear hunting it is a question of the one who discovers the bear being the owner (e·wa, e·wata), and having the right to the head, breast, heart, and skin; also, according to another testimony, to the upper part of the spine. The next shares fall to those who first touch the bear with a weapon (knife or lance), eventually killing it, and in the following order.
>
> Number I gets the left hind-quarter of the bear
> Number II gets the right hind-quarter
> Number III gets the left fore-quarter
> Number IV gets the right fore-quarter
>
> . . .The discoverer of the bear may just as well be a woman as a man.

Indeed, it often happens that a child discovers the bear, and so gets the main portion. . . . He who by himself both discovers and shoots the bear gets the whole animal for himself and his family.

In her monograph on shamanism, Merete Jakobsen declares that "the encounter with the spirit of the bear is very significant in the process of becoming an agakkoq [medicine man]" (1999, 55), and hostile bears are often viewed as the incarnation of evil shamans. From this perspective, the blind man's act of killing the bear is a display of his good medicine power.

Rémi Savard (1966, 140–48) makes the argument that the killing of a young man's first polar bear calls for a village feast and celebration—a rite of passage into manhood. Saladin d'Anglure takes this even further, insisting that the first polar bear taken by a young man is proof of his sexual virility: "The bear, like the hunter, was valued for his predatory and reproductive qualities, that is, his powers of vision, rapid movement, and force that are also associated with sexual potency" (Saladin d'Anglure 1990, 189).

Walter Ekblaw ([1928] 1961, 11) adds that among the Polar Eskimos in Greenland, a boy became a man and could take a spouse after killing his first polar bear. Could this tale then be a coming-of-age story? Today young Greenlandic men still take pride in wearing bearskin pants, visible proof of their masculinity and virility, but alas for them, sometimes women do also (see fig. 12).

While this whole argument that killing a polar bear is a puberty rite seems fully plausible, there is little evidence of it implicit in the Blind Man and the Loon narrative. We need to be critical. Only in the stand-alone sequel of the Sun-Brother Moon-Sister is the young man's sexual potency explicitly realized, and this sequel can only be found in a few regional variants of the Eskimo subtype, notably in Group B.

Rémi Savard draws attention to a passage in which Knud Rasmussen (1929, 179) observes that a young Inuit man must never eat the meat of his first big game kill. It is expected that he will give it all away to the elders. Of course in the tale itself there are no elders except the blind man's mother or grandmother. Still, the young man openly violates this taboo when his sister sneaks some of the bear meat to him. Is he aware of this cultural taboo when he partakes?

If Savard's view of the first-kill taboo is correct, then the blind man's mother or grandmother may be entirely justified in withholding the meat from him. After all, she is the one who discovers the bear, and by rule she is the one who should receive its meat. In most variants we are not told whether this is the first polar bear the boy has killed. But in Davidialuk's variant, it is fairly clear that the blind man is an experienced hunter and has already taken other bears: "He remembered well the sound of a wounded bear from his old hunting days before he was blind" (Seidelman and Turner 1994, 125–28).

In variants of the Eskimo subtype, it would seem as if the wicked mother or grandmother is acting selfishly by lying to the young hunter and that she is violating one of the cardinal rules for sharing meat.[3] By being the first to spot the bear, she is clearly entitled to parts of it, even the choicest parts, but clearly she is not entitled to all of it. In the Nunavut area, they have a special name for the kind of person who is stingy with food, especially in times of scarcity. They call such a person Iqattattuq (Bennett and Rowley 2004, 441).

Other customs and taboos seem to be egregiously violated in the story. As Kleivan and Sonne remind us,

> Misfortunes affecting the individual or the community were usually traced back to breaches of taboo . . . The polar bear, a large and relatively rare quarry, was the object of especially many rituals. They can probably be considered an offshoot of an age-old circumpolar bear cult. The head was brought into the house to stay there for a prescribed number of days. In order to please the bear, blubber was smeared inside its mouth, while its nose was stoppered and its eyes closed with moss and lamp dregs, so that it would not be bothered by the smell and sight of human beings. (1985, 20)

There was also a taboo on women working with knives or needles for several days after the kill. Readers familiar with Eskimo variants of the Blind Man and the Loon will quickly realize that the wicked mother or grandmother doesn't observe any of these rituals or taboos.

Traditional values, coded taboos, and social rules such as these permeate the story of the Blind Man and the Loon, but are taught largely through inversion and reversal. They are conspicuous in their absence from the texts but fully visible in the ethnographic record. Part of the power of the story is that it so vividly teaches the tragic consequences of violating these widespread but unstated norms subsumed in hunting rituals, the incest taboo, child care, respect for the handicapped, and food sharing. When we hear the story or read it or see it, we are connected to that power.

Symbolic and Ecological Dimensions: Loons and Water Bugs

Loons are considered the oldest living birds on the earth, with some fossils dating back twenty million years (Klein 1985, 127). There are four distinct species of loons in North America—the common loon, the red-throated loon, the arctic or pacific Loon, and the yellow-billed loon—but these species are seldom distinguished in the oral narrative tradition, or, more tellingly, they simply get left out in translation. All four species breed and nest in Alaska. In the version of the tale I collected on July 10, 1983, from the late Abraham Luke, living in Dot Lake, Alaska, the pair of loons which assist the blind man in restoring his sight are identified in the Tanacross language as *tsalbet* (common loon) and *daadzen* (arctic or pacific loon).

The latter name is intriguing from a semiotic standpoint, since the derivation of *tsalbet* in the Tanacross language is morphemically similar to the name for the pacific or arctic loon in Gwich'in, *ts'aɬvit* or *ts'alvit* (see chapter 4). Etymologically, the word *ts'alvit* means "almost to the point or tip of the arrow" (Benveniste 1953). This strong association of the loon with the blind man's shooting of the moose with his bow and arrow begs the question: what is the metaphorical connection between the arctic loon and the tip of the hunter's arrow? One could speculate that the northern Dene implanted arctic loon feathers on the shafts of their arrows to insure that the arrows would fly as straight and true as the blind man's did, and that the arrows would somehow "see" their targets. Robert McKennan (1959, 52; 1965, 36), however, noticed in the 1930s that both Gwich'in and Upper Tanana hunters preferred to fletch their arrows with three or four hawk or eagle feathers.

In the Indian subtype, there are a substantial number of variants, including Maggie Gilbert's, in which the cruel wife offers her husband a cup of water full of bugs. She thinks at this point that he is still blind, but he only pretends to be. Although this final insult leads directly to her own death, the woman is actually offering her husband ordinary loon's food (see chapter 4, note 8). Along with fish, aquatic organisms are an important part of the loon's diet (Dunning 1985, 79), and Catharine McClellan (1975, 536) tells us that when the Inland Tlingit shaman finishes his vision quest, the first food he eats is that which his spirit animal suggests to him. However, by rejecting these water bugs and tossing away the water his wife offers to him, the blind man seems to abandon his symbolic association and identity with the loon.

Insects swallowed in water are mentioned by Hinrich Rink ([1875] 1997, 49–50) as a form of witchcraft among Greenlanders. The belief is that once swallowed, insects would eat the entrails of the victim and reappear out of his body greatly enlarged in size. Though this motif of offering the blind man insects in his drinking water is generally found only in the Indian subtype, an Inuit variant collected at Barrow by Spencer and Carter (1954, 67) has the grandmother offering her grandson water containing caribou hair and worms.

Religious Dimensions: Ritual and Belief

The tale obviously reenacts healing through the magical act of diving under water and rising again several times. There is a cleansing associated with the water deep in the lake, and with repetition. Nevertheless, in most of the Greenlandic variants the ritual does not involve the blind man diving down with the loon but rather allowing the loon or another kind of bird to drop excrement into his eyes or to touch his eyes with its wing feathers. In some Greenlandic variants the helping bird actually does both. It drops excrement into his eyes and then wipes them clean with its wing feathers.

Still, the tale's power does not stop there. It also establishes a bond of kindness and respect between men and birds that stimulates our imagination and kindles our emotions. The reciprocity between the boy or the man and the loons recalls an ancient ritual and articulates a special kind of world view. This enlightened world view, achieved through diving down underwater or touching the eyes with droppings or feathers, allows a peek at the shaman's supernatural world and belief system.

In both Inuit and Na-Dene cultures, every shaman has a protective spirit, and it would seem that the loon in our story is just such a spirit. If that is the case, the blind man or blind boy is viewed by Native audiences as a shaman. For those who might miss the point, Maggie Gilbert even identifies the blind man in her Gwich'in variant as a "medicine man" and a "dreamer" just before the loon approaches him, emphasizing this by pronouncing it in English (see chapter 4, lines 81–82).

And as we have already seen, several of Knud Rasmussen's Canadian Inuit sources for "The Blind Man and the Loon" were either shamans, married to a shaman, the acknowledged son of a shaman, or learned their stories from an uncle who was a shaman. Jean Malaurie's source, Pualuna, in northern Greenland, was a former shaman. This is hardly a coincidence.

In Greenland, the helping spirits to *angakkoqs* (represented in our story by loons or other birds) are recognized as *toorneq*, *tôrnaq*, or *toornarsuuk* (see Jakobsen 1999, 66–69). On Canada's Baffin Island they are called *torngat* or *tuurngait*. Farther to the west, they are known as *turñnrat* or *tuunbaq*.

E. J. Peck's comprehensive list of 347 *torngat* in Cumberland Sound on Baffin Island includes one loon-like spirit (#198) named Aullaqtaq. Aullaqtaq "makes short flights to various places. Like a large bird. Black and white. Good spirit. Brings light on the back of his head from heaven, the world boundary, and the land. Light being considered a means of life, a bringing light is the cause of healing and blessing" (Laugrand, Oosten, & Trudel 2005, 448). Birket-Smith too cites an eighteenth century Danish missionary report of an East Greenlandic shaman who used a loon as his tôrnaq ([1924] 1976, 453).

Animal guardian spirits are also an integral part of northern Dene religious belief. The Gwich'in, for example, call them *yitsochii* (McKennan 1965, 78). The folklorist James Teit (1900, 381–82), working with the Thompson Indians of British Columbia, once described and illustrated a shaman's pipe whose stone stem was inlaid with a loon's necklace design. And working with Northern and Southern Tutchone and Inland Tlingits throughout the Yukon Territory, ethnographer Catharine McClellan noticed that it was commonly the case that "shamans had loons for spirit helpers" (McClellan 1975, 170). These shamans were known to go down to the beach and talk to loons as part of their vision quest.

Medicine power certainly enables the blind man to talk and

communicate with the birds. McClellan adds that several Southern Tutchone shamans had the practice of symbolically "going under the water" to retrieve a lost soul. In the actual ritual, shamans would lie down under a blanket and remain motionless for several hours or days. While under their blankets, the shamans sent their spirit helpers off on long journeys (McClellan, 1975, 543). In the tale of the Blind Man and the Loon, this shamanistic ritual seems to be reflected in the loon's diving under water with the blind man to restore his sight.

In the Alaskan village of Minto, on the Tanana River downstream from Tanacross, the Swedish folklorist Anna Birgitta Rooth recorded a variant of the Blind Man and the Loon story during the 1960s that was accompanied by a medicine song. Performed by Moses Charlie and transcribed by Håkan Lundström, this song has been used magically to heal anyone in the community with sore eyes (Rooth 1976, 25–26; Lundström 1980, 135–36)—yet another example of how the tale acquired new power after it became localized.

A parallel example underscoring this traditional belief system, according to one Sahtu Dene storyteller, is that "if a person owned a strong medicine power on the raven, this person could talk to ravens and ravens could talk to the person, sometimes predicting the future. And if this person had a strong enough medicine, he could transfer himself into a raven and stay with the raven for a while. Later, he could come back to being human again" (Blondin 1990, ii). This world view is also pervasive among the Eskimo, where Pacific Loons are actually known to sing songs in Yup'ik (Andrew 2008: 170–73).

Ethnographic reports further amplify the archaeological connection between this tale type and an in situ ritual complex. As early as 1897, Edward Nelson (1899) observed Eskimo men wearing loonskin caps in their sweat baths, and in 1976, Thomas Johnston, the late ethnomusicologist, published a photograph of a Point Hope dancer wearing a loonskin headdress and performing the box-drum dance. Johnston (1976a, 16–17) wrote: "The loon, a long-beaked bird, is found throughout the Arctic, particularly at Point Hope where it has long been a source of special interest. Its great diving powers are thought to aid the shaman in his long dive to the ocean floor to communicate with the whaling spirits."

Anecdotal as it may be, we would be remiss not to observe that the Nunamiut Eskimo of Anaktuvuk Pass, Alaska, have a story about a loon's bill amulet. As told by Elijah Kakinya (Bergsland 1987, 272–74), the pacific loon's bill was used by a woman at Point Barrow to save her son from a voracious sea monster with a big mouth. Froelich Rainey (1947) and Kaj Birket-Smith (1959) have also commented on the use of loon heads as Iñupiat hunting amulets, while Lorraine Koranda has stressed the importance of the loon in the Iñupiat Messenger Feast:[4]

> On a band fitting snugly around the dancer's head was fastened a dried loon head with beak. Loon feathers decorated the flaps which fell over the dancer's ears. This headdress was used in the Messenger Feast ceremonial dances and in colorful loon dances of the north coast, in which the dancer used birdlike motions to imitate with good humor the proud movements of one of the most elegant of the world's birds, the Pacific (or Arctic) Loon." (Koranda 1972, 12)

Psychological Dimensions

Dan Merkur has written at some length about the Blind Man and the Loon story, which he sees as a symbolic description of an Inuit shaman's initiation ritual. He writes: "The psychotherapy that Inuit shamans achieved through their visions was available in their society only to initiated shamans. The therapeutic insights were placed in the public domain, however, in the myths that shamans narrated openly about the moon god" (2005, 129). In order to postulate this theory of the story, Merkur accepts the fact that the Blind Man and the Loon is inextricably linked to the Sun-Sister Moon-Brother story, one of its sequels.

But this carries the very same flaw advocated in the psychosexual theory of Savard and Saladin d'Anglure. The Sun-Sister Moon-Brother sequel sometimes stands by itself and is also strictly limited to the variants in only one area: the Nunavik-Nunavut region of the central Canadian arctic (see map 1, Group B). In nearly all other regions, the blind man is not associated with the moon at all.

Merkur also suggests that the blind man's killing of the bear has "echoes" of "an Oedipal killing of the father" (2005, 131), which strikes me as a highly imaginary comparison, not grounded at all in the ethnographic literature. What makes the bear a Freudian father figure? Even more strangely, Merkur thinks that the blind man's helping spirit is not the loon so much as the bear. He argues that in traditional Inuit belief the polar bear's spirit is regarded as the most powerful spirit from which shamans obtain their helpers, citing the existence of the widespread polar bear cult that extends from Canada into Greenland (1985, 227; 1991, 228, 240).

Rémi Savard, in his doctoral dissertation (1966, 126–54), takes the approach that the principal theme revealed in variants of "The Blind Man and the Loon" is the differentiation of the sexes, not just biologically but socially. This is supported in the sequel about the people without anuses and/or vaginas. Taken together with the Sun-Sister Moon-Brother incest tale, which often appears in Group B variants, Savard sees a strong structural and symbolic connection between eating taboos and sexual taboos.

In "The Blind Man and the Loon," there is certainly a transgression by the blind man when he eats the meat of the polar bear, his first kill. But Savard pushes the envelope when he says the blind man achieves a high level of intimacy with his sister by accepting the bear meat she has hidden up under her parka, against her bare skin.

This is followed by a second major transgression when (in the Sun-Sister Moon-Brother sequel) he has sex with her in the dark, and she in turn marks him with lamp soot and then serves him her severed breasts on a platter. In the structuralist terms of Claude Lévi-Strauss, who emphasizes the incest taboo as the very foundation of kinship and culture, Savard believes the two stories taken together are a parable on the gender-based origins of humanity and the emergence of culture. Again, provenance is the key: such a view remains suspect in that it relies narrowly and only on Group B variants.

Dimensions of Social Justice: Violence and Revenge

Audiences everywhere usually find themselves cheering for the underdog. This is true for folktales as well as novels and Hollywood movies. In the Indian subtype we see a man triumph over old age, blindness, and spousal abuse. In the Eskimo subtype we see a youth triumph over blindness, child abuse, and greediness. Just recently, and tellingly, the Lumaajuuq story (Group B) has been used in a workshop for psychiatrists and social workers coping with intergenerational abuse in Inuit communities (Crawford 2007).

In Euro-American society we expect healing to occur through acts of apology and forgiveness, often accompanied by compensation adjudicated through courts of law. However, we must be open to the fact that in other cultures healing and justice are sanctioned through acts of violent revenge. Revenge, as most Americans found in the killing of Osama bin Laden, helps to bring closure.

In many Eskimo variants the evil mother or grandmother blinds the young man using witchcraft right at the beginning (see for example, SB 2274, collected by Knud Rasmussen, appendix C). And Rink informs us that violent revenge was "the duty of the nearest relative" among Greenlanders whenever witchcraft was practiced, and that "capital punishment, as the result of deliberation and decree, was inflicted upon witches, and upon such individuals as were obviously dangerous to the whole community, or at least suspected of being so" ([1875] 1997, 35). This kind of subtext generally escapes a western reading audience.

Birgitte Sonne (1982, 1988) writes at length about the cruel and violent side of Greenlandic Eskimo history, noting especially how much of a culture shock it was for Knud Rasmussen when he began to hear stories from the East Greenlanders about the bloody murders and other crimes that marked their recent past. In light of this, Rasmussen admits he had to reassess the historical value of the folklore he was collecting from them:

> for these tragedies, recounted by eye-witnesses, demonstrate that the old Eskimo legends to a far greater extent than has hitherto been believed, are the Eskimos' own history, which has been handed down by oral tradition to subsequent generations It has been thought that the greater number of the legends, which reveal appalling cruelty, were the outcome of imagination. . . .The many heartless things that are spoken of: "Men who eat their wives;" "Orphans who are ill-treated;" "Remorseless massacres of women;"—subjects that are very frequently treated of in Eskimo legend,—are undoubtedly all experiences that have been conscientiously repeated from generation to generation. (Rasmussen 1908, 288–89)

So too in the 1950s Jean Malaurie (1985, 188), another collector of the Blind Man and the Loon, found that among the Polar Eskimos there were many stories circulating about cruel acts of murder and revenge, often after "a month to several years" had passed. This is in close keeping with the "slow burn" style of retaliation by the blind man that helps characterize the Eskimo subtype (see chapter 1).[5]

Emic Dimensions

As we have seen, there is a wealth of speculation among scholars and collectors, but a lot more can be learned about the story by comparing comments made by the storytellers. The eye-for-an-eye kind of justice displayed among the Inuit performers of "The Blind Man and the Loon" seems to have been an integral part of the northern Dene ethic as well. In Peter Kalifornsky's Dena'ina variant (1991) from Kenai, Alaska, the blind man gouges out the eyes of his wife in retaliation for her cruelty and then abandons her. The blindness is not only literal but figurative. In an endnote to his telling of the tale, Kalifornsky says: "In this story, blindness is a metaphor for unawareness. The man and woman are each blind to one another at different points in the story, and, being incapable of being aware of each other at the same time, they eventually separate to seek happiness with someone else" (1991, 148–49).

And after performing the story for me in his native Tanacross language and in English, Kenny Thomas Sr. explained that the blind man Yamaagh Telcheegh indeed felt guilty about killing his wife, but he wanted to get even with her for the way she lied to him, and most importantly, he had every right to do so. Thomas added that the two loons in the story were medicine people, which explains why nobody in his region of the upper Tanana River hunts loons today (Thomas 2005, 214–15). This same hunting taboo holds for the Gwich'in and other northern Dene, but we should be aware that both loons and loon eggs continue to be hunted for subsistence by Inuits in northern Alaska and Canada, particularly on St. Lawrence Island and in the village of Noorvik.[6]

In the Yup'ik community of Tununak, on Nelson Island, Alaska, elder Andy Charlie offers an interpretation of the story that lies at the opposite end of the spectrum from that offered by Kenny Thomas Sr. While Thomas is critical of the woman for betraying her blind husband and thinks she deserved what she got when he took revenge and killed her, Charlie is quite critical of the blind boy killing his grandmother. He claims the boy made a terrible mistake by taking revenge on her. Following his performance of the story in Yup'ik, Charlie offers an extended commentary on it, saying: "Even though you are very angry and upset, don't seek revenge; don't recompense with evil," and "if someone offends you, let it go in one ear and out the other, pretending it never happened" (Charlie 1997, 25). For Charlie, the right thing for the boy to do after he found out that his grandmother blinded him would simply be to avoid her.

Final Reflections

It is quite surprising that the same story (or regional oicotypes of it) can lend itself to such diametrically opposite messages, emically formulated by elders who know the story extremely well in their own Native languages. Is this the result of broad ethnic differences between Dene and Yup'ik world views, or is it the product of differences in individual values? There is no definitive answer. The framework of the story has universal appeal, but at the very same time it must be decoded with local or regional or ethnic values, and these social values and standards of behavior have many personal permutations. In this sense the tale is polygenetic.

As Raymond Jones and Jon Stott astutely remind us, "the recognition of similarities in stories from different cultures, however such similarities have arisen, should not lead us to minimize the importance of the differences in these tales. Even if a tale has migrated from one culture to another, the receiving culture gives details and provides emphases that reflect its own beliefs" (2006,xi).

In one of the semi-literary retellings of the story, as delineated in chapter 2, the tale of the Blind Man and the Loon is clearly targeted toward juvenile readers (see Toye and Cleaver, 1977), and in the popular film adaptation of the tale called *The Loon's Necklace* (Crawley, 1949), the motif of violent revenge inflicted by the blind man on his cruel wife has been completely expunged. In this retold version the blind man is betrayed by an old hag, and in the end she is transformed into a screeching owl.

In Western culture children are taught that using violence to get even with someone who has offended you is not only morally unjust, it is also illegal. The state holds the exclusive right to inflict capital punishment. So a radically different ethic and sensibility is being employed in these literary and media retellings. The story is projected through a different cultural prism, with different standards for social behavior and a different kind of rhetoric.

An elegant aesthetic feature of the Eskimo subtype is the parallelism between the blind man's healing through repeatedly diving underwater with the loons and the wicked mother's death through repeatedly diving underwater as she is towed by the narwhal or beluga. And in the Indian subtype told by Maggie Gilbert there is poetic justice and symmetry in the way that the wife is killed with the moose's femur, a bone that comes from the very animal that she so selfishly stole from her husband.[7]

The blind man's mother is also something like Captain Ahab in Melville's novel *Moby Dick*. Ahab is killed by being pulled to sea by a whale with a tangled harpoon line wrapped around his neck. The wicked mother of the blind man has the harpoon line wrapped around her waist or her foot. Thus the blind man's miraculous physical healing, akin to Christian baptism by immersion, is only a prelude to the much deeper-seated spiritual and emotional healing rooted in achieving social justice. This is not the compassionate justice and forgiveness of a Jesus or a Ghandi or a Martin Luther King Jr. It is the retributive justice of oppressed individuals who need to be released from their rage and their anger. In most of Native America it is not enough for the blind man to regain his eyesight through the magical powers of the loon and the ritual of diving down. This would indeed be a happy ending, but "The Blind Man and the Loon" does not end happily.

Whenever the beaten-down protagonist overcomes adversity and wins, as in the outcome of this tale, both the performers of the tale and their audiences have an excuse to celebrate. We celebrate not only the boy's or man's renewed vision and his wholeness as a subsistence hunter; we also recognize and celebrate his right to social justice, to redemption from undeserved suffering. When we witness social justice, it makes us happy, and when we are happy we begin to be healed. We undergo a catharsis. The world itself becomes whole again. I believe this is the very real power of the story, the medicinal power that keeps it alive and kicking in oral tradition.

Conclusion and Afterword

The Folktale as Hypertext

"The Blind Man and the Loon" is constructed much like a hypertext. That is, it has embedded links to many symbolic cognitive domains in Eskimo and Indian culture. Its complex, immediate links to material culture (especially historic and late prehistoric subsistence hunting technologies), to kinship rights and obligations, to spirituality (shamanistic dreaming and healing), and to notions of personal and social justice are a total revelation. Each variant provides continuity with the past and each performance contributes to cultural survival.

On a computer, such links or "pages" are activated by a mouse click. But in the world of face-to-face oral transmission or in folk art, these links are activated by the life experience and cultural knowledge of the audience. After Roland Barthes, variants of the Blind Man and the Loon story operate as open-ended "writerly texts." That is, as listeners or readers we are encouraged to find links and connections of our own making. Of course these links are not visually underlined or highlighted in blue as they are on the world wide web, but they are still there as key words and word sequences, subtle mnemonic devices waiting to be triggered in performance.

Sportscasters enrich the narrative of their play-by-play by calling up all sorts of statistics and anecdotes about the players and the environmental setting for the games. They tell us the temperature, which way the wind is blowing, and the condition of the quarterback's injured thumb and his pass completion percentage. As storytellers they appear to be omniscient, but they are often simply adding statistics and context by reading from a computer screen linked to a database or set of databases, or being prompted by other hidden observers known as spotters. This is the backstory. With remote cameras and wireless microphones they are able to jump directly into and out of the game to interview players and coaches and add a library of anecdotes from their biographies. In this way radio and television audiences have a richer intellectual experience than those who attend the sporting event in person and who experience it viscerally. Similarly, with folktales, much of the performance context, storyteller's life history, and linguistic nuances can be supplied with authority by the folklorists who record them in the field.

Storytelling as Cartography

The storyteller is also a cartographer. And the story of the Blind Man and the Loon is a cognitive map of ancient Indian and Eskimo cultures, plotting systems of knowledge, emotion, belief, and value. While hearing or reading the tale of the Blind Man and the Loon, we are able to spelunk our way into another world, crawling on our hands and knees. This world we enter is prehistoric and paleolithic. It is a graphic mindscape and a spiritual geometry that galvanized much of the ancient polar world and continues to generate a wealth of art and narrative performance, even today, especially today. In a very tangible sense, the great panoply of folk art, commercial art, fine art, music, films, and audio recordings all ride in the slipstream of the folktale. Through intertextuality, this remarkable tale connects storytellers and audiences from many disparate languages and cultures into a virtual artistic community.

Each individual variant is embedded within a local community and a local language. It is also embedded within a region and embodies the social values and subsistence technologies of those regions. Finally, as my two maps show, all of the oral variants taken together are embedded in space and in time within the sweeping cultural history and prehistory of North America and Greenland. They show us how the world is connected intellectually.

Social Dynamics

For years we have heard people complain that once a folk song or traditional story circulating in oral tradition has been recorded and written down it becomes fixed and static and loses most of its oral qualities. This is a popular superstition about folklore itself. But as I demonstrated in chapter 2, the process of redaction for the Blind Man and the Loon story has produced many semi-literary variants and variants of variants in print, not to mention other media such as film, radio, video, CDs, and the Internet. We have seen the tale morph and mutate and replicate itself hundreds of times since it was first recorded by Wittus Frederick Steenholdt and published by Hinrich Rink. Even when corrupted, it is almost as though the text has a life and an afterlife of its own, apart from its many individual "authors." It refuses to be standardized. It is a vibrant, protean piece of culture, a life force.

The richness of folktales is that they collectively augment human intelligence and store it for quick retrieval. This enhances both their educational and entertainment value. "The Blind Man and the Loon," for example, offers practical and symbolic solutions to complex social problems such as the breakdown of the nuclear family and the destruction and loss of kinship rights and obligations. It is a vehicle for thought and reflection, a meditation on traditional values, beliefs, and behaviors, a tool for processing information, and a rich ethnographic database. Yet it must be rhetorically decoded to be untangled and understood. To borrow the words of Internet pioneer Douglas Engelbart, we could say each iteration of the story effectively "downloads" a community's "collective IQ."[1] This happens more in oral performance than in print because live audiences tend to consist of local social networks.

A Classical Tale

It is hard to know whether the story of the Blind Man and the Loon is better known in oral tradition, in film, in the graphic arts, or in print. But the story's openness to wide-ranging local and individual interpretations and reinterpretations is certainly one hallmark of a classic. Yet a "classic" may be defined along several other lines as well. As a noun a classic is "a work considered to be of the highest rank or excellence" and "having lasting significance or worth, enduring." As an adjective, it suggests "formal, refined, and restrained in style" as well as "simple and harmonious, elegant."[2]

The tale of the Blind Man and the Loon radiates all of these special qualities, and it has inspired a wealth of elegant art, language, and sound, delighting the senses. It is a bright thing of wonder in our social galaxy. Because of this, the Blind Man and the Loon is an oral and a written and a mediated classic, a collective masterpiece of the North performed thousands of times by hundreds of storytellers in hundreds of places through the ages.[3] Nevertheless we must not regard it merely as a relic or fossil of the distant past. We can still hear it. We can still see it. It continues to live, to resonate, and to be performed in our own time, here, now, today.

Appendix A

Paradigm of Tale Traits

A) Cast of Characters (dramatis personae)
    A1 Man alone
    A2 Man and wife and
        a) son
        b) daughter
        c) children
        d) old hag
    A3 Boy and
        a) mother
        b) mother and sister
        c) stepmother and sister
    A4 Boy and grandmother and
        a) sister
    A5 Man and wife and lesbian mother and
        a) sister
B) Special Identity of Protagonist
    B0 None—trait absent
    B1 Extremely good hunter
    B2 Medicine man
    B3 Coyote trickster
C) Cause of Blindness
    C0 Not given, blind at the outset
    C1 Brought on by old age
    C2 Cruel deliberate act by
        a) mother

b) grandmother

c) wife

d) stepmother

C3 Accidentally when eyes are hit with strips of rawhide

C4 Sorcery [often combines with C2 or C3]

C5 Eye juggling and failure of magic charm

C6 Snow blindness (natural cause)

D) Animal(s) Hunted and Killed

D0 None—trait absent

D1 Buffalo

D2 Bear

a) polar

b) brown or grizzly

c) black

D3 Caribou

D4 Moose

D5 Deer

D6 Trout/Salmon

D7 Wolves

D8 Several species

E) Woman's Betrayal

E0 None—trait absent

E1 Lies about accuracy of the blind hunter's shot, abandons him, and keeps the meat for herself

E2 Lies and withholds meat from blind hunter but stays near him, feeding him something else

E3 Withholds meat or fish from blind hunter

E4 Abandons blind hunter to starve to death

F) Helper, Offers Aid

F0 None—trait absent

F1 Sister

F2 Son

F3 Daughter

F4 Little bird

G) Number and Kind of Diving Birds

G0 None—trait absent

G1 One

a) loon

b) goose

           c) mulgi

           d) gull

           e) owl

           f) species unidentified

    G2 Two

           a) loons

           b) geese

           c) divers

           d) water birds

    G3 Several spring birds (species unidentified)

H) How Vision Is Restored

    H1 By diving underwater according to talking bird's instructions

           a) once

           b) twice

           c) thrice

           d) four times

           e) five times

           f) six times

           g) numerous times

    H2 By rubbing dirt or powder in his own eyes

           a) thrice

    H3 Goose or bird strikes his face with wings one or more times

           a) after dropping excrement on eyes

    H4 Naturally after a long period of time

    H5 Bird or supernatural being cleans his eyes

           a) by washing them in water and scraping them with a feather

           b) by removing bird excrement from them with hands

           c) by rubbing them

           d) by licking them

    H6 Borrows eye(s) from

           a) owl

           b) coyote

I) Reward Given to Bird

    I0 None—trait absent

    I1 Decorates Loon with white markings made from

           a) clay

           b) dentalium shells

           c) ivory arrowheads

d) beads

e) his own tears of joy

12 Promises to put fish in the lake for Loon to eat

13 Sharpens Loon's bill

J) Woman's Final Insult

J0 None—trait absent

J1 Offers him a drink of polluted water

a) with bugs

b) with worms

J2 Offers him spoiled, burned, or distasteful food

J3 Lies to him about

a) her source of meat

b) her intentions to feed him

J4 Curses him

K) Revenge Taken against Woman

K0 None—trait absent

K1 He returns and kills her on the spot, then

a) abandons his children to die

b) kills his children also

c) kills all children except helper

K2 He ties her to a harpoon line and she is dragged to sea by

a) beluga whale

b) salmon

c) walrus

d) seal

e) narwhal

K3 Miscellaneous other reprisals, including

a) abandonment

b) setting her adrift at sea without a paddle

c) blinding her

d) choking her to death by stuffing roots in her mouth

L) Fate of the Woman

L0 None—trait absent

L1 She is transformed into

a) a narwhal

b) a beluga whale

c) an ant

d) an owl

e) a stone

L2 She dies a violent death

M) Sequels (may be multiple)

    M0 None—trait absent

    M1 Boy and his sister undertake a long journey to live elsewhere

        a) visiting the clawed people who eat the sister

        b) visiting the people without anuses and/or vaginas

    M2 Boy and his sister are transformed into

        a) the moon and the sun (after committing incest): Sun-Sister Moon-Brother is another distinctive tale type

        b) wolves

    M3 Man recounts his adventures and hardships to others

        a) after which Cormorant delivers olachen and Raven transforms people into stone

    M4 Man dies after

        a) talking to owl-wife

        b) children are helped by wolves

        c) he remarries

    M5 Man invites other tribes for feast

    M6 Man remarries, is betrayed by brothers-in-law and rescued by sea lions

    M7 Man and his brother are pursued by a rolling head

    M8 Boy is transformed into a loon

    M9 Man becomes the Traveler and goes around the world "fixing" all the hostile animals so they are friendly to humans

Note: The traits for Maggie Gilbert's Gwich'in variant in chapter 4, for example, may be charted as: A2c B2 C0 D4 E1 F0 G1a H1b I0 J1a K1a L2 M3.

Appendix B

Annotated Bibliography of Variants

Part 1. Variants Collected from Oral Tradition

Akadlaka, Marcel. "A Blind Son." In *How Kabloonat Became and Other Inuit Legends*, edited and illustrated by Mark Kalluak, pp. 46–51. Yellowknife: Department of Education, Government of the Northwest Territories, 1974. Akadlaka, from Eskimo Point (Arviat) NWT, was handicapped, not from blindness but from a childhood paralysis of his arms and legs. He died in 1971. An ink drawing accompanies the English text. A separate edition from the same publisher entitled *Inuit unipkatuangi* contains the same story in Inuktitut syllabics. Reprinted in Dale Blake, *Inuit Life Writings and Oral Traditions: Inuit Myths*, pp. 8–14. (St. Johns, Newfoundland: Educational Resource Development Co-operative, 2001). Inuktitut text here is in Roman.

Amaunalik. "The Blind Boy and his Sister (The Genesis of the Narwhal)." In Erik Holtved, *The Polar Eskimos: Language and Folklore*. 2 vols. København: C. A. Reitzels, 1951. Volume 1 (pp. 152–65) contains the Inuit transliteration. Volume 2 (pp. 59–64) has the free translation. Collected by Holtved at Thule, West Greenland, in 1936–37. Amaunalik performed 79 tales and 105 drum songs. Born in 1907, she was the mother of nine children. She learned the stories from her grandmother. Her mother came to Greenland from Baffin Island in the 1860s. For Holtved's biographical sketch and photo of her, see 1:13–15. Rasmussen (1908) also collected a variant at Thule.

Andre, Eliza. "The Blind Man and the Loon." In Michael Heine, Alestine Andre, Ingrid Kritsch, and Alma Cardinal, eds. *Gwichya Gwich'in Googwandak: The History and Stories of the Gwichya Gwich'in*, p. 324. Tsiigehtshik: Gwich'in Social and Cultural Institute, 2007. Eliza Andre was from Tsiigehtchik

NWT. English only. Eliza's Gwich'in audio recording is shown later under Other Archival Variants.

Barr, Emily. "A Blind Man and the Loon." In *Tales of Eskimo Alaska* edited by O. W. Frost, pp. 62–67. Anchorage: Alaska Methodist University Press, 1971. Collected by Martha Barr from Emily Barr at Cape Espenberg, Kotzebue Sound, Alaska. Emily Barr was about eighty years old when the story was collected in 1970. She was born at Shishmaref and raised in Kivalina and Point Hope, then moved to Cape Espenberg after she married.

Billum, John, and Molly Billum. "Nadosi Ts'akae: Ant Woman and the Blind Man." In *Atna' Yanida'a: Ahtna Stories*, pp. 47–54. Anchorage: National Bilingual Materials Development Center, 1979. Bilingual text transcribed in Ahtna by Molly Billum, with English translation by Millie Buck. John Billum was a resident of Chitina (Chitna), Alaska, and a past president of the Chitina Native Corporation.

Blondin, George. "Regarding a Blind Man." In *Legends and Stories from the Past*. NWT: Education, Culture, & Employment, n.d. An abbreviated internet variant written by a Dene elder and scholar. Although he has "a bad wife" who breaks several taboos and deserts him, the blind man takes no revenge on her after he is healed. Published online at http://www.ece.gov.nt.ca/Divisions/kindergarten_g12/Legends/Legends/wholebook.pdf.

Blue, Annie. "Cikmiumalria Tan'gaurluq Yaqulegpiik-llu / Blind Boy and the Arctic Loons." In *Cungauyaraam Qulirai: Annie Blue's Stories,* pp. 2–17. Fairbanks: Traditional Council of Togiak and the Alaska Native Language Center, 2007. Bilingual in Yup'ik and English, with audio CD. Unusual variant in that the blind boy turns into a loon at the end. An autobiographical piece about Annie Blue is included in the introduction by Eliza and Ben Orr.

Boas, Franz. [5 variants]. [Storytellers are anonymous]. "Origin of the Narwhal." In *The Central Eskimo*. Sixth Annual Report, Bureau of Ethnology, 1884–85, pp. 625–27. Washington: Smithsonian Institution, 1888. Reprint 1964, University of Nebraska Press, pp. 217–19. First version collected by Boas in Cumberland Sound or Davis Strait, Baffin Island, 1885.

———. [Storyteller is anonymous]. "Origin of the Narwhal." In "The Eskimo of Baffin-Land and Hudson Bay: From Notes Collected by Capt. George Comer, Capt. James S. Mutch and Rev. E. J. Peck," *American Museum of Natural History Bulletin* 15, no. 1 (1901):168–71. This version was collected by Comer, Mutch, or Peck on Baffin Island.

———. [Storyteller: NEg·ê]. "The Blind Man Who Recovered His Eyesight."

In *Kwakiutl Tales*, 2:447–52. New York: Columbia University Press, 1910. Collected by Boas on the British Columbia coast. The English-only text contains Kwakiutl personal and place names. Available for viewing online at Google Books. Not included in Boas and Hunt's 1905 collection *Kwakiutl Texts*.

——. [Storyteller: Henry Tate]. "The Blind G·it-q!ấ°da." *Tsimshian Mythology*. Washington: 31st Annual Report, Bureau of American Ethnology, 1916, pp. 246–50. Collected by Boas from Tate at Port Simpson, British Columbia, in 1914 and rewritten into standard English. Available online at Google books. The original non–standard English text for this version has been edited and published by Ralph Maud in *The Porcupine Hunter and Other Stories: The Original Tsimshian Texts of Henry W. Tate* (Vancouver: Talonbooks, 1993), pp. 65–70.

——. [Storyteller is anonymous]. "Hāntl'ēkunas" (Good with bow and arrow). In *Indian Myths and Legends from the North Pacific Coast of America: A Translation of Franz Boas' 1895 Edition of Indianische Sagen von der Nord-Pacifischen Küste Amerikas*, translated from the German by Dietrich Bertz; edited and annotated by Randy Bouchard and Dorothy Kennedy, pp. 474–476. Vancouver: Talonbooks, 2002. Owikeno Kwakiutl version. English text is titled "Hāntl'ēkunas" (Good with bow and arrow), after the name of the blind man. On p. 656 Boas adds a paragraph comparing Eskimo and North Pacific coast variants. First published 1895.

Brean, Alice. "The Loon and the Blind Man." In *Athabascan Stories*, pp. 29–35. Anchorage: Alaska Methodist University Press, 1975. Alice Brean is a Native author from Tanacross, Alaska. Text is in English.

Bruce, Ellen. "Dinjii Dèe Ehdanh Ts'aɬvit hah (Blind Man and the Loon)." In *People of the Lakes: Stories of Our Van Tat Gwich'in Elders (Googwandak Nakhwach'ànjòo Van Tat Gwich'in)*, by the Vuntut Gwich'in First Nation and Shirleen Smith, pp. 19–20. Edmonton: University of Alberta Press, 2009. Although the text appears under a bilingual title, the tale is in English only, based on a 1980 oral recording. Bruce, a Gwich'in-speaking elder of Old Crow YT was born near Rampart in 1911 and became an ordained Anglican Church priest in 1987. She married Robert Bruce Sr. and they had three children of their own and adopted four more.

Charlie, Andy Jr. "Iingilnguq Tunutellgek-llu: The Blind Boy and The Two Arctic Loons." In *Ellangellemni: When I Became Aware*, edited by Eliza Cingarkaq Orr, Ben Orr, Victor Kanrilak Jr., and Andy Charlie Jr., pp. 6–25. Fairbanks: Lower Kuskokwim School District and the Alaska Native Language Center, 1997. This bilingual Yup'ik and English version was recorded in Tununak, Nelson Island, Alaska. Editors have included a rare storyteller's commentary and rich annotations.

Chimovitski, Makari. "The Blind Boy and the Loon." In Kaj Birket-Smith, *The Chugach Eskimo*, p. 151. Copenhagen: Nationalmuseets publikationsfond, 1953. Collected by Birket-Smith when the storyteller was age eighty-six. Chimovotiski, who spoke a little Russian and almost no English, was born in Nuchek, Prince William Sound, Alaska. His photo and a biographical note appear on pp. 2–3. This is the only known Alutiiq-based variant.

Curtis, Edward S. [Storyteller is anonymous]. "The Adventures of Hántliqŭnŭs." In *The North American Indian*, Vol. 10: The Kwakiutl. Reprint New York: Johnson Reprint Company, 1970, pp. 255–62. Collected by Curtis in English from an anonymous source. The text is annotated as "a Wikeno myth." The Wikeno or Oweekeno First Nation has a population of roughly one hundred on the Wannock River near the headwaters of Rivers Inlet, British Columbia. Curtis was a controversial photographer and filmmaker, as well as a collector of folktales. Text was originally published in 1915. This text is available online at http://curtis.library. northwestern.edu/curtis/viewPage.cgi?showp=1&size=2&id=nai.10. book.00000336&volume=10#nav.

Davidialuk, Alasua Amittu. "Lumak." In *The Inuit Imagination: Arctic Myth and Sculpture*, by Harold Seidelman and James Turner, pp. 125–28. New York: Thames and Hudson, 1994.Davidialuk, who wrote the text, was a prolific Inuit storyteller and artist from Pavungnituk, Québec, who lived from 1910 to 1976. There is a biography of him by Marybelle Myers called *Davidialuk* (Montréal: La Fédération des Coopératives du Nouveau Québec, 1977). A gifted artist, Davidialuk also made at least five stone-cut prints of scenes from the story (see listing at the end of chapter 5).

Dick, Charlie. "The Man Who Was Helped by Loon." In *Dene Gudeji: Kaska Narratives*, edited by Pat Moore, pp. 310–29. Watson Lake, Yukon: Kaska Tribal Council, 1999. Illustrated with black and white drawings by William Atkinson. Charlie Dick is a trapper and member of the Crow Clan who has lived at Frances Lake, Pelly Banks, Pelly Lakes, and Ross River, Yukon Territory, and Lower Post, British Columbia. Text appears in bilingual form.

Dorsey, George A., and Alfred L. Kroeber. [3 variants]. [Two of the three storytellers are anonymous]. "The Deceived Blind Man D," "The Deceived Blind Man K," and "The Deceived Blind Man and the Deserted Children K." In *Traditions of the Arapaho*, pp. 282–93. Chicago: Field Museum Columbia, Publication 81. A.S., Vol. 5, 1903. Texts were collected from the Southern

Arapaho in Oklahoma (*D* for Dorsey) and from both the Southern Arapaho in Oklahoma and the Northern Arapaho in Wyoming (*K* for Kroeber). The D text was collected from Cut-Nose. An owl, rather than a loon, restores the blind man's sight, in each case. Available online at Google Books.

Farrand, Livingston. [Collation of several storytellers]. "The Blind Man Who Was Cured by the Loon." In "Traditions of the Chilcotin Indians." *Memoirs of the American Museum of Natural History* 4 (1900):35–36, 52. Collected by Farrand at Chilcotin River, British Columbia, in 1897 during the Jesup North Pacific Expedition. Apparently, the text is a collation from several storytellers. Reprint, AMS Press, 1975.

Gilbert, Maggie. "The Blind Man and the Loon." Tape recorded in Gwich'in by Craig Mishler at Maggie's house in Arctic Village, Alaska, April 21, 1973. Transcribed by Kenneth and Caroline Frank and Fannie Gimmel. See chapter 4 in this volume for a biographical sketch and transcribed text. Hear it performed online at http:///www.uaf.edu/loon/audio/.

Hawkes, E. W. [Storyteller is anonymous]. "The Son Who Killed His Mother (The Story of the Narwhal)." In *The Labrador Eskimo*, Anthropological Series, Geological Survey, Ottawa, Memoir 91, No. 14, pp. 157–58. Ottawa: Canadian Geological Survey, 1916. Tale was collected by Hawkes on Labrador Coast in 1914. Reprint, Johnson Reprint Corp., 1970.

Heyes, Scott. [Storytellers are the artists Daniel Annanack and Tivi Etok]. "Lumaajuaq." In "Melting Ice: Evaporating Traditions? Inuit Connections to Place in a Changing Environment," pp. 13–14. Paper presented at the International Conference: Common Ground, Converging Gazes: Integrating the Social and Environmental in History, Paris, 2008.

Holm, Gustav. [Storyteller: Nakitilik]. "Den Blinde, som fik sit Syn igjen." In *Sagn og Fortællinger fra Angmagsalik / Legends and Tales from Angmagsalik,* edited by Hinrich Rink, pp. 31–31. Kjøbenhavn: F. Dreyer, 1887. Collected by Holm from the widow Nakitilik at Angmagsalik, East Greenland, in 1884–85. English translation by Johan Petersen appears in *Meddelelser Om Grønland*, 39, no. 1 (1914):250–51. Reprinted in William Thalbitzer, ed., *Østgrønlandske Sagn og Fortællinger, Ammassalik* (East Greenlandic Myths and Tales, Ammassalik). *Det Grønlandske Selskabs Skrifter* 19, no. 2 (1957):240–41. Original by Holm archived in Rink's papers at Danish Royal Library as NKS 2488, VIII, 4°, pp. 59–62. The blind man's name here is Inik rather than Tutigaq. Sonnesbase Document SB 1121. Danish text available for download from Google Books.

Ipellie, Arnaitok. 1997. "Lumaajuq." *Inuktitut Magazine* 81:63–68. . Bilingual in Inuktitut and English, including both Qaluijaaqpait (Roman orthography) and Qaniujaaqpait (syllabics). Written by an Iqaluit, Nunavut elder as learned from his father, accompanied by his own introduction. May be viewed online as PDF file at http://www.itk.ca/publication/magazine/inuktitut/back-issues/inuktitut-magazine-1997-81.

James, Jimmy Scotty. "The Blind Man and the Loon." In *My Old People's Stories: A Legacy for Yukon First Nations. Part II: Tagish Narrators*, by Catharine McClellan. Edited by Julie Cruikshank. *Occasional Papers in Yukon History* 5, no. 2 (2007): 421–22. Tale was collected in English by McClellan from James in Carcross, Yukon Territory, on December 6, 1950. A brief biographical sketch and photo of James, an Inland Tlingit, appears on pp. 356–57. Available online at http://www.tc.gov.yk.ca/fr/pdf/mcclellan_opyh_5(2).pdf.

Jenness, Diamond. [Storyteller is anonymous]. "The Blind Hunter." In *The Corn Goddess*. Ottawa: National Museum of Canada Bulletin 141 A.S. No. 39 (1956):46–47. Collected by Jenness from an anonymous Sekani storyteller in northeastern British Columbia.

Johnson, Minnie, and "JE." "The Story of the Blind Man and the Loon." In Frederica de Laguna, *Under Mount Saint Elias: The History and Culture of the Yakutat Tlingit*, part 2, pp. 888–89. Washington: Smithsonian Institution Press, 1972. First variant collected by de Laguna from Johnson at Yakutat on July 22, 1952. Second variant collected from "JE" on March 3, 1954.

Kalifornsky, Peter. "Kił Ch'u Dujemi: The Man and the Loon." In *A Dena'ina Legacy: K'tl'egh'i Sukdu: The Collected Writings of Peter Kalifornsky*, edited by James Kari and Alan Boraas, pp. 144–49. Fairbanks: Alaska Native Language Center, 1991. Bilingual, facing-page Dena'ina and English texts are written by Kalifornsky himself, with a short exegesis. English text only is reprinted in the anthology *Our Voices: Native Stories of Alaska and the Yukon*, ed. James Ruppert and John W. Bernet (Lincoln: University of Nebraska Press, 2001), pp. 323–24. Also reprinted as "The Man and the Loon" in *The Last New Land: Stories of Alaska Past and Present*, ed. Wayne Mergler (Anchorage: Alaska Northwest Books, 1996), pp. 551–54. Peter lived most of his life on the Kenai Peninsula and Lower Cook Inlet, Alaska.

Kappianaq, George Agiaq. In John MacDonald, *The Arctic Sky: Inuit Astronomy, Star Lore, and Legend*. Toronto and Iqaluit: Royal Ontario Museum and Nunavut Research Institute, 1998. Recorded on audio cassette at Igloolik, Northwest Territories, in December 1986 and archived both at the Igloolik Research Centre and in Yellowknife as IE-071. Kappianaq is an Amitturmiut from the northern Foxe Basin. Story is subsumed in the first half of "The Sun and the Moon," which appears in English translation on pp. 211–18 and is transcribed in Inuktitut by Leah Otak, pp. 240–48. English version is reprinted verbatim in John Bennett and Susan Rowley, eds., *Uqalurait: An Oral History of Nunavut* (Montreal: McGill-Queen's University Press, 2004), pp. 161–66.

Kara of Ammassalik. "La grand-mère qui est remorquée par un narval (The grandmother who was towed by a narwhal)". In Paul-Émile Victor, *La civilisation du phoque,* 2:169–72. Paris: Raymond Chabaud & Armand Colin, 1993. Told by Kara of Ammassalik in 1936. Summarized in Sonnesbase SB 23.

Keats, Della (Puyuk). Untitled. *Journal of Alaska Native Arts.* January–February (1985):8. Transcribed by Luci Abeita. Keats was a traditional healer from Noatak, Alaska. She may have learned the tale from Jenny Mitchell (see later).

Keenainak, Tapea. [Storyteller is anonymous]. "Lumaaju." In *Interviewing Inuit Elders*, 1:201–4, edited by Jarich Oosten and Frederic Laugrand. Iqaluit: Nunavut Arctic College, 1999. Bilingual text with interlinear English translation. Story told to Keenainak by an anonymous elder. Keenainak is the mother of three children at Iqaluit, Nunavut, and is a member of the Baffin Divisional Education Council. The text may be viewed at http://www.nac.nu.ca/publication/vol1/PDF/stories/stories_lumaaju.pdf.

Keithahn, Edward L. [Storyteller is anonymous]. "The Wicked Mother." In *Alaska Igloo Tales*, pp. 69–70. Lawrence, Kansas: U.S. Indian Service, 1944. Collected by Keithahn at Shishmaref, Alaska. Illustrated by George Aden Ahgupuk. Reprint, Alaska Northwest Publishing, 1974.

Koyina, Laiza. *Dǫ weda goòle xè Teèt'o si (The Blind Man and the Loon).* English version translated from the Dogrib by Mary Adele Football. Yellowknife: Northwest Territories Department of Education, 1983.

Krauss, Michael E. [2 variants]. [Storyteller: Lena Nacktan]. "Blind Man and Loon." In Eyak Texts. Unpublished typescript, 1970, pp. 105–6. Dictated to Krauss in Eyak by Lena Nacktan in Cordova, Alaska, on July 9, 1963. Manuscript housed at University of Alaska, Rasmuson Library, Fairbanks. Anna Nelson Harry's version (Krauss 1982) is also included here, pp. 71–82. Both texts are annotated by Krauss.

———. [Storyteller: Anna Nelson Harry]. "Blind Man and Loon." In *In Honor of Eyak: The Art of Anna Nelson Harry,* pp. 85–89. Fairbanks, Alaska Native Language Center, 1982. Recorded on tape by Krauss in Yakutat, Alaska on May 27, 1965. Anna Nelson Harry was one of the last speakers of Eyak, and the transcription is in Eyak orthography with English verse translation appended by a free prose translation. Before her work with Krauss, Anna Nelson had been a key respondent for Frederica de Laguna and Kaj Birket-Smith, contributing heavily to their ethnography, *The Eyak Indians of the Copper River Delta, Alaska*, published in Copenhagen in 1938. A short biography of Harry is included in Krauss's introduction, pp. 14–19.

Kreutzmann, Jens. "Erneq arnaminik avataqartoq." In *Oqaluttuat & Assilialiat*, edited by Kirsten Thisted and Arnaq Grove, pp. 71–74. Nuuk: Atuakkiorfik, 1997. Greenlandic variant of SB 207, collected by Hinrich Rink. Original archive version at Danish Royal Library is in NKS, 2488, II, 4°.

———. "Sønnen som bugte sin mor som fangeblære" (The son who used his mother as a hunting bladder). In *Fortællinger & Akvareller (Tales and Watercolors)*, edited and translated by Kirsten Thisted, pp. 71–74. Nuuk: Atuakkiorfik, 1997. Danish version of SB 207, collected by Hinrich Rink.

Kroeber, Alfred L. [Storyteller is anonymous]. "The Origin of the Narwhal." In "Tales of the Smith Sound Eskimo," *Journal of American Folklore* 12 (1899):169–70. Collected by Kroeber from a Smith Sound, Greenland Inuit visiting New York during the winter of 1897–98. Kroeber (1899:318) says that in Greenland the moon is called "Anningat" or "Aningaut." Variants of this name are attached to the blind boy or blind man in many of Knud Rasmussen's Canadian versions. Reprinted in Tristram Coffin's edition of *Indian Tales of North America* (Austin: University of Texas Press, 1961), pp. 131–32; also in Stith Thompson's *Tales of North American Indians* (Bloomington: Indiana University Press, [1929] 1967), p. 195. Thompson erroneously attributes the text to Boas rather than Kroeber, changes Kroeber's title, and omits the second and concluding page of Kroeber's tale.

Kublu, Alexina. "Aninganga qaqsaurmut tautuliqtitaq: Brother receives sight from a loon." In *Interviewing Inuit Elders*, 1:162–81. Iqaluit: Nunavut Arctic College, 1999. Text written in Inuktitut by Kublu, as learned from her father, Michel Kupaaq Piugattuk, with interlinear English translation. A five-part online series of texts completes the full tale. These may be also viewed and downloaded individually or as a package from: http://www.nac.nu.ca/publication/vol1/stories.html. Kublu was born in Igloolik and teaches interpreters and translators at Nunavut Arctic College in Iqaluit. She received her Bachelor of Education degree from the Nunavut Teacher Education Program and has taught in the communities of Arctic Bay, Cape Dorset, and Arviat. She is married to the linguist Mick Mallon and is the mother of two daughters. As of this writing she is the Languages Commissioner for the Territory of Nunavut.

Kupaaq, Michel. "L'incestueux Frère-Lune poursuit Soeur-Soleil" (The inces-
tuous Brother-Moon chases Sister-Sun). In Bernard Saladin d'Anglure,
Être et renaître Inuit: Homme, femme ou chamane, pp. 106–41. Paris:
Gallimard, 2006. Collected by Saladin d'Anglure in Igloolik, Nunavut,
in 1972 or 1973, and translated into French. Includes extensive commentary and notes interspersed with text. The healing bird here is a
red-throated loon. Michel Kupaaq died in 1997. Original manuscript is
at Laval University, Québec.

Kusugaq, Thomas. "Aningaat," transcribed and translated by Alex Spalding
in his *Eight Inuit Myths/Inuit Unipkaaqtuat Pingasuniarvinilit*. Canadian
Ethnology Service, Paper No. 59. Ottawa: National Museums of Canada
Mercury Series, 1979. Collected in Inuktitut by Spalding at Aivilik, Repulse
Bay, Nunavut, from Thomas Kusugaq in 1950. Kusugaq collaborated with
Spalding to create *Inuktitut: A Multi-dialectal Outline Dictionary*.

Lowie, Robert H. [2 variants]. [Storyteller is anonymous]. "The Blind Dupe."
In "The Assiniboine." *Anthropological Papers of the American Museum of
Natural History* 4, no. 1 (1909):204–5. Collected by Lowie in northeastern Montana. The bird that restores the blind man's sight here is not a
loon but a gull.

———. [Storyteller: Panayū's]. "The Blind Dupe." In "Shoshonean Tales."
Journal of American Folklore 37 (1924):78. Collected by Lowie in southwestern Colorado in 1912 from the Southern Ute storyteller Panayū's. No
bird intervenes to restore the man's eye sight; he heals himself.

Luke, Abraham. "The Blind Man and the Loons." In Craig Mishler, *Born
with the River: An Ethnographic History of Alaska's Goodpaster and Big
Delta Indians*. Alaska Division of Geological and Geophysical Surveys,
Report of Investigations 86–14, 1986, pp. 64–70. Tape recorded by the
author from Abraham Luke of Dot Lake, Alaska, at Kelly's Motel in Delta,
Alaska, on July 10, 1983. A brief life history of Abraham Luke is included
on pp. 113–16. Luke performed this in the Tanacross language with some
code-switching to English, then retold it in nonstandard English. Only
the English telling has been published.

Luke, Howard. "Old Blind Man and the Loon: Dodzenee." In *Howard Luke: My
Own Trail*, ed. Jan Steinbright Jacskon, pp. 24–25. Fairbanks: University of
Alaska Press, Alaska Native Knowledge Network, 1998. English rendering
of Lower Tanana Athabaskan variant included in Luke's autobiography.

Lytzen, Carl. [Storyteller is anonymous]. "Narhvalen [Narwhal] (monodon
monecerus)." Reported by Colony Manager C. Lytzen from the Native oral
story. In *Grønlandske Sagn [Greenland Legends]-kalâtdlit oKalugtuait*, 2nd

ed. (Anders Nyborg, Rungsted Coast, 1973). Unpaginated. Reprographic republication of the Danish text and the Greenlandic text. SB 548. First published 1879.

Malaurie, Jean. "Pigtail and Narwhal Tusk." In *The Last Kings of Thule*, translated from the French by Adrienne Foulke, pp. 100–101. Chicago: University of Chicago Press, 1985. Collected by Malaurie from Pualuna at Siorapaluk, north of Thule, Greenland, in 1950–51. Biographical sketch on pp. 51–55, portrait on p. 107. Originally published as *Les derniers rois de Thulé* (Paris: Plon, 1955).

Mason, J. Alden. [Storyteller: Snake John]. "Blind Coyote and His Wife." In "Myths of the Uintah Utes," *Journal of American Folklore* 23 (1910):301. Collected by Mason at White Rocks, Utah. No birds intervene to restore Coyote's eye sight—he heals himself.

Mayokok, Robert. "The Blind Man and the Polar Bear." In *Eskimo Stories*, pp. 14–18. Nome: *Nome Nugget*, 1960. Ending is surprising in that the blind man "held no grudge against his selfish old mother" after his eyesight is restored. Mayokok was an Iñupiaq sketch artist and storyteller from Wales who illustrated many books written by non-Native authors, as well as his own. He was born in 1903 and died in 1983. A life history sketch has been published by Susan W. Fair, "Robert Mayokok: Second Generation Iñupiaq Illustrator from Wales Alaska," in *Eskimo Drawings*, ed. Suzi Jones, pp. 127–35 (Anchorage: Anchorage Museum of History and Art, 2003). Another short biography appears on the website http://www.calacademy.org/RESEARCH/anthropology/eskimo/mayokok.htm.

McIlwraith, T. F.[Storyteller is anonymous]. "The Fortunes of *Qwn·a*." In *The Bella Coola Indians*, 2nd ed., 1:661–62. Toronto: University of Toronto Press, 1992. First published 1948. Collected in English by McIlwraith among the Nuxalk First Nation on the Bella Coola River, British Columbia, between 1922 and 1924. For more about McIlwraith, see John Barker and Douglas Cole, *At Home with the Bella Coola Indians: T .F. McIlwraith's Field Letters, 1922–1924* (Vancouver: University of British Columbia Press, 2004).

Metayer, Maurice. [Storyteller is anonymous]. "The Blind Boy and the Loon." In *Tales from the Igloo*, pp. 92–98. Edmonton: Hurtig Publishers, 1972. Collected and translated into English by Metayer from an anonymous storyteller on the Coppermine River, Northwest Territories. There is also a French edition of Metayer's book, *Contes de mon Iglou* (Montreal: Editions du Jour, 1973). The tale is reprinted in Raymond Jones and Jon Stott, eds., *A World of Stories: Traditional Tales for Children*, pp. 351–54. (Don

Mills, Ontario: Oxford University Press, 2006). This reprint contains a color reproduction of a painting by Agnes Nanogak. A pairing of the text with Agnes Nanogak Goose's 1975 interpretive painting of "Blind Boy" at the Winnipeg Art Gallery (a different image) can be found online at http://www.virtualmuseum.ca/Exhibitions/Holman/english/storytelling/blind_boy.php3

Millman, Lawrence. [Storyteller: Ken Annanack]. "The First Narwhal." In *A Kayak Full of Ghosts*, pp. 36–37. Santa Barbara: Capra Press, 1987. Collected in English from the schoolteacher Ken Annanack of Pangnirtung, Baffin Island, c. 1981, as told to his daughter.

Mitchell, Jenny (Aluniq). "The Blind Boy and the Loon." In Charles Lucier, "Noatagmiut Eskimo Myths." *Anthropological Papers of the University of Alaska* 6, no. 2 (1958): 96–98. Collected by Lucier from Mitchell at Sisualik, Kotzebue Sound, Alaska in 1952 and translated by Della Keats (see earlier). Lucier was married to an Iñupiaq woman and was active in Eskimo drumming and dance groups. He now resides in Eugene, Oregon.

Monroe, Paul. "The Blind Boy and the Mulgi." In Edwin S. Hall Jr., *The Eskimo Storyteller*, pp. 245–47. Knoxville: University of Tennessee Press, 1975. The story was translated by Martha Burns or Herbert Onalik, but the original Iñupiaq text was not preserved. Collected by Hall from Monroe at Noatak, Alaska, in 1965, when Monroe was seventy-three or seventy-four years old. He married Mary Jones and fathered ten children, but when Hall met him he was a widower and lived alone in a log cabin, carving wooden bowls and spoons. A brief autobiography appears on pp. 103–6.

Morice, A. G. [Storyteller is anonymous]. Untitled. In "Notes Archaeological, Industrial, and Sociological on the Western Denés, with an Ethnographical Sketch of the Same." *Transactions of the Canadian Institute* 6 (1892):171–72. Collected by Fr. Adrian Morice, an Oblate missionary priest, from an anonymous Carrier storyteller at Stuart's Lake, British Columbia. Available online at Google books.

Nastapoka, Abraham. "How the Tuulliik cured the Blind Man." In *Tumivut, atuagait inuit nunavimmiut iluqqusinginnuangajut* (*Tumivut, the Cultural Magazine of the Nunavik Inuit*) 6 (1995):21–22. Recorded in Inukjuak, Nunavik, Québec in 1967. Transcribed by Jacob Oweetaluktuk and translated by Johnny Nowra. Unusual in that the loons lick the blind boy's eyes and dive with him to restore his sight. Also, the variant seems truncated in that he is not abused by his stepmother and does not seek revenge once his sight is restored.

Netro, Joe. "Man with No Eyes." In *A Book of Indian Legends and Storys from*

Old Crow, Yukon Territory, pp. 7–8. N.p.: 1980. Written in English by a Gwich'in elder. Copy at the University of Alaska Consortium Library, Anchorage. The author was a member of the Old Crow village council and a store owner.

Norman, Howard. [Storyteller: Pioopiula] ."How the Narwhal Got Its Tusk." In *Northern Tales: Traditional Stories of Eskimo and Indian Peoples*, pp. 83–86. New York: Pantheon Books, 1990. Told by Pioopiula to Michael and Severance Rosegood in 1975. Translated by Severance Rosegood. Provenance is Greenland. In this rendition there is no loon or other bird to restore the blind boy's sight. Instead, he is healed by his eccentric aunt after she is transformed into a narwhal.

Norton, Nora Paaniikaaluk. "The Woman Who Made Her Son Blind." In *Folktales of the Riverine and Coastal Iñupiat*, ed. Wanni W. Anderson and Ruth Tatqaviñ Sampson, pp. 175–86. [Kotzebue]: Northwest Arctic Borough and National Endowment for the Humanities, 2003. Iñupiaq text collected from Norton, of Selawik, Alaska, on September 9, 1968. Transcribed by Angeline Ipiilik Newlin and translated by Michael Oakiq Atoruk. Norton was born in 1910 around Shungnak and moved to Selawik with her parents in the 1920s. She was the mother of four children and married Edward Iñuġuk Wood, a reindeer herder, freighter, and store-keeper. Reprinted in English (with a revised translation) in Wanni W. Anderson, *The Dall Sheep Dinner Guest* (Fairbanks: University of Alaska Press, 2009), pp. 228–31.

Nungak, Zebedee, and Eugene Y. Arima, trans. "Lumaaq." [Storyteller: Aisa Qupiqrualuk]. In *Unikkaatuat Sanaugarngnik Atyingualiit Puvirngniturng-mit: Eskimo Stories From Povungnituk, Quebec*. National Museums of Canada Bulletin 235, Anthropological Series 90, 1969. Collected by André Steinmann, c. 1958–59. pp. 49–51. Reprinted as *Inuit Stories-Povungnituk-Légendes Inuit* by the NMC in 1988. This bilingual Inuit syllabic and English edition contains photographs of five soapstone carvings made by the storyteller. English-only version reprinted in W.H. New, ed., *Canadian Short Fiction*, 2nd ed. (Scarborough, Ontario.: Prentice Hall Canada, 1997), pp. 23–24. Reprinted again in Stacey Day, *Tuluak and Amaulik: Dialogues on Death and Mourning with the Inuit Eskimo of Point Barrow and Wainwright, Alaska*. (Minneapolis: Bell Museum of Pathobiology, University of Minnesota Medical School, 1973), pp. 153–54. Can also be read online at http://www.canadianstudies.ca/NewJapan/myths.html.

Nutaraaluk, Lucassie. Untitled. In *Interviewing Inuit Elders*. Vol. 4, *Cosmology and Shamanism*, pp. 66–67. Edited by Bernard Saladin D'Anglure.

Arviat: Nunavut Arctic College, 2001. The translated story is told as part of a discussion called "Encounters with Inurajait: Human-like Beings." Nutaraaluk, the son of a shaman but a practicing Anglican, was interviewed on tape in Iqaluit in 1998. Ironically, his own grandfather, almost like the blind man's mother, died after tangling his foot in the line of a harpoon and being dragged into the ocean by a walrus.

Oonalik. "How Soolook's Vision Was Restored by a Loon." In Clark M. Garber, *Stories and Legends of the Bering Strait Eskimos*, pp. 33–38. Boston: Christopher, 1940. Collected by Garber from Oonalik at Wales, Alaska.

Petitot, Émile. [2 variants]. [Storyteller: Sylvain Vitoedh]. "Tchia: Le Jeune Homme" and "Ta-Édin-Yan (La Viel Aveugle)." In *Traditions Indiennes du Canada Nord-Ouest*. Paris: Maisonneuve Frères, 1886, pp. 84–88; and 226–29. First variant of the tale is from the Loucheux (Gwich'in); second variant is from the Hare. Stories collected by Oblate priest Father Petitot from Sylvain Vitoedh at Fort Good Hope, Northwest Territories, in 1870 and published in French. The French texts are available at Early Canadiana Online: http://www.canadiana.org. The 1888 edition of Petitot's book (see next entry) has original Dene texts in both languages. Both variants in the 1886 edition of Petitot's book have been republished and translated into English in *The Amerindians of the Canadian North-west in the 19th Century, As Seen by Émile Petitot*. Vol. 2. Edited by Donat Savoie. (Ottawa: Department of Indian Affairs and Northern Development, 1970). The texts appear on pp. 176–80.

———. *Traditions Indiennes du Canada Nord-Ouest: Texts Originaux et Traduction Litterale*. Alençon: E. Renaut-De Broise, 1888. The two variants of the story appear on pp. 245–49 and pp. 392–96. Available on microfiche from University Microfilms, Pre-1910 Canadiana, Ann Arbor. These are the same two variants included in the 1886 edition except that Native language texts are included with parallel column literal French translations. The orthography used by Petitot is idiosyncratic.

Qupalorâsewk. In Hans Lynge, "Ulâmieq." *Meddelelser Om Grønland* 90, no. 2 (1955):115–19. Told by Qupalorâsewk in Northwest Greenlandic. Notable variant since the blind man's mother is a lesbian who steals his wife. Summarized in SB 767.

Rasmussen, Knud. [6 variants]. [Storyteller: Arnâluk]. "How the Narwhal Came." In *The New People: Polar Eskimo*, pp. 169–70. Part 1 of *The People of the Polar North: A Record*, edited by G. Herring and compiled from the Danish originals. London: Kegan Paul, Trench, Trübner and Company, 1908. Recorded from the Inuit storyteller Arnâluk, an old woman living at Thule in western Greenland. An ink sketch of her is included on p. 182. Holtved (1951) also collected a Thule variant.

———. [Storyteller: Ivaluardjuk]. "How the Moon Spirit First Came." In *Intellectual Culture of the Iglulik Eskimos*, translated from the Danish by W. Worster, pp. 77–81. Vol. 7, part 1 of *Report of the Fifth Thule Expedition, 1921–24*. Copenhagen: Gyldendalske Boghandel Nordisk Forlag, 1929. Reprint, New York: AMS Press, 1976. Collected by Rasmussen from the Inuit storyteller Ivaluardjuk at Repulse Bay, on Hudson's Bay, Nunavut, in 1921. Ivaluardjuk, whose photo appears in figure 7, was an old man with a long white beard who served as Rasmussen's expert geographer, drawing a detailed map of the region. He was also a noted singer. Once widowed, he had remarried to his adoptive daughter.

———. [Storyteller: Kibkârjuk]. "The Blind Man Who Regained His Sight." In *Observations on the Intellectual Culture of the Caribou Eskimos*, translated from the Danish by W. E. Calvert, pp. 108–9. Vol. 7, part 2 of *Report of the Fifth Thule Expedition, 1921–24*. Copenhagen: Gyldendalske Boghandel Nordisk Forlag, 1930. Reprint, New York: AMS Press, 1976. Recorded as "The blind man who regained his sight" by Rasmussen from the Pâdlermiut woman Kibkârjuk, whom he called "one of my best storytellers." Recorded at an inland village near Yathkyed Lake and the Kazan River, Nunavut, in the winter of 1921–22. Kibkârjuk was the oldest wife of the shaman Igjugârjuk. Her photo appears in figure 11.

———. [Storyteller: Ikinilik]. "The Sun and the Moon." In *The Netsilik Eskimo: Social Life and Spiritual Culture*, pp. 524–26. Vol. 8, part 2 of *Report of the Fifth Thule Expedition, 1921–1924*. Copenhagen: Gyldendalske Boghandel Nordisk Forlag, 1931. Reprint, New York: AMS Press, 1976. Collected by Rasmussen from the elder Ikinilik at Itivnârjuk, a fish camp on the Back River in the spring of 1923. The Back River flows from Aylmer Lake northeast through Garry Lakes and Franklin Lake to the Arctic Ocean, Nunavut. It is a long river, 1077 kilometers (673 miles), very remote and expensive to access. Ikinilik, a man who talked at length about the Inuit religion and world view, smoked a pipe and sat on soft caribou skins while he talked. Rasmussen says he was "the best singer at Itivnârjuk" and "a clear-headed, elderly man, well-versed in all the traditions of his tribe." See the photo of him in figure 10.

———. [Storyteller: Nâlungiaq]. "The Tale of the Sun and Moon." In *The Netsilik Eskimo: Social Life and Spiritual Culture*, pp. 232–36. Volume 8, part 1 of *Report of the Fifth Thule Expedition, 1921–1924*: The Netsilingmiut. Copenhagen: Gyldendalske Boghandel Nordisk Forlag, 1931. Reprint, New

York: AMS Press, 1976. Collected by Rasmussen at Malerualik from the Inuit woman Nâlungiaq, who was about forty-five years old, had two children, and was married to Inûtuk, her third husband. Her photos are included in figure 9. She points out that "the sun and the moon murdered their mother, and though they were brother and sister, they [incestuously] loved each other. For that reason they ceased to be humans" (pp. 209–210). Rasmussen stayed with this family for over six months. When visited by him in 1923, the Netsilingmiut were scattered between Committee Bay, Victoria Strait, and Somerset Island. Most Netsilingmiut now live in or near the modern government-built settlements of Taloyoak and Pelly Bay on Boothia Peninsula, and Gjoa Haven on King William Island, Nunavut.

———. [Storyteller: Netsit]. "The Blind One and the Loon." In *Intellectual Culture of the Copper Eskimos*, translated by W. E. Calvert, pp. 204–7. Vol. 9 of *Report of the Fifth Thule Expedition*, 1921–24. Copenhagen: Gyldendalske Boghandel Nordisk Forlag, 1932. Reprint, New York: AMS Press, 1976. Includes transliteration and translation. Collected by Rasmussen from the twenty-five-year-old Inuit storyteller and poet Netsit on the Coronation Gulf, Nunavut, in 1923. Netsit, raised by a shaman, was Rasmussen's companion when traveling by dog sled. His photo appears in figure 8. Rasmussen says he tried but failed to elicit additional versions of a Greenlandic story he called "Aningait, the blind, who was ill treated by his grandmother."

Robinson, Gordon. [Storyteller : a Haisla man]. "Numas (Old Man)." In *Tales of Kitamaat*. Kitimat, pp. 31–33. British Columbia: Northern Sentinel Press, 1956. Written in English by a Haisla man; Haisla is a branch of the Kwakiutl, coastal British Columbia. Robinson's photo and a biographical sketch are included on pp. iv–v.

Rollinmud, Stanley. *The Blind Man and the Loon: Wîschasta îstarhûrhe cha, mnotha cha gichi*. Morley, Alberta: Stoney Cultural Education Program, 1973. Text in Stoney (Assiniboine). Illustrated and compiled by Shirley Crawler, Elaine Twoyoungmen, and Mary Jane Chiniquay Jr. This variant may be related to the one recorded by Robert Lowie and published in 1909.

Rooth, Anna Birgitta. [3 variants]. *The Alaska Expedition 1966: Myths, Customs and Beliefs among the Athabascan Indians and the Eskimos of northern Alaska*. Lund: CWK Gleerup, 1971. Rooth collected three Athabaskan variants in nonstandard English along the Tanana River in 1966, all untitled: (1) from Peter John of Minto, pp. 184–86; (2) from Moses Charlie of Minto, pp. 135–38 (includes a medicine song for curing blindness);

and (3) from Frank Sam of Northway, pp. 310–11. Peter John was born in Rampart in 1900, married Else Albert, and had four children. He became the traditional chief and spiritual leader of the Doyon Region of Interior Alaska from 1992 until his death in 2003. He is the author of the book, *The Gospel According to Peter John*, edited by David J. Krupa (Fairbanks: Alaska Native Knowledge Network, 1996). A biographical sketch of Peter John appears online at: http://www.tananachiefs.org/corporate/chief_john.html. Moses Charlie was about eighty years old when Rooth interviewed him. He was born in Tanacross and married Bessie David of Kokrines before settling in Minto. They had ten children. Frank Sam, also about eighty years old, when interviewed by Rooth, was a young father when the ethnographer Robert A. McKennan met him in 1929–30.

Sowdloapik, Josephee. [Storyteller: Sowdloapik; the English text is condensed]. "The Years I Started Remembering." In *Stories from Pangnirtung*, foreword by Stuart Hodgson, pp. 67–68. Edmonton: Hurtig Publishers, 1976. Sowdloapik was a sixty-five-year-old woman from Qikiqtarjuaq (Kekertukdjuak), a village on the east side of Baffin Island. The book includes a colorful illustration of a scene in the story by Germaine Arnaktauyok.

Spencer, Robert F. [Storyteller is anonymous]. "The Blind Man and the Loon." In *The North Alaska Eskimo*, Bureau of American Ethnology Bulletin 171, pp. 396–97. Washington: Smithsonian Institution Press, 1959. Collected by Spencer from an anonymous Iñupiaq storyteller at Point Barrow in 1952–53.

Spencer, Robert F., and W. K. Carter. [3 variants, two of them are summarized]. "The Blind Man and the Loon: Barrow Eskimo Variants." *Journal of American Folklore* 67, no. 263 (1954):65–72. Collected by Spencer or Carter from Tukúminaroak and others at Point Barrow in 1952. Authors say they collected eight variants altogether. Essay analyzes the distribution of the tale and regional variants. One of these variants is reprinted and discussed in Claude Levi-Strauss's *The Naked Man: Mythologiques, Vol. 4* (Chicago: University of Chicago Press, 1990), see pp. 201–5.

Swanton, John. [2 variants]. [Storyteller: Walter McGregor]. "How One Was Helped by a Loon." In "Haida Texts—Masset Dialect," *Memoirs of the American Museum of Natural History* 14, no. 2 (1908):353–62. Swanton collected the story from McGregor in Skidegate, Queen Charlotte Islands, in 1901. In a footnote, Swanton says "This is a Tlingit story," but it was told to him in Haida.

————. [Storyteller: Abraham]. "The Blind Grisly-Bear Hunter." In "Contributions to the Ethnology of the Haida." *Memoirs of the American Museum of Natural History* 5, no. 1 (1909):212. Collected by Swanton from Abraham in Masset, Queen Charlotte Islands, in 1900–1901. An abstract appears in English under the title.

Teit, James A. [2 variants]. [Storytellers: Dandy Jim and anonymous]. Both variants are titled "The Blind Man and the Loon" and appear in "Tahltan Tales," *Journal of American Folklore* 34, no. 133 (1921):226–27; 227–228. Each variants was collected by Teit, one of them from the storyteller Dandy Jim at Telegraph Creek, British Columbia. Both are entitled "The Blind Man and the Loon," but they are distinguished as Version a and Version b. Teit acknowledges Dandy Jim as the principal Tahltan storyteller in his preface to "Kaska Tales," *Journal of American Folklore* 30, no. 118 (1917):427–73.

Thomas, Kenny Thomas Sr. *Crow Is My Boss: The Oral Life History of a Tanacross Athabaskan Elder*, edited by Craig Mishler, pp. 203–6. Norman: University of Oklahoma Press, 2005. Recorded in English by Mishler from Thomas at Tanacross on October 30, 2000. Appears as the first episode of a cycle about the world traveler, Yaamaagh Telcheegh, and includes a rare storyteller's commentary.

Vaudrin, Bill. [Storyteller is anonymous]. "The Loon Story." In *Tanaina Tales from Alaska*, pp. 15–18. Norman: University of Oklahoma Press, 1969. Collected in English by Vaudrin at Pedro Bay or Nondalton, Lake Iliamna, Alaska, from an anonymous storyteller. Vaudrin's text has been copied in the *Bristol Bay Native Corporation Annual Report for 2002*, an online PDF file at http://www.bbnc.net/index.php/our-people10/media/annual-reports/. The person who contributed the story to the report, Elizabeth Blahuta, a Dena'ina Athabaskan from Nondalton, admits she got it directly from Vaudrin's book, "but I'm sure I heard the story when I was small. . . . My dad says it's a respect story."

Part 2. Semi-literary Variants

Armour, Drew. "The Blind Man and the Loon." *The Beaver*, Outfit 315, no. 1 (Summer 1984):8–12. Author describes the text as "a précis of one of the great Inuit monomyths." Armour, an associate professor of medicine at Dalhousie University in Halifax, includes some commentary and color examples of graphic art inspired by the story (created by Pitseolak Ashoona) but does not provide his source for the text.

Bastian, Dawn, and Judy Mitchell, eds. "Blind Boy." In *Handbook of Native*

American Mythology, pp. 54–55. New York: Oxford University Press, 2004. Text is a redaction based on three sources: Kroeber 1899, Seidelman and Turner 1994, and Nungak and Arima 1988.

Bayliss, Clara K. "The Origin of the Narwhal." In *A Treasury of Eskimo Tales,* pp. 43–48. New York: Thomas Y. Crowell Co., 1922. An abridgment and rewriting of Boas's text of the same title in *The Central Eskimo* (1888). This version omits the son's remorse after revenge is taken on his wicked mother, and it expunges the brother-sister sequel in Boas. Almost comically, the loon perches on the rooftop of the blind boy's hut.

Bierhorst, John, ed. "The Blind Boy and the Loon." In *The Dancing Fox: Arctic Folktales*, pp. 125–31. New York: William Morrow and Company, 1997. Bierhorst defends his redaction of seven scholarly sources, listed in the endnotes, as providing "the full range of incident, imagery, and sheer storytelling skill." Rink, Rasmussen, and Boas are all credited as sources in the introduction.

Bruchac, James, and Joseph Bruchac, eds. " The Blind Boy and the Loon." In *The Girl Who Helped Thunder and Other Native American Folktales*, illustrated by Stefano Vitale, pp. 86–89. New York: Sterling Publishing, 2008. Story is "retold" by the editors, who point out the moral right at the beginning, just in case you miss it. Acknowledged sources include Metayer (1972) and Hall (1975).

Caswell, Helen. "The First Narwhal." In *Shadows from the Singing House*, illustrated by Robert Mayokok, pp. 41–47. Rutland VT: Charles Tuttle Company, 1968. Stories are all "retold" by Caswell. Adapted from a Greenlandic text since the protagonist is named Tutigaq, and both Rink and Rasmussen are listed in the bibliography.

Dobrindt, G. H. "The Legend of the Old Man and the Loon." *Ballads and Epic Poems of Indian Stories and Legends*. N.p., 1983. Author acknowledges Chief James Mason of the Saugeen Indian Band (Chippewa) as his source but has heavily rewritten the original text with flowery description. No betrayal and no vengeance motifs. This is one of the rare variants attributed to Algonquin-speaking peoples.

Dwyer, Corinne. "The Loon's Necklace." In *Loon Legends: A Collection of Tales Based on Legends*, illustrated by Mark Coyle, pp. 7–23. St. Cloud MN: North Star Press, 1988. A lengthened yarn with no acknowledged sources.

Leechman, Douglas. [2 variants; only the 1952 edition is different from the others]. "The Loon's Necklace . . . and Whence It Came: A Legend of the Pioneer Days in British Columbia." *Forest and Outdoors* 27, no. 1 (1931):24–25. It is difficult to tell whether this is an oral or literary variant. No storyteller is acknowledged, and it is entirely in English, but it includes many local place names from the Nicola Valley, British Columbia, and seems to be an oral version embellished by the author.

———. "The Loon's Necklace." *The Civil Service Review* 15, no. 4 (1942):372–75ff. Copy on file in Douglas Leechman Collection at the British Columbia Archives, MS-1290, box 19, file 11, Victoria. This closely follows the 1931 version.

———. "The Loon's Necklace." In *Folk-lore of the Vanta-Kutchin*. Ottawa: National Museum of Canada Annual Report for the fiscal year 1950–51. Bulletin 126 (1952):81–82. Abbreviated summary collected in English by Leechman from Effie Linklater in Old Crow, Yukon Territory. It is difficult to tell what the original oral version was like.

———. "The Loon's Necklace: A Legend of the Interior Salish." In *Native Tribes of Canada*, pp. 258–64. Toronto: W. J. Gage & Company, 1956.This published variant apparently derives from the script for the film *The Loon's Necklace* but is condensed from Leechman's 1931 and 1942 versions.

———. "The Loon's Necklace: A Legend of the Interior Salish." In Philip Penner and John McGechaen, eds., *Canadian Reflections: An Anthology of Canadian Prose*, pp. 247–52. Toronto: Macmillan Company of Canada, 1964. Another condensed version, virtually identical with the 1956 edition.

Lynch, Kathleen, compiler and illustrator. "The Blind Boy and the Loon." In *Northern Eskimo Stories*, pp. 21–26. Anchorage: Adult Literacy Laboratory, Anchorage Community College, 1978. Lynch credits two print sources: Maher (1969) and Barr in Frost (1971), thereby redacting a literary version with an oral one. This is a spiral-bound booklet designed to teach literacy to adult Alaska Natives.

Macfarlan, Allan A. "The Loon's Necklace." In *North American Indian Legends*, pp. 329–33. Mineola NY: Dover Publications, 1968. Apparently reprinted from Macfarlan's *Indian Adventure Trails* (New York: Dodd, Mead & Co., 1953). The blind medicine man is named Dark Night, who wards off attacking wolves with his magic bow. Attributed to the Iroquois.

Maher, Ramona. "The Blind Boy and the Loon." In *The Blind Boy and the Loon and Other Eskimo Myths*, pp. 17–30. New York: John Day Company, 1969. A redaction. Borrowing from several sources, Maher says that "motifs and characters from separate variants complete and enrich the story."

Melzack, Ronald. "The Origin of the Narwhal." In *Why the Man in the Moon Is Happy and Other Eskimo Creation Stories*. pp. 26–33. Toronto: McClelland and Stewart, 1977. Reprinted in Lorrie Anderson et al., eds., *Storytellers' Rendezvous: Canadian Stories to Tell to Children*, pp. 4–6. Ottawa: Canadian

Library Association, 1979. Retold by Melzack, a Canadian psychologist and professor emeritus at McGill University in Montreal.

Millman, Lawrence. "The First Narwhal." In *A Kayak Full of Ghosts: Eskimo Folktales*. pp. 36–37. Northampton MA: Interlink Books, 2004. This redaction derives from Pangnirtung resident Ken Annanack around 1981, a valid oral source. And the story line here conforms remarkably well with documented oral traditions within the Group B region. However, in his introduction to the volume, Millman confesses that "I've strived for readability rather than word-for-word accuracy. I've pared down localisms. Sometimes I've spliced together two or more versions of the same story. I've cut, polished, even recast" (2004: 15).

Momaday, N. Scott. Untitled rendering. In *The Way to Rainy Mountain*, p. 58. Albuquerque: University of New Mexico Press, 1969. See Section XVII, which begins, "Bad women are thrown away." This Kiowa-based variant by a Pulitzer Prize–winning author is totally naturalistic, without any magical restoration of sight to the blind man by intervening birds and without any witchcraft on the part of his wife.

Oosten, J. G. "The Incest of Sun and Moon: An Examination of the Symbolism of Time and Space in Two Iglulik Myths." *Études/Inuit/Studies* 7, no. 1 (1983):143–51. Retitled "The Myth of the Sun and the Moon," this edition is an abridgment of the variant told by Ivaluardjuk to Knud Rasmussen (1929) at Repulse Bay in 1921. Oosten does not acknowledge Ivaluardjuk as the storyteller and does not inform the reader that he has rewritten and condensed Rasmussen's English text.

Parker, Janet, and Julie Stanton, eds. "The Blind Boy and the Loon." In *Mythology: Myths, Legends, and Fantasies*, pp. 471–72. Willoughby, Australia: Global Book Publishers, 2005. Story is a "retelling" based on variants from Hall, Rink, and Nungak and Arima.

Petrone, Penny. "Origin of the Sun and the Moon." In *Northern Voices: Inuit Writing in English*, pp. 14–16. Toronto: University of Toronto Press, 1992. Petrone reprints Oosten's (1983) derivative condensed version, presuming it to be authentic, but retitles it again.

Quitsualik, Rachel. "Glutton." *Nunatsiaq News*. August 8, 15, and 22, 2003. The only known text in which the blind man kills the bear with a spear instead of a bow and arrow. The Inuit author from Pond Inlet on Baffin Island precedes the story with a long essay on the evils of gluttony, carefully distinguishing it as hoarding rather than simply overeating. May be viewed online at http://www.nunatsiaqonline.ca/archives/30829/news/editorial/columns.html.

Rink, Hinrich. "Den Blinde, som fik sit Syn igjen." In *Eskimoiske Eventyr og Sagn*, pp. 51–54. Kjøbenhavn: C.A. Reitzels Boghandel, 1866. Danish text. This is the earliest known published version, a redaction based on eight texts written by Greenlanders and Labradoran Eskimos. Available online at Google Books and the Internet Archive. A translation of Rink's notes to the text appears in chap. 1, p. 36.

———. "The Blind Man Who Recovered His Sight." In *Tales and Traditions of the Eskimo*, pp. 99–105. Edinburgh: William Blackwood and Sons, 1875. Reprint, Mineola NY: Dover Publications, 1997. The Blind Man is named Tutigak. This is the English translation of the 1866 Danish edition. Available online at http://www.sacred-texts.com/nam/inu/tte/tte2-002.htm.

Rowan, Carol, ed. "Lumaaq." In *Unikkaangualaurtaa (Let's Tell a Story): A Collection of 26 Stories and Songs from Nunavik, with Activities for Young Children*. Westmount, Québec: Avataq Cultural Institute, 2006. Editions in English, French, and Inuktitut. Written for toddlers and young children. Available online at http://www.northerndelightstea.com/en/nunavik/legends/09.php.

Smelcer, John E. "The Blind Man and the Loon." In *A Cycle of Myths*, pp. 57–60. Anchorage: Salmon Run, 1993. pp. 57–60. Appears here as an Eyak story but in another book, *In the Shadows of Mountains: Ahtna Stories from the Copper River* (Chugiak: Salmon Run Press, 1977), Smelcer introduces the same text as an Ahtna story and claims "it teaches a moral lesson: 'Don't be greedy and be kind to those less fortunate.'" Smelcer is himself an Ahtna but does not cite his source for the text.

Toye, William. *The Loon's Necklace*. Illustrated by Elizabeth Cleaver. Toronto: Oxford University Press, 1977. Reprint, 1990. The author says the stories are "retold."

Part 3. Commercial Media Variants

Arnaquq-Baril, Alethea Ann. *Nunavut Animation Lab: Lumaajuuq*. Film. 7 minutes, 36 seconds. Ottawa: National Film Board of Canada and the Inuit Broadcasting Corporation, 2010. Available for viewing online at http://www.nfb.ca/film/nunavut_animation_lab_lumaajuuq.

Bissell, Keith. *How the Loon Got Its Necklace: A Legend of the Salish Tribe of Indians from the Interior of British Columbia*. LP record. Montreal: CBC Radio Canada International, 1974. Composed in 1971 for a string quintet and percussion.

Crawley, Frank Radford "Budge." *The Loon's Necklace*. 16 mm film, 11 minutes. 1949. Released in French *as Le Collier Magique* (1950). One of the most influential of all variants. Restored and made into a video in 1981. Credits: Producer/Director: Radford Crawley for Crawley Films; Writer: Douglas Leechman; Storyteller: George Gorman/François Bertrand. See Leechman (1931, 1942, 1956). Distributed in VHS format by Encyclopedia Britannica Educational Corporation, Chicago IL 60604. It may be viewed online at http://www.youtube.com/watch?v=DfUmSFVncPk or at http://avtrust.ca/masterworks/2001/en_film_2.htm.

East of England Broadband Network. The Blind Boy and the Loon. Animated cartoon strip. 9 minutes, 30 seconds. 2011. Available for viewing online at http://myths.e2bn.org/mythsandlegends/textonly2982-the-blind-boy-and-the-loon.html.

Hills, Peggy (McGuire). "How the Loon Got Its Necklace." 12 min. 34 sec. Compact audio disc. In *The Storyteller's Bag*. Mississauga, Ont.: Chamber Music Society of Mississauga, 2006. Classical music by Keith Bissell; text by Mark Brownell. Dramatic reading by professional actors Lorne Cardinal and Cheri Maracle. Attributed to both Salish and Ojibway oral tradition but without documentation. Apparently based the Crawley film and Macfarlan's version, vilifying wolves. See Bissell, 1974.

Hoedeman, Co, dir. *Lumaaq: An Eskimo Legend*. Film, 8 minutes. Ottawa: National Film Board of Canada, 1975. Lumaaq legend is converted from Davidialuk's sketches to an animated cartoon strip. The film may be viewed online at http://www.youtube.com/watch?v=QSVm-Fg3ltI.

Lindner, Banjo Dan. *The Loon's Necklace*. Music compact disc. South Strafford VT, 1992.

Pheasant, Kenny. Maang Donaabkowaaginim: The Loon's Necklace. *Anishinaabemdaa*. Compact audio disc. 4 mins. Anishinaabe Native language version; from Manistee, Michigan. n.d. May be previewed online at: http://www.anishinaabemdaa.com/cdrom.htm.

Worthy, Barbara, ed. *Legends, Vol. 2: Inuit Legends*. Compact audio disc. Canadian Broadcasting Corporation, North Radio One (CBC Audio), 2003. Contains "Lumaajuuq: The Story of the Blind Boy" in Inuktitut and English. Original music performances by Celina Kalluk, Madeleine Allakariallak, Elisha Kilabuk, and Orla Osbourne. English performance is on disc 1, Inuktitut is on disc 2, but they are mislabeled. Available for purchase online via http://www.cbcshop.ca/legends-vol-2-inuit-legends-2-cds-english-inuktitut.html

Part 4. Greenlandic Variants Listed in Sonnesbase (SB)

See http://tors.ku.dk/biblioteker2/eskimologi/datasamlinger/sonnesbase. Original texts are in Kalaallisut (Greenlandic) unless otherwise noted. Danish summaries compiled by Birgitte Sonne. Sonnesbase is formatted in askSam and may be freely downloaded.

DANISH ARCHIVES COLLECTION ABBREVIATIONS

KRH: Knud Rasmussens arkiv på Hundested Bibliotek (Knud Rasmussen's Archive in Hundested City Library).

KRKB: Knud Rasmussens Arkiv (Det kongelige Bibiliotek). (Knud Rasmussen's Archive. The Royal Library, Copenhagen).

NKS 2488, I–IV, 4° + V–VIII: Ny Kongelig Samling. Rink's samlinger, Det kongelige Bibiliotek (The New Royal Collection. Hinrich Rink's Collection, The Royal Library, Copenhagen).

NKS 3536: Rasmussen samling på Det kongelige Bibiliotek (Knud Rasmussen's Collection. The Royal Library, Copenhagen).

Danish Archival Variants (location for each variant is shown in brackets):

1) SB Document 149: collected by Peder Kragh, 1823–28, Danish summary by Christian Berthelsen; newly translated by Thisted (1999); the ending is apparently missing—fragmentary. Told from the first person point of view by the blind man.
   [NKS 2488, VI, pp. 152ff.; recopied as NKS 2488, II nr. 40]

2) SB Document 167: copied by Wittus Frederick Steenholdt, collected by Peder Kragh, 1823–28 (actually 1827), Danish summary by Christian Berthelsen. A handwritten booklet entitled *"Samling of Grønlandske Fortællinger* (Collection of Greenlandic Tellings) clean-written by Wittus Frederick Stenholdt, 1827." This is the oldest variant of the story that has been preserved, and even so it seems to have been a fair copy. Published here for the first time in appendix D.
   [NKS 2488, VI, pp. 40h-43h; recopied as NKS 2488, II nr. 60, 1857–1862]

3) SB Document 168: collected by Peder Kragh, 1823–28, Danish summary by Christian Berthelsen.
   [NKS 2488, II nr. 62]

4) SB Document 207: written by Jens Kreutzmann, 1859, Danish summary by Christian Berthelsen; full version translated to Danish and published in Thisted (1997). Also published in full in Kalaallisut in Thisted and Grove, *Oqaluttuat & Assilialiat* (1997).
   [NKS 2488, II nr. 103]

5) SB Document 324: told by Jonasine Nielsen (Saattoq: Upernavik), Danish translation by Apollo Lynge, revised by Signe Åsblom.
[Original handwritten text: KRKB 3: Record from the Danish Literary Expedition to Greenland 1902–04, Eskimo legends]

6) SB Document 1121: told by Nakitilik. Written by Gustav Holm after an oral translation by Johan Petersen. Published in Danish by Gustav Holm (see earlier citation).
[NKS 2488, VIII nr. 4, pp. 59–62]

7) SB Document 1375: unknown storyteller (Tasiilaq/Angmassalik/ Ammassalik)—published in Danish in Knud Rasmussen, *Myter og Sagn fra Grønland, I /Myths and Legends from Greenland I* (1921), pp. 312–17. Reprinted by Nordiske landes Bogforlag, 1979. First written by Sofie Jørgensen, summarized; in the Hundested Library. Original handwritten text.
[KRH box 52, no. 2, notebook 413: najagît kanganisaranilo". Transcript: KRH, box 52, no. 2, notebook 424: "Ningânilât."]

8) SB Document 1496: told by Cecilie Olsen/Sísê/Sissili (Sisimiut/ Holsteinsborg). Transcribed and translated by Karolina Platou Jeremiassen—see appendix C in this volume.
[KRKB 1, 7 (19). Dagbøger fra den litterære Grønlandsekspedition 1902–04/Danish Literary Greenland Expedition" (1902–04)]

9) SB Document 1544: told by Arnâluk/Arnaaluk (Agpat/Appat: Avanersuaq /Thule). Published in English in Knud Rasmussen's *The People of the Polar North: A Record* (1908:162–72).
[Original handwritten text: KRKB 1, 5(14): Records from the Danish Literary Greenland Expedition 1902–4. Rasmussen's fair copy: KRKB 3 Eskimoiske Sagn/ Eskimo Legends, 4, Records from the Danish Literary Greenland Expedition 1902–04: "Uluâ"/Uluaa. Typewritten manuscript: KRH, box 51, no.33.]

10) SB Document 1608: told by Silas (Ilimanaq /Claushavn: Ilulissat/ Jakobshavn), summarized. Published in Danish in Knud Rasmussen, *Myter og Sagn fra Grønland, III /Myths and Legends from Greenland III* (1925), pp. 201–205. Reprinted by Nordiske landes Bogforlag, 1979.
[Original handwritten text : KRKB, no.3: Records from the Danish Literary Greenland Expedition 1902–04. Transcript: NKS 3536, IV, 4°, 9.]

11) SB Document 1732: unknown storyteller (Neria: Paamiut/ Frederikshåb), Danish translation by Christian Berthelsen.
[NKS 3536, I, 4°, volume 5, page 2v-3h]

12) SB Document 1838: written by Jakob Lund, 1863, Danish translation by Christian Berthelsen from early original. The Lund variant appears

under the title "Nerdlerit tagpigssitânik" (The geese which gave him back his sight).

[NKS 2488, III 80h–83v nr. 330]

13) SB Document 1847: written by Amos Daniel, 1863, not translated or summarized (illegible handwriting)

[NKS 2488, III, 4°, page 187h–197v, no. 344]

14) SB Document 1895: told by Gert Lyberth (Maniitsoq/Sukkertoppen), Danish translation by Signe Åsblom.

[Handwritten text: KRKB 5, 1, (5)]

15) SB Document 2176: told by Matînarujuk/Matiinarujuk (Nuuk/ Godthåb). Transcribed and translated by Karolina Platou Jeremiassen—see appendix C in this volume.

[KRKB, 1, 4(12), Dagbøger fra den litterære Grønlandsekspedition 1902–04/The Diaries of the Danish Literary Greenland Expedition 1902–04, no.10]

16) SB Document 2224: told by Gaba Olsen, Gâba, Gaaba, Gabriel (Kuuk: Upernavik), no translation or summary.

[KRKB, 1, 5(13), Dagbøger fra den litterære Grønlandsekspedition 1902–04 / The Diaries of the Danish Literary Greenland Expedition 1902–04, no.10]

17) SB Document 2274: told by Kuania/Kuannia/Kuaannia (Illuluarsuit: Sydøstgrønland?). Transcribed and translated by Karolina Platou Jeremiassen—see Appendix C in this volume.

[KRKB, 1, 7(20), Dagbøger fra den litterære Grønlandsekspedition 1902–04 / The Diaries of the Danish Literary Greenland Expedition 1902–04]

Part 5. Other Known Variants

Andre, Eliza. "Blind Man and the Loon." Recorded in Gwich'in by Louie Goose at Tsiigehtshik, NWT, 1974. CD-R Redbook audio. Cat. No. N-1992–253: 0566. Committee for Original Peoples' Entitlement: Oral History Project Fonds. Prince of Wales Northern Heritage Centre, Yellowknife. This is not the original field recording but one edited later for radio. Broadcast on CHAK-AM radio, Inuvik, the same year. Née Eliza Sam, she married Chief Hyacinthe Andre in 1928 and was the mother of twelve children. She died in 1977. A translation has been published in Michael Heine et al., eds. *Gwichya Gwich'in Googwandak: The History and Stories of the Gwichya Gwich'in* (2007).

Anonymous. Labrador Version, in German, collected by Moravian missionaries, n.d. NKS 2488, IIII, No. 303: The New Royal Collection—Hinrich Rink's Collection, The Royal Library, Copenhagen. Translated into English by Birgitte Sonne. Text is included in Appendix D.

Blondin, George. *Legends and Stories from the Past.* n.d. Online English version by a Sahtu (North Slavey) Dene elder born in 1923 in the Northwest Territories near Great Bear Lake. Blondin is a former wilderness guide, miner, and trapper as well as author of *When the World Was New: Stories of the Sahtú Dene* (Yellowknife: Outcrop, the Northern Publishers, 1990), which contains many additional stories and his autobiography. The text "Regarding a Blind Man" is online at the NWT government's Division of Education, Culture, and Employment, Curriculum Services: ww.ece.gov. nt.ca/Divisions/kindergarten_g12/Legends/Legends/story2.pdf. This version appears to be abridged and cleaned up for children, since there is no revenge taken by the blind man against his wife, but it is impossible to tell if this was the result of the storyteller's intentions or those of the web page editor.

Bruce, Ellen. "Blind Man." Tape 4-3-A (VI-I-96T). Recorded in Old Crow, Yukon Territory, April 22, 1980. Transcript CYI T0065. Council for Yukon Indians, Whitehorse. Translation published in Vuntut Gwitchin First Nation and Shirleen Smith, *People of the Lakes: Stories of Our Van Tat Gwich'in Elders/ Googwandak Nakhwach'ànjòo Van Tat Gwich'in* (2009).

Demit, Ellen. Ruffed Grouse Story (Blind Man and the Loon)/Tsaan'tuug. Recorded by Gary Holton on January 20, 2001 in Healy Lake Village. In this story the blind man assumes the identity of a ruffed grouse. Mp3 audio file in the Tanacross language. Fairbanks: University of Alaska Native Language Center Archive. See online reference http://www.uaf .edu/anla/item.xml?id=ANLC3658.

Moses, Leo. How the Loons Got Their White Markings. Recorded and translated from the Yup'ik by Frank Hunter, 1975. Unpublished English typescript in the personal collection of the author, 3 pp. Leo Moses was born in Kashunak about 1935 and now lives at Chevak. He is a carpenter and member of the Army National Guard, also a former member of the Advisory School Board and president of the Chevak village council. He says he learned many good stories in the steam bath, an important place for Yup'ik socializing.

Pete, Shem. "Blind Man and the Loon." Untranscribed tape recording by linguist James Kari in Dena'ina in 1977. 6 mins. Ti #1266. Jim Kari personal collection, Fairbanks, Alaska. Shem Pete is the Dena'ina storyteller and singer featured in the encyclopedic place name book, *Shem Pete's Alaska.* He lived for many years at Nancy Lake, Alaska, and in the village of Tyonek. He died in 1989.

Stoeri, David. Blind Man and the Loon. A "witch woman" replaces the blind man's wife in this audio variant told by a fourth grade teacher to young school children at the Summit School in Winston–Salem NC. Attributed to the Ojibwa in northern Michigan but clearly a semi-literary version with several songs. 12 min. 30 sec. Posted on the web on March 19, 2012. M4a audio file may be downloaded at http://summit.nc.schoolwebpages .com/education/components/docmgr/default.php?sectiondetailid=32 21&fileitem=2452&catfilter=ALL.

Thomas, Kenny Sr. "Yamal Telcheegh." Videotape performance by Tanacross, Alaska elder. Recorded in English by Mishler from Thomas at Tanacross on October 30, 2000. This is the basis for Thomas's written version, shown above (Thomas 2005), and forms the first part of a longer cycle of stories. The video contains a wealth of nonverbal communication, including a bent wrist demonstrating the loon's dive under water with the blind man (Image 18). Author's personal collection. See it online at http://uaf.edu/loon/video/.

Titus, Walter. "Blind Man and the Loon." Tape recorded in English and Lower Tanana by Karen McPherson at Minto, Alaska, on August 31, 1972. Oral History Collection, Rasmuson Library, University of Alaska, Fairbanks. Tape H91-12-68. Available on compact disc through many Alaska libraries as part of the Songs and Legends series, Volume 93, Track 2. The English version is about 7 minutes; the Lower Tanana language version is less than 3 minutes. Titus was born in Nenana in 1909 and moved to Minto when he married in 1923. He learned the story from his grandmother Sarah. See other Minto versions in Rooth (1971). The Loon is rewarded with a beaded necklace, which is found only in Group F. Hear it online at http://uaf.edu/loon/audio/.

Unka, Ellen. "The Old Man and the Loon." Recorded and translated by David M. Smith, December 8, 1971. Unpublished English Ms. in possession of David M. Smith and the personal collection of the author. Ellen Unka was a resident of Fort Resolution, Great Slave Lake NWT and told the story in Chipewyan, having heard it on the radio. She was in her 70s at the time and also spoke Dogrib and Slave. The target animal is a moose, making this variant a member of Group G.

Wright, Arthur. The Blind Man and His Faithless Wife. In Frederick Blount Drane's "A Circuit Rider on the Yukon." pp. 266–770. Unpublished English typescript, Frederick Drane Collection, Folder 15, Box 7, Rasmuson Library archives, University of Alaska, Fairbanks. Wright, a half-blood Athabaskan mission worker stationed on the Tanana River, wrote this story for *The Alaska Churchman* Episcopal Church magazine and published it in February 1921.

Appendix C

Knud Rasmussen's Greenlandic Variants

Knud Rasmussen collected ten Greenlandic (Group A) variants, but only two (SB 1375 and SB 1544) have been published to date, the former in Danish and the latter in English. The three texts that follow here are apparently the first in his collection ever to be published in Greenlandic (Kalaallisut).

Texts have been transliterated into the new Kalaallisut orthography by Karolina Platou Jeremiassen (KPJ) of Nuuk and translated by her, then edited by Craig Mishler. In contrast to most Eskimo languages in Canada, Kalaallisut or Greenlandic is written with the Roman alphabet rather than the Inuktitut syllabary. For a detailed description of the orthography and a pronunciation guide, see http://www.omniglot.com/writing/greenlandic .htm. Respecting the look and feel of the longhand originals, we have not attempted to reconfigure these transcriptions from paragraphs into lines. The original page numbers are shown here in parentheses.

1. Oqaluttuaq utoqqannguamik Ulûak (SB 1496)[1]

Utoqqannguarooq paneqarlunilu erneqartoq, ukiilerpunngooq kisimiillutik, taamaallutinngooq taassuma utoqqannguup erni piniartigillualivillugu sinngagilerpaa: taamaallunigooq ernerata alissani iteqqumiittoq issing-ernialeraa arnaata piaaralugu isaasigut serparpaa tappingersillugulu. Qatanngutaatagooq arnap nalligingaaramiuk ullut tamaasa pisuttuuttarpaa, arnaataligooq taanna erninnguani piaaralugu immaaranguaq nerisittar-paa tassa sinngaginermit, najaataligooq arnamik terlinganit nerisittarpaa.

Ilaannigooq ukiumi nanorsuup siornga meqqoqanngitsorsuup igalaanngua-tigut ameramininnguakkut itsuarpai, arnaatalu ernermi pisissia tigutippaa, namminerlu nanorsuarmut nalaartillugu, erneratalu pisissini qilugamiuk (page 1) piseriarpaa, pisorpallariallartoq arnaa oqarpoq: "Aa eqqut pisippat." (Eqqut tassa umernerngup sinaakkutaa ameq) taannalu nanorsuaq uppeqaaq toqulluni.

Taassumalu pisinnittup sianiginngilaa tappiitsuugami. Arnaatalu najaatalu amiialerpaat, naammassigamikku igalerput, qalammatalu taanna erninngua pilerpoq: "Sunaana sumit uusuarnersuaq naamavara." Arnaata oqarfigaa: "Uilunnguinuku orsuutigissikkikka," ernilu uilunnguanik tunillugu nerisassaanik, namminnerlu nanoq nerillugu. Ukiorsuaq taanna nanorsuaq nerisarilerpaat, taannalu nerisissanagu taassuminnga.

Najannguatagooq nalligivallaaleraangamiuk tunuminut tigutilluni pisuttuuttarpaa, ilaannigooq upernalillaraa pisuttuaqatigalugu unillutik qummut qiviarniariartoq eqqorluinnarlugu

(page 2)

isaasigut anarpaat, anallarmani isini allarteriaramigit qaammaallalluni, kingullermik allarteriaramigit qangali ueratarpoq. Angerlaleramik najannguata oqaluttuutilerpaa nanorsuaq pisarigaa, namminnerlu nerisarigamikku oqarfigalugulu tappiitsuusaaginnaqqullugu tunumigullu tigutilluni ingerlappaa. Taamaalisimallugulu illuminnut eqquppaa arnartik igasoq nanuliorluni. Qalammata arnaata aasit uilunnguanik tunivaa nerisassaanik, aasit taanna oqalulerpoq: "Sumit una uusuarnersuaq naamavara?" Taamalu oqarluni nannup neqai uusut tikkuarpai. Aasiilli arnaa annilaangaarluni uisalerpoq oqarfigalugulu: "Tassa nannuttarsuarpit neqaa neriniarit." Taannalu nerilerpoq naammatsilluaramilu aatsaat soraarpoq.

(page 3)

Upernallarmanngooq qilalukkat ingerlaalillarmata arni pilerpaa, alermik noqitsigiumallugu qeqqagut pitullugu avataralugu. Arnaata akueraa tamaanillu qilalukkat annersioramigit anginertarsuat naalippaa. Taannaqami arnaata noqquserpaa, kiisagooq artulersalerlugu arpasaqattaartalerpoq qaarsorsuakkut sissap tungaanut qilalugarsuullu nusullugu aallaruppaa, taannalu arnaa suaartaleqaaq: "Ulugaa kiputissaraa," oqalukkaluaramilu tusarneqaqnngilaq, kiisalu qilalugarsuup nusullugu imaanut morsuuppaa, qilalugarsuarlu pueriartoq nuitsiariarluni allamik oqassanani: "Ulugaa kiputissaraa," kiisamigooq taamaalluni ipivoq. Taamaallaanngooq ernerata arni naalliutsimmani taamaalillugu akiniarpallarujaa.

Naavoq.

Oqaluttuartoq Sicelia Olsen allattoq Frederik Olsen.

(page 4)

1. A story about an old woman named Ulûak (SB 1496)

Once there was an old woman who had a daughter and a son. They were going to stay over the winter all alone. Even though the old woman had the benefit of her son's hunting, she became jealous of him. While her son tried to dry a piece of skin[2] he took from the urine bucket, she purposely splashed him on his eyes with it, so he lost his sight. His sister felt sorry for him, and she walked with him every day. While his mother fed him just a little bit on purpose because of jealousy, his little sister gave him food whenever their mother turned her back.

Once during the winter, a polar bear with no skin on its forehead looked inside through their little window, made of a piece of skin. So the mother took her son's bow and handed it to her son, while she aimed at the polar bear. Her son straightened his bow and arrow

(page 1)

and shot the target. There was a falling noise, whereupon his mother said, "You hit the edge." (*The edge is the frame of their window, made of skin*).[3] Then that big bear fell down and died, but the one who shot the arrow didn't know a thing, since he was blind.

The mother and his sister started to take the skin off the bear. When they finished, they started to cook, and when the meat was cooked, the son said, "What is it I'm smelling? It smells like meat." The mother answered, "It is just some common mussels," and she gave her son a bit of mussel to eat, while she and her daughter ate the meat of the bear. Through the entire winter they ate the meat of the bear, but she never gave the son even a bite of it.

When his sister felt sorry for him, she would take him out to walk, letting him hold her shoulder from behind. Once, in the springtime, while they were out walking, they stopped to rest, and a bird made droppings on him just as he looked up,

(page 2)

and they hit him right in his eyes. As he wiped his face, his sight brightened up. The second time he wiped his eyes; he opened his eyes.

On their way home, his sister told him that he did catch the bear, and that they had been eating the meat; she also told him to pretend to be blind, and let him hold her shoulder as they walked.

She went inside the house, still having him right behind her, while their mother was cooking the bear meat. When she finished cooking, she gave her son some mussels as usual, and he began to talk. "Where is the smell

193

of meat coming from?" As he said that, he pointed to the meat; his mother didn't know what to do and was quite surprised, while she said, "That is the meat of the bear that you killed. Go on and eat." And he began to eat, and he ate and ate until he was full.
(page 3)

In the spring, when the belugas were on their way, he told his mother to hold the rope, with the rope tightened up around her waist. She agreed to do that, and the son found a biggest beluga to catch and harpooned it. His mother used all her strength to hold the rope and the beluga as well. She began to run toward the beach, trying to keep up with the beluga. The beluga hauled her down to the sea, while she yelled, "Ulugaa, hand me something to cut the rope with!" But no one heard her. The beluga was still hauling her away, and when it dove under the water, she would go under, and when it appeared on top of the water, she would also appear, while shouting out, "Ulugaa, hand me something to cut the rope with!" At last, she drowned. Her son took revenge on his mother for all the suffering she had caused him. The end.

The storyteller: Sicelia Olsen. The writer: Frederik Olsen
(page 4)

2. Uluak (SB 2176)[4]

Uluagooq pinerrareqaaq. Nunaqarfini ajorsarfiginagu ukiivigisarpaa—ukiivigigaangamiuk qimallaaraa ajorsarfiginagu. Nunaqarfissaminik ajorsarfissaminik ujaarleraluallaaraaq. Ujaarlerluni ilaanniaasiit nuusarnut ukiivissippoq. Taanna ukiivigiumagamiuk. Ingammik tassani piniagassanik amerlanaarsilerpoq. Kalippallaalillaraangami qasuersaarluni uninngasarpoq. Uninngagaluaraangami ingammik puisitarsui amerlavallaallaraat.
(page 1)

Ilaanniaasiit angusimallarluni tikikkami ileqqumisut innarpoq. Sinikkami iteriallarami tappingersimallarluni. Ippassaralaajummat taama angumatigaluni kiisa arnakasia qujaannarpoq erni tappingersimammat. Sunaaffa namminikasik taama periallarsinnarlugu. Piniartituarillugu tappingiinnaqaaq.

Arnakasini anigaangat najaa oqaluleraraaq: "Allap pinngilaatit arnakasimma pivaatit. Qanoruna isillugu iliorfiginiassavarput." Taamalu saperlugu iliorfiginissaa.
(page 2)

Ilaanni taamaalluni ukiuinnaleqaaq. Ukiorissilluni issitsisimaleraa ilaanniaa ullaakkut iterami kamissimalerluni aaqqatai (nillernermut?)

seqquloriallarmat sunarsuaruna isileqaaq—taaka pinialeriarlugu nanorsuaq puttummigami igalaasakkut. "A—qanoruna piniassuarpununa," kipunngersaarpallaaleqimmata angutitaat oqarpoq: "Pisissera qaanermiittoq qaassiuk." Najaata tunniuppaa. Najaata tunniummagu oqarfigaa "Narlortinniaruk tungaanut piseriaraluassaqaara." Piseriaramiuk qanga pisorpallannguarsi, soorluuna allamut tugani. Aatsaat najaa oqarnialeriallartoq

(page 3)

arnakasiata taliinnarminik inerterpaa oqaqqunagu. Oqarfigeriarlugu oqarpoq: "Sunaana piseqaajuk, eqqut piseqaat eqqut piseqaat, nanorsuakasik pissillarluni taamak aallaannaqaaq." Arnakasiata panni aneqqugamiuk isaannarminik Marluullutik aneriallaramik—eeq—nanorsuakasik uppissimallartoq, kiisa kisimik marluinnaallutik uitsatilerput. Arnakasia oqalulerpoq: "Ernersuara oqarfiginiaqinagu—uagut taanna nutaartugariinnassavarput." Pilareeramik iseramik

(page 4)

soorlu tamaani pinngitsut. Isaannarminik iqaqquinnaqaa paniata iga kukuppaa igalertullarami qalammata nutaartukasipput pisaqarnikunnguakkulullu minillugu, ilisimagaluarlugit nerisut tipersualu naamagaluarlugu.

Tassannga ullaanngorami ualileraa arnakasia uernalerpoq, sinileriarmat najaata anini oqaluutilerpaa: "Uutsissutissavakkit nannuttarsuarnik." Qulissunnilu piareersarlugu. Soorlu immaralaannguaq qulissilluni, qalakkamiuk nerisippaa naammattumik soorlu sungaqanngitsoq mamarsangaarami naammatsillannguarsinnarpoq, qangali qujanan022uarsi tassa taamaalillugu nerisilerpaa arnakasini sinissiisarlugu tassa nerisaritilerpaa, taamaaseruttoraa kiisa aasaatiinnaqaa nerisaralugu (upernaatiinnaqaa).

(page 5)

Tuullingit ingerlaalillarmata oqalulerpoq: "Taaka tatsit atarnanut aanniarallannga." Najaata kisigiallaat (nangaagaluarluni) ingerlakkamiuk tatsit atarnanut pissutiinnaqaa. Pissummani oqarfigiinnaqaa: "Tassa illit angerlarniarit uanga tuullippalaarnissaanut aliannaassaanga." Najamilu qimakkaani taannaqa tassani utaqqilerpoq. Utaqqeruttuleriarlugillu qanga tuullippalaarsuarmit tusarnissi ilimagileriarnagu aarimmi nipaa tusarpaa, a-aliannaalerami tassani immaqa uisasuugaluaruni. Aggerpalukkamik qulangiullutillu aappaa qarlorluni,

(page 6)

meriarami oqarpoq: "Kanna inuusuttutsiaq immaqaliaa oqaatsigut ilisimagaluarunigit kingumut silap qaamanera takoqqissagaluarpaa uunga tatsip sinaanut nerfallarluni." Nerfallariallartoq avannaatungaanut mikkaluarlutik kingumut aggerpaluinnaleqaat timmillutik, qulangeriarlugu timmeqaa

kiinaannaatigut. Qangali kissaallannguarsi, aamma aappaata kingulliulluni timmeqaa, kingumut nermallattaariarlutik avannamuinnarsuaq tuullippalaarlutik aallarput. Tatsimut poriarluni kiinnani allarterniarlugu
(page 7)
ila tupinnakasinguna, silarsuup qaamanersua taamak takuaa inuusukkallaramiluunniit tappissutsimigut tappinnerulersimalluni misigaaq, aa—angerlaannassagaluarluni aamma isumaliulerpoq: "Arnakasimma aamma kingumut taama isissavaanga." Massa tassa tassa uteqqilerluni seqernup tarriffissani qulangeriannguallaraa najaa nuivoq qianngarmi anini naakkigalugu. Ania isumaliulerpoq uilluni pissagaluaruni tipaatsuallappallaassaqimmat tappiitsuusaaqqilerpoq kisianni tikilluainnalermani oqarfigaa:
(page 8)
"Sooq qiavit,atigissarsiumaleqagit qernersuatsiamik seeqqinissarsiumaleqagit (takisuut) qasigissamit pinnersuattaamit?" Taama oqarniariartoq massilerami: "Soqaat sulingusaqaat tappissingusaqaat?" Taavaana najaa nuannaalermioq angerlaallugu aallaruppaa—imminnut oqaluuttuannguarlutik ingerlajualerput.—Ingerlaniarlutik ania oqarpoq: "Uisallunga iseraluaruma arnakasimma taama isilluni tappingersissavaanga." Najaa maarami: "Ataguliaa takujumaarpatit perpassuit akip ataani." Illulu nuissagamikku aleqami (kukkusaq, najami) tunua tigullugu ania palungasoq tappiitsuusaarluni isernialeriarluni arnakasia maarami: "Sila silarsuaq
(page 9)
taamaasigaangat tammarluni iserumaatsuugaluaq tassaluaasiit iluamik nerisassaqarminak." Qaaqqummani oqarpoq: "Illermiinngulaarnaqaaq akimut ingitsinnga." Akimut ingitsimmani sikilluni qinilerpai ii—pissaqaraanni, nariorlugu eqqaa mikialersoq, makilluni arnakasini oqaluttoq tassaluaasiit nerisassaqarminak qinileriallarami ippatit ataani—ii—pissaqarami nanorsuakasissuup neqaa qaa panertoq, taamatullu takullugit makileriarami arnakasini oqarfigaa: "Makkumi suut, akip ataani?" Taamaasiniariartoq arnakasia tupallarluni oqarpoq: "Suleqaat sulingusaqaat uigisaqaat?"
(page 10)
Misigileriallaraa ernersuani uittaritsiarami. Tassa ajoqutinnguaarulluni angalavataalerpoq. Kingumut piniartigileramikku ingammingaasiit piniagassaminut ajorsanngippallaaleqaaq. Taamaasillarluni arnakasimmi aappassaaneernissaa siooragilerpaa, aappassaaneerpani naveerluinnassagami. Kiserngoruteriaraangamik panialu erneralu oqaluleraat, "Kingullermik taamaaseriarpatit tassa uinnaveersaaginnassaatit," najaa oqalulerpoq. "Avatartariumasuusaarniariuk qilalukkamut annermut," Ilaannaasiit qilalukkat avannamukaalermata aarimmi qilalukkamik naalittalerpoq nunaminngaanniit

najaata noqittariaramigit, ilaanniaasit arnap qatanngunni angut oqa-
luffigilerpaa: "Illit anaanat oqaluffiginiariuk aqagumut kingoraarlunga
avatartaaniaqqullugu.
(page 11)
    Taamaasillugu terliseriarniarniassavarput." Tikikkamik tamaani soorlu
oqaasissaqanngitsoq, kiisami angut qatanngunni aamma qasukkullugu:
"Pisinnaaguit kingoraassagaluarpat ullorluunniit ataaseq" arnakasia oqarpoq: "Sulimi pisinnaagaluarpunga." Unnummat arnakasia sinilluanngilaq
pilerinermut aqagumut avatartaajumalluni. Ullaaralaannguaq taavaana
makittareermioq. Sukatersinnaasani tamaasa sukatilerlugit taavalu erni
aallaleriarmat aallaqatigaa, taava piffissaminnut pigami arnaata erni oqarfigaa: "Angisuumik naalillariaanak minnersiorlugit uiannguamilluunniit
naalinniarsarissaatit." Ernera oqarpoq:
(page 12)
    "Sullungami annersiussavakka?" Qilalukkat avannamukarlutik nalliutil-
laraangata minnersiorlugit naalittarai ilaanni puiarpalummata tusaleriallaraa
uinngiakujoorpaluttoq angingaarami annilaarnaannarpoq, tassa kingull-
ersiorajukkamik puinersikulammersussagaatik aarimmi pueriallarami
aappalaartorsuaq angingaarami arnaa oqarpoq: "Tamanna naalillariaanagu."
"Sullugumi naalissavara piniarniannginnakku naalinnianngilara," naak
naalikkumallugu massa qamaruttulerianngualларluni aarimmi puileqaat.
milaasuinnaat piniassalluni qinillarluni aarnuersarai, ilaanniaasiit anner-
suaq puillarmat naalippaa, arnakasia maarami oqarpoq:
(page 13)
    "Sooruna tamassarsuaq naaleqaajuk?!" Taamaaseriarmat aleq aallar-
poq. Iperaruloorluni, taanna arnaq tutsinnerani qaporujuinnarpoq taamalu
arnaq taanna sillimalluarmat qilalugaq annermik aallarsaalerpoq. Taava
utoqqannguaq nikuingajattalerpoq, taannalu tukerluarami soorlu qeri-
innakasillartoq. Kingullermik masseriarami qillaallaannarpoq taavalu
nusuleramiuk tukerami qimallugu ammut aallarpoq oqalullunilu: "Uluaak
sugaluttuaqaarmaana, quuit ataanni annavit ataanni pinngorsarniarakkit"
taava nusukkamiuk aallaruppaa, nuigamilu oqalulerpoq: "Quuit ataanni
annavit ataanni pinngorsarniarakkit. Uluak
(page 14)
sugaluttuarimmaana?"
    Aarimmi angerlarmat najaata isigileriallaraa kisimiilluni angerlartoq,
aperivaa: "Naammi arnakasiit?" Akivaa: "Qilalukkap avatartaraa."
    Taava arnakasitsik toqummat ernummataarullutinngooq nuna taanna
najulerpaat arnakasimminnik ajoqutaarullutik, tassagooq Uluap ukiivini

nunagalugu saarnalisarfiginnguarujaa.

Tassunga naavoq.

Den 21.juni 1902
Godthåbshavn
(Matiinarujuk)

(page 15)

2. Uluak (SB 2176)

Uluak was a very competent hunter. He would spend a year in a settlement without suffering in need. He would try to look for a place where he wouldn't be so successful in hunting. Once, while looking for a place to spend the winter, he found Nuusaq. The area he settled in had lots of game. If he was exhausted from dragging his catches, he would stop to get some rest. But even though he stopped to rest, he would end up having more killed animals than before.

(page 1)

Once, after another successful day of hunting, he went to sleep as usual. When he woke up, he was blind. Just yesterday and days before with lots of kills, his mother was only grateful for the fact that her son had become blind. It turned out that she was the one who actually made him go blind. Their only hunter could not see any more. Whenever their mother left the house, his little sister would start talking: "No one else but she did it; how can we take revenge?" But they didn't have the courage to do anything to her.

(Page 2)

Then the winter came. Once, in a cold winter morning, after he pulled his sealskin top boots on, he heard a noise from outside. What in the world was entering their house?—while they were trying to find out what it was, a polar bear suddenly appeared through their window—"Oh, what are we going to do with it?!"

Hearing them sound very frightened and scared, the only man in the house said, "Hand me my bow over by the entrance." His little sister handed it to him. When she handed it to him, he said, "Aim at the bear for me. I'll try to hit it." He shot an arrow at the bear, and the noise that came afterward revealed that he had hit the target. As his little sister opened her mouth to speak,

(page 3)

her mother shut her up by waving her arms. Then she said to her son, "What have you hit, you have hit the edge of the window. You hit the edge, and

the polar bear jumped up and ran off." Then the mother commanded her daughter to go outside without saying a word, just by using her eyes. They both went out, and there it was—a dead polar bear. There they were, busy with butchering the animal. The mother started to speak: "Don't tell my son about it—we'll have the meat for ourselves." They went inside the house.
(page 4)

With her eyes, the mother commanded her daughter to cook the meat. The daughter cooked the meat; and so they ate the meat, without sharing it with the one who shot the animal, although he was aware of them cooking and could smell the food.

Another day began, and during the afternoon, the mother became sleepy. When she was asleep, the sister said to her brother, "I will give you a piece of meat, the meat of the bear you have caught." She went to heat the meat, while she cried quietly. When it was done, she fed her brother, who seemed like one with no mouth at all, so fast he ate, and he ate until he was full. What a blessing! She continued to feed her brother whenever their mother was asleep. And so on they lived, living off the meat of the bear. The spring came along.
(page 5)

When the common loons began their migration, he said, "Take me to the lake." His sister unwillingly took him up to the lake. When they arrived, he said, "You go home. I will stay here waiting to hear the sound of loons." And when she left him, he started to wait. He waited a long time. Just as he wasn't sure of hearing those loons, he heard them approaching. Ooh, he was so cheerful to be hearing them again.

Two loons approaching started to twitter,
(page 6)
and they said, "Look at the young man down there. If only he could understand our language, he would perhaps be able to see the daylight again. If only he would lay down right by the lake."

When he laid down as they were flying north, they returned. As they flew over him, one of the loons made droppings on him, and they hit him right on his face. The second loon did the same thing, and they turned off again to fly away to the north. As he bent over to clean his face,
(page 7)
what a pleasant surprise. He saw the daylight again, even more clearly than in his younger days before he went blind.

After decided to go home, he started to think, "My old mother will probably do the same thing to me again." At sunset, his little sister arrived to guide him home. She was feeling sorry for her brother and therefore crying. Her brother thought that if he opened his eyes, it would make her too excited, which made him pretend to be a blind man a bit longer. When she was really close, he said to her,

(page 8)

"Why are you crying? Do you want to have new pair of skin pants from a spotted seal, with very black spots?" While he said that, she raised her head, saying, "What happened to you? Can you see again?" His sister was so happy while taking him home; they talked while walking home.

While they were walking, her brother said, "If I go in with my eyes open, then my mother will probably do the same thing to me again." His sister mumbled, "You will see how much food there is under the other side." When they were approaching the house, he was walking behind his sister, holding her shoulder, still pretending to be blind. When they entered the house, their mother said, "When the weather is so

(page 9)

calm like today, you wouldn't want to go inside, though you don't have anything to eat as usual." When she asked him to come, he said, "I'm tired of being in bed. Bring me to the other side." When she helped him move to the other side, he looked down under, and ooh, there was plenty of food. He smelled in that direction and the area around it. He sat up straight while his mother was saying that he, as usual, had nothing to eat. He looked around and found a piece of polar bear meat, dry on the top, and while getting up, he said to his mother: "What about those, under the other side?" As he said that, his mother looked at him, quite surprised, and she said, "What are you doing? Did you open your eyes?"

(page 10)

She sensed that her son was sitting with his eyes open. So he began to go on his hunting trips again with no handicap. When they once again had him as their hunter, he was fully successful in hunting. But then, he began to fear that his mother once again would make him go blind. When they were alone, the daughter and the son would talk. "If she tries anything, you should keep your eyes closed." His sister said, "You should ask her to hold the rope, next time you catch the biggest beluga."

Then once, when the belugas were on their way north, he harpooned them, while his sister was on land, holding the rope. Then the sister told her brother, "Go and tell your mother to be the one who holds the rope tomorrow instead of me,

(page 11)

so that we, without her knowing it, can take our revenge." When they returned, it was as if she had nothing to say to them. At last the brother thought that his sister would be tired and said, "If you can manage it, maybe you should substitute for my sister, even for a day." Their mother said, "I still can, I presume." That night, the mother did not get much sleep. She was so excited for the next day, when she would be the one with the rope. The next morning, she was quickly awake. She tightened everything that can be tightened and went along with her son when he took off hunting. And then when they arrived at their destination, the mother told her son, "Don't catch a big beluga. Make sure you catch a little one, maybe a young one." The son said,

(page 12)

"Why should I catch a big beluga?" When belugas were on their way up north, he harpooned the little ones. When they could hear them breathing he heard a whispering sound. It was so big that it was scary. Naturally, the biggest belugas follow the little ones. After they waited a long time for them to breathe, a red beluga came up and it was so big. The mother said, "Don't catch that." "Why would I catch it? I don't even want to catch it. I certainly won't." Even so he had it in his mind to catch it, as they waited along for them, they came up to breathe, the bigger ones only. He observed them and their breathing before he made a move. And then, when the biggest one came up to breathe, he harpooned it. His mother screamed and said,

(page 13)

"Why did you harpoon it?!" As she said that, the rope took off. She followed along, and there was a splash when she hit the water. And as the woman tightened up the rope she was holding, the beluga went further out while dragging her along. Then the old woman almost stood up, and when she sat her feet firmly on the ground, it was as if she was frozen.[5] The last time she tried to stand up, there was only a shiny object that showed up. Then as the beluga dragged her along, she lost her place on the ground, and was on her way down, while she talked: "Uluak, what are you doing to me? Under your urine, under your feces, I have brought you up." Then it hauled her away. When she appeared again, she said, "Under your urine, under your feces, I have brought you up. Uluak

(page 14)

what are you doing to me?"

As he was on his way home, his sister saw him coming back alone and asked him, "Where is your mother?" He answered, "She is the bladder to a beluga."

After their mother had died, they lived without any worries in their land, and it was told that Uluak spent the rest of his life on the land where he had decided to spend the winter.

That is the end.

21th of June 1902
Godthåbshavn [Nuuk]
(Matiinarujuk)

(page 15)

3. (Ulúnga)—Ulorâ

Kuannia[6]
Østgrønlandske Sagn (SB 2274)

Ningiorajigooq marlunnik ernutaqarluni, najagiinnik, ania piniartigalugu, kisimiillutik. Ernutaa angimmaqateqanngilaq nakeqigami. Ernutaa ilaanni qajartorami natsersimalluni tikippoq. Najaata anini tikilermat ornippaa, oqarpoq: "Ningiormagooq seeqqinissaa."

"Avatassara,"
(page 1)
ania oqarpoq. "Usikattassaagooq," najaata oqarfigaa. Aamma ania qajartorami ussuararsimalluni tikippoq. Ernutaata anneerarsimasoq takugamiuk ningiuni oqarfigaa: "Anneerarsimavoq." Oqarmat ningiua aammaarluni oqarpoq: "Natsissaragooq." Angusoq oqarpoq: "Alissaragooq." Tassa ameeramiuk ningiuata nallorpaa, erisassagamiuk. Tassa erisarlugu ineramiuk oqaluuppaa: "Kilippatit pilerpatsit qaqigissanngilat, kisiat utertippatit qaqingissavat isaangit tappingissavoq."
(page 2)
Kipigamiuk inermat soraaruppaa, illuata tungaanut utertillugu suli ineri-arnagu (tappingerluni) qaaqilluni kittorarpoq, isaagut noqqarlugu. Tassa tappingerpoq. Illup iluanut iserami aneqqinngilaq.

Uninngalersoq qaammaqqutaata eqqutaa nannup nerilerpaa. Ningiuat oqarpoq ernutsi pillugu: "Pisissaqiuk!" taava taamungaannaq pisisserarpaa, ningiua oqarpoq. "Eqqutaa piseqaat!" Soorlu nanoq qamannga pinerluni nanunnguusallartoq,
(page 3)
ningiua aneriarami pilaannalerpaa nanorsuaq. Tassa uutsisini (qulis-siut) pivaa. Uutassani aggoramiuk uulerpaa. Arnaq ernuttani pilerpaa:

"Oqaatigillariaananga pingasuukkaluarutsigu erniinnaq nungussavoq." Ner-
ileraangamik oqummigassaq ataaseq nuilaaminut nakkaatittarpaa animinut
tunniussassani. Ningiuat oqartaraaq: "Una aqqaqaa." Oqartaraaq najaa:
"Kaaqigama nungulertoqaara!" Inimiikatalluni ania oqarpoq qaqqamut
pisuttuarumalluni, najami tunumigut eqilluni ingerlattassammani
(page 4)
tatsip (taseq) sinaanut. "Kisianni seqineq tarrippat aajumaarparma." Nerlerit
qulaaqqutileqaat. Qulaaqqutilerlugu nerlerit ilaat oqarpoq: "Inutsiaq kanna."
Tatsip sinaanut meraqaat. Inuk pivaat: "Saallutit suluttassaqaatsit." Sulut-
taramikku isai isaqquminnik qullingiarterpaat isai taama ippinnanngillat
sunaaffa nerlermik angakkuunerigamik. Najaata ornikkamiuk nannumaa-
siit neqaanik tunivaa, kaannissaa mianerileramiuk aqquppaa, qaammagu
ullaarullugu majuuteqqippaa. Tatsimaasiit sinaanut ilivaa.
(page 5)
   Nerlerit qulaaqqutileqaat aammaaqqillutik, ilai oqarput: "Inuk aakanna,"
taamannak oqaramik sinaanungaasiit meraqaat. Ilaat oqarpoq: "Saallutit
suluttassaqaassi." Suluttareeramikku isaqquminnik qullingiarteramikku, isai
qasilliallaqaat, taanna nerleq oqarpoq: "Kisiaq ullut pingatserpata uikkumaarputit." Unnummat ilanngaavoq, noorparmat najaata aavaa najaniaasiit
tunuagut eqillugu aterpoq. Isiinnartoq najaataasiit nannup neqaanik iisas-
saanik tunivaa,
(page 6)
perlernaveersimaannartillugu. Ningiua maangaannaq qungujuttarpoq, ernuttani ajorniutigalugu tappingermat. Qaammanaasiit akikkut anini majuuppaa.
Tatsip sinaanut ilivaasiit. Nerlerit qulaaqqutileqaanaasiit, ilaat oqarpoq
. . . (Gentagelse).
   Qasillaallammat oqarput: "Atileruit uikkumaarputit." Atileramik najaata
innaarsuit allortaleramigit, isigilerpaa
(page 7)
soorlu anini isigalugu allortalersoq, tikikkami uillatsiariallartoq nannup amia
paattorsimasoq takuaa—isilerluni. Ueriallartoq paap qaani nannup isigai.
Iserami illermut ingippoq, isersimalerlunilu oqarpoq: "Unnuaq sinnattorama
nannup amia paap silataani paattorsimasoq." Aanarsua oqarpoq: "Tap-
pingiutikasiit." Sallulluni aanarsua tupigutsannermik pisassaajunnaarpoq.
(page 8)
"Unnuaq sinnattorama paap qaani nannup isigai." Aanarsua oqarpoq:
"Tappingiussuatit pillingissaraatit." (Nannup amia tappingerneranut
ajoqutaatinniarlugu) tassa uippoq, amaqqinnut uikkama unikkaarakku
amarikasia uisaallaqaaq, nerisassaanik arnaq aniata nerisassaanik aalleqquaa.

Eqqussimmat nerileraluarpoq mamarilluarnagit, amaruni uumiginermut ilumini. Aammaarluni qajartulerami angumaleqaaq. Najani maligualerpaa imannak: "Sooruna amaqqivut qilalukkap nassatariinnanngilaa?" Najaa piumanngilaq amaqqini ungaginermik.

(page 9)

Najani aammaarlugu manigulerpaa: "Toqullaruma perlerlutik toquin- nassagaluarputit." Najaa kiisami angerpoq: "Qilalukkap nassatarissavaa." "Amaqqivut sooruna nunaqqatitsinnut tusarliutaanianngilatit qilaluartu- tit?" ernutaata pivaa. "Noqinneq artoqaara." "Uanga noqikkumaarpara illit qitikkut qilersimaannarumaarputit, isigisarniarimma qilalukkamik naalinnikkaangama artorneq ajorikka." Ningiua oqarpoq: "Qaa qaa,"

(page 10)

tusaamasaanissaminut pileritsalluni. Qaammagu akikkut (ullaakkut) nun- artaanut pipput. Qilalukkat anileqaat. Qilalukkat qaqortut uiallaqimmata amaruata inakkaluarpaa quluumik naaleqqullugu. Qernertat puillaraangata isigiinnararai ernutaata. Erntaa oqartarpoq: "Angivallaaqaaq,"—kiisami angisooq puimmat naaleqaa. Amaruata noqiinnaleqaa. Ernutaata ikiunnguar- nagu isiginnaarlugu noqiinnalermagu nuluagut akkerpaa. Avammut amarua arpalluni aallarpoq immap tungaanut. Arpariakasalluni imaanut

(page 11)

nakkarpoq. Avammut nuulluni pueqaaq taanna inukasik kingornagut (nillikaannaqaaq) puttallaannaqaaq, qilalugaq puttallaannartoq taanna ulungaarluni arnakasik. Qilalugaq puttalluinnanngilaq. Aammaarluni avammut nooqqilluni nueqaaq [————] pingajussaanik nueqqimmat suli amuarlugu qaanut ingippoq: (aamma ulugaarluni taamak—*husk hans mundtlige udmåling af dette*)—kiisa tasamunga qilalugaq aanngarpoq. Tas- saniiginnarlutik ajorileramikku ernutai tunumut aallarput.

(page 12)

Timerpaqalutik illut tikikkamikkit najaa illup qingaagut itsuarpoq. Ania oqarpoq: "Unagooq imileqaaq." Illup iluaniittut oqarput: "Iserlunigooq imerli." Isermat aniata utaqqigaluarlugu aninngimmat iserpoq, nungoreeraat neril- lugu. Aniata toqorarlugit nunguppai, sunaaffa ataasikasik pinnagu. Aqajarui siittarluugit najami saanii aallaruppai puumut ikillugit. Ingerlaleriartoq najaa oqarpoq: "Soorluuna uummalersunga." Taanna najaa nikueriallartoq illuanik aqullaartaannarpoq.

(page 13)

Aammaarluni nikuinneq ajormat uterluni ilakasiat nanillugu toqukkamiuk aqajarua siillugu nanivaa seqquata quliaqutaa. Najaminut . . . aallarutite- qqippaa.[7] Ingerlariaramik najaa oqarpoq: "Pisukkunnarsisunga." Najaa

nikueriallarpoq pisulluni aallaannarujuk. Najaa pisulluni qasuleraangat aniata nammaliuteqqittarpaa. Aammaasiit (inuit) illut allat iseqqeriallaraat unnuami isigisaat qaariallarmat tarraannanngorput, oruluusaannarami ilakasiat
(page 14)
kapeqaa tarraannaammata. Kaperiarmagu tarraannakasik aanaaleqaaq. Ilai taakkua tarraannakasiit oqarput: "Kapeqaa!"

Qaammagu qimaannarpaat tunumut. Illut siumortaraat attakuani neqit anarnittut nereriaraluaramikkit anarneqimmata soraaginnarput, milluannaammata sunaaffa iteqanngitsorsuugamik neqit miluaannanngorlugit issingertaraat. Taakua ilaannik ania nuliarpoq. Nulia illaaqalerpoq erneriallartoq itilimmik (kiaavilimmik) angutip sakia (bedstemor) takori. . . .[8]
(page 15)

3. (Ulúnga)—Ulorâ

Told by Kuannia
East Greenlandic Tale (SB 2274)

There was an old woman with two grandchildren, a brother and sister, where the brother was their hunter. The grandson was an excellent hunter, and no one was like him. The grandson took off on one of his hunting trips and returned with a ringed seal. His sister came to meet him on his way and said, "Our grandmother wants to make skin pants out of the skin."

"That is for my bladder float,"
(page 1)
the brother said. "That is for his bladder float," the sister told her grandmother. Once again, he went on hunting in his kayak and returned with a bearded seal. When the granddaughter saw him coming with a bearded seal, she said to her grandmother, "He has caught a bearded seal." When she said that, once again her grandmother said to her, "That is my skin-anorak."[9]

The one who caught the bearded seal said, "That is for my rope."[10]

When she took the skin off the seal, she cut it in pieces, so that she could scrape the pelt off. When she finished working with it, she spoke to the skin: "If he begins to cut you in thin slices, you shall not burst, but when he takes you back, then you shall burst, and then his eyes will be blinded."
(page 2)

When she cut the last piece, she returned it to their house. The skin was not finished, and it burst and hit the man right on his eyes and blinded him. He became blind. When he entered their house, he did not leave again.

As he stayed inside, a polar bear began to eat the edge of their window.

The grandmother said to her grandson, "Shoot it with your arrow!" and then he guessed the location of the bear and shot his arrow. "You hit the edge!" The polar bear made its last breathing noise as it died,
(page 3)
and the grandmother went outside and started to butcher the bear. Then she cooked the sliced meat. She said to her granddaughter, "Do not tell him about this. If we three share the meat, soon there won't be anything left to eat." When they ate, the sister would drop a bite of meat and hide it under her clothing, so that she could give it to her brother. Their grandmother would say, "You eat way too fast." And the sister would answer, "It is because I was so hungry that I ate so fast!" When the brother was tired of being inside the house, he told his sister that he would like to go for a walk, and that his sister could take him outside and hold him while they walked.
(page 4)
"To the side of the lake and you can come back and get me after the sunset." The geese flew above. As they flew over him, one of them said, "There is a man down there." Then they landed by the lake. They told the man, "Place yourself in front of us, and then we will spread our wings and wave them." After they did that, they wiped his tears with their wings, and he didn't feel anything. It turned out that those geese were shamans. When his sister came to him, she took a piece of bear meat to him, and when she thought that he might be hungry, she took him home, and the next morning, she took him back to the lake again. She left him beside the lake.
(page 5)
The geese were flying toward him, just like the last time, and one of them said, "There is a man down there." As they said that, they landed near the lake just as they did last time. One of them said, "Place yourself in front of us, and we will spread our wings and wave with them." After they did that, they wiped his eyes with their wings. He felt a soreness in his eyes, and then one of the geese said, "You should first open your eyes on the third day." At night, he slept, and in the morning his sister came to get him, and he held his sister as usual on their way home. When they entered the house, his sister gave him a bit of the bear meat as usual,
(page 6)
to prevent him from being hungry. Their grandmother would sit and smile at the air, thinking of her grandson, and the fact that he became blind. Once again, in the morning, his sister took him to the lake, and as usual placed him by the lake. The geese were flying toward him, and one of them said . . . (Repeating)[11]

When he felt the soreness again, they told him, "You can open your eyes on your way home." When they were on their way home, his sister jumped over some uneven ground. She saw her brother,
(page 7)
as if he was looking at his own way, jumping just like herself. When they were approaching home, he opened his eyes a bit and saw the skin of the polar bear, stretched right outside the house. As he was entering the house, he saw the feet of the bear on their entrance. When he came inside the house he sat down, and a while after, he said, "I had a dream last night; I dreamed that there was a polar bear skin outside the house." His grandmother said, "That was the cause of your blinding." She was lying and surprised over his words.
(page 8)
"I had a dream last night; I dreamed that there were polar bear feet on our entrance." His grandmother said, "The causes for your blinding are tormenting you." (She blamed the polar bear skin, saying that it was the cause for her grandson's blindness.) Then he opened his eyes. "When I opened my eyes, I told my grandmother about what I have seen."[12]

His grandmother got busy. She told his sister to bring some food in to her brother. When she returned, he started to eat; but he didn't enjoy his meal because he was furious at his grandmother.

When he was in his kayak again, he began to catch plenty of animals. Then he told his sister, "Why don't we let a beluga take our grandmother down into the ocean?" His sister did not agree; she did not want to harm her grandmother.
(page 9)
Then he tried once again by saying, "If I die, you will die of starvation." So his sister agreed at last: "The beluga will take her down to the ocean." "Grandmother, why won't you become famous among our fellow villagers by catching a beluga?" the grandchild said. "It is too heavy for me to drag." "I will drag it. You should just stay there with a rope around your waist. You have seen me catching belugas, and you know that I never had any trouble dragging them in." Their grandmother said, "Yes, let us do that,"
(page 10)
liking the idea of becoming famous. And the next morning, they came to the place where they would hunt. Finally, the belugas appeared. When the white belugas appeared, the grandmother told her grandson to aim at a smaller one. When the belugas came up to breathe, the grandson would just stand there and watch them. The grandson said, "It is too big,"—and when

the biggest one came up, he harpooned it. The grandmother began to drag it. Her grandson stood there and watched, with no intention of helping her, and after a while, he kicked her from behind. The grandmother started to run down to the beach. She ran and ran, straight into the water.
(page 11)

A bit further out on the sea, the beluga showed up, and right after that the grandmother showed up as well, shouting, "Uluak." The beluga went down under again. It came up to breathe a bit further out [————][13] The third time it came up she had pulled her way to the beluga, and sat on it, while shouting "Uluak": (once again, still shouting "Uluak" — *remember his oral version of this*)[14] — then the beluga went down under and did not appear again. The grandchildren were feeling uncomfortable staying in their home, so they decided to move.
(page 12)

When they had been walking from the coast for a long time, they came to a place with houses, whereupon his sister looked inside through a hole. Her brother said, "She wants to drink." Those inside the house said, "Tell her to come in and drink." When she came in, her brother stood outside, waiting for her. When she didn't come out again, he entered the house and saw that they had eaten his sister. So he killed all of them except one. He cut open their stomachs and collected his sister's bones and put them in a bag. On his way, his sister said, "It is as if I am becoming alive again." Then she stood up, but she had difficulty staying up.
(page 13)

When she tried to get up and failed once again, her brother went back and found one last person still alive and killed him. Then he opened the person's stomach and found a piece of his sister's knee bone and put it in the bag along with the other bones. As he was walking, his sister said, "I want to walk." And she stood up and started to walk. When she got exhausted, her brother would take her up on his shoulder. Once again, they came to a place with houses and went in. They realized that those people that they had seen during the night became shadows at daylight. When the brother became anxious and uncomfortable being around them, he stabbed one of them,
(page 14)

since they were only shadows. The stabbed shadow started to bleed. The other shadows said, "He stabbed him!"

The next morning they left them and went on with their journey. They saw some meat under the houses, and the meat smelled pretty bad. They

tried to eat it, but because of the smell and because the meat was all dried out, they stopped eating it. It turned out that those people who lived in the village were people without anuses, and therefore they ate their food by just sucking on the meat. The brother found himself a wife among them. And his wife became pregnant and gave birth to a son with an anus. The man's mother-in-law, the grandmother saw . . .[15]
(page 15)

Appendix D

The Steenholdt Text and Additional Variants from Hinrich Rink's Collection

A. The Wittus Frederick Steenholdt Text

Prefatory note: This is the oldest known variant of the tale of the Blind Man and the Loon even though it could be thought of as a tale of the Blind Man and the Geese. It was written by Wittus Frederik Steenholdt in 1827 and ended up in the collections of Peder Kragh and the Greenlandic scholar Hinrich Rink. The original manuscript is handwritten in Greenlandic (Kalaallisut) and apparently was never published until now (see fig. 3 on p. 31). It is untitled and identifiable internally only by the number 25a. English translation by Karolina Platou Jeremiassen. Referenced as SB 167. Additional documentation in section B.2 later.

25a. Tutigaq was a very competent hunter who caught many seals and walruses. Once, when he wanted to make a robe from a piece of skin, he couldn't find the piece of skin he wanted to make a robe of. His mother had cursed it. She thought that it was someone else's piece of skin. When he stretched it out, there was a little bubble (on the skin), and when the bubble burst open it sprayed on his eyes.

Still working on the skin, he began to have a hard time seeing things around him. After he slept, he woke up and couldn't see at all. From that moment on, he was blind. Those they had spent the summer with left during the autumn to spend the winter elsewhere. They wanted Tutigaq to come along, but he refused, not wanting to be a burden.

They ended up building a home at the place. There were only the three of them to spend the winter. They only ate mussels at that place. Tutigaq's mother had the habit of giving him a spoonful of mussels.[1]

When the days got shorter, Tutigaq said to his little sister, "Sister! The

211

days are shorter. That makes the animals travel around. Bring my arrows inside from the boat." His little sister went out and brought them in. Tutigaq prepared his arrows. He kept the arrows near himself when he went to sleep.

One night, a polar bear came to visit, putting its head through the window. He said to his little sister, "Sister, give me my arrows; aim at its cheek. When his sister aimed at its cheek, he shot the arrow into the air. There was the sound of a bump.

Tutigaq shouted and said, "That's a man knowing how to shoot an animal." His mother said, "What did you hit?" Saying that to her overjoyed son, although he could hear the bear roar. Then his mother said to his little sister, "Bring him some mussels," although it was bright outside.

They went out, taking their ulus.[2] On her way out, his little sister told him, "You caught a polar bear." When they came out, they started butchering the animal. When they finished butchering, they began to cook, and when they finished cooking, they began to eat while they were preparing mussels.

When they were cooked and brought inside, Tutigaq said, "Where does the smell come from?" His mother said, "It is mussels which I cooked, using the bouillon as a fat; that is where the smell comes from." They ate, and when they were full, their mother fell asleep. When she fell asleep, his little sister gave her big brother a piece of the polar bear meat, and said, "Hide and eat." Then he ate. They lived like that, where she gave her big brother a piece of polar bear meat only at night. But when there was no more meat, she stopped.

Then the spring came. While they were leaving, he said to his little sister, "Sister! The lake ice is probably melting; take me there!" His little sister took him there, holding his hand. She left him by the lake. While staying there, he heard the sound of geese. When he made them come, one of them said from above, "Can you see him down there?" It turns out that they were worried: "Look up and hold your eyes open." He looked up, holding his eyes open. He could feel his eyes getting warm. Then the goose said, "Don't open your eyes!" When the sound of their wings got further away, he opened his eyes a bit and saw a man who was about to fly, right by the lake. He closed his eyes again. When he opened his eyes again, he could see everything.

When he could see very clearly, he started to wait for his little sister. Then his little sister appeared, keeping her hands warm by putting them in her coat, near her neck. He shouted to her: "Sister! Don't you come up here, I will provide you with clothes!" His sister answered, "Who else will come?" When she got near, she could see that his eyes were black. Then they walked down, and when their house appeared, he could see the skin of the polar bear, hung up to dry.

When they came in, his mother pointed at him, and was very glad. Her son asked her, "Where did the skin outside come from?" His mother replied, "That is made of many old skinpieces." So they left it there. When the spring came, and the sea ice began to melt, the narwhals came, and he started to hunt the narwhals. He usually took his little sister with him. When they came to the seaside, he would bind a rope around her waist and shoot at the narwhals with his harpoon, then he would help his sister up. Once they came to the seaside he asked his little sister, "Would you miss your mother?" His little sister replied, "No, I wouldn't miss her at all." Then Tutigaq said, "I will ask her if she can help me tomorrow; don't volunteer."

The day after, he said to his mother, "Now go hunt for your daughter." His mother: "Yes, I can help you." They left, and when they arrived at the seaside, he bound a rope around her waist. Many narwhals came, and his mother said, although it was a little one, "A kid" (baby narwhal). When he came to them, they would go under. Then a narwhal with a kid appeared, when it came toward him he prepared to harpoon it. Although his mother wanted him to catch a small one, he harpooned the biggest one. And he said, "I'm so angry," holding his fist ready.

His mother prepared to hold still; her son ignored her. He pushed her. When the narwhal went under, his mother could not be seen from the shore. It took her along under the water. After a while, the narwhals appeared, and when one of them appeared, a shining object was visible, and after a while when his mother appeared, she said, "My ulu," while making a twist of her hair.

It is said that that was the reason why the beluga turned black. Tutigaq's mother turned into a black narwhal, with her hair becoming a narwhal tusk. She had an amaut[3] made of sealskin that turned into the narwhal's skin, and the spots of the sealskin became the spots of the narwhal.

Tutigaq went home, and when he came home, he was sad for murdering his own mother. Then they went into the land.[4] While they walked, his little sister became thirsty. When they could see a house, he said to his sister, "Go down there, I will wait." Then he began to wait [a long time]. When he got tired of waiting, he went down to look for her. When he looked through the window, he could see that she was dead. He came into the house and took her. When he got out, he put her on his shoulder and continued. While walking, he felt as if she became alive again. While he was still walking, she began to move, and he put her down. She was herself again. Still walking, they could see a house. They went down and looked inside through the window; there was nobody. The fire was on, and the lamp was also provided with fat; they went inside. When they got inside, a plate near the lamp got filled by itself with food from the pot, splashing. They ate from it.

It turned out that they were toorneq, the helpers of a shaman.[5] Tutigaq found a wife there, and his little sister found a husband. When they went to bed, Tutigaq would lie nearer to his wife, but he felt something wet. It turned out that by accident he made his wife burst open. Then he worried again, and they left again. While still walking they could see another house.

They went down and could see lots of meat outside the house. It turned out that the people living there were people without anuses. Their anuses were in their stomach; they only ate bouillon from the meat and threw the meat outside. They stayed there. The excrements from those with anuses would be smelled and used as a perfume.

Tutigaq found himself another wife. His little sister found a husband. Tutigaq had a child with a normal anus. The grandmother, who was over-joyed, stuck a hole in herself where the anus would be and killed herself.

When they had worries again, they left. They came into their home where Tutigaq became a great shaman. With helpers. Once while he was on a spiritual journey, he saw an ingnek; then he came there, right outside them.[6] When he went inside he said, "Guess who I am?" None of them knew who he was. "Haven't you heard of someone far away, who used his mother as a harpoon-float?"[7] The others said, "No." Tutigaq said, "I am Tutigaq, who used his mother as a harpoon-float."

Then he began to tell about his frustrations, telling them about his trip to the land far away, about his mother and how he used her as a harpoon-float. He slept there. The next evening he left, taking his partner to visit his homeland. They travelled, and by dawn, he let his partner seek shelter, while he continued. He first arrived the day after. He stayed there for many days. But when his partner was on his way home, his partner sought shelter, because he was not yet a real shaman. But Tutigaq became a great shaman. From that point he left, and on his way to Amerla, he took off on a spirit journey one night.[8]

That is the end.

B. Hinrich Rink's Eight Variants of the Blind Man and the Loon as Located in Sonnesbase (SB), with Provenance

1. Document SB 149: collected by Peder Kragh, 1823–28, summarized by Christian Berthelsen; fragmentary version, the ending is missing:
   [NKS 2488, VI, pp. 152ff.; recopied as NKS 2488, II nr. 40]

2. Document SB 167: copied by W.F. [Wittus Frederik] Steenholdt, collected by Peder Kragh, 1823–28 [actually 1827]. This tale text is included a booklet entitled *Samling de Grønlandske Fortællinger* [Collection of Greenlandic Tellings]. Detailed Danish summary in Sonnesbase by Christian Berthelsen:
   [NKS 2488, VI, pp. 40h–43h; recopied as NKS 2488, II nr. 60, 1857–62]

3. Document SB 168: collected by Peder Kragh, 1823–28, summarized by Christian Berthelsen:
   [NKS 2488, II nr. 62]

4. Document SB 207: written by Jens Kreutzmann, 1859, summarized by Christian Berthelsen, translated and published in Kreutzmann (1997a, 1997b):
   [NKS 2488, II nr. 103]

5. Document SB 1838: written by Jakob Lund, 1863, translated by Christian Berthelsen from early original. The Lund variant appears under the title "Nerdlerit tagpigssitânik" (The geese which gave him back his sight):
   [NKS 2488, III 80h–83v nr. 330]

6. Document SB 1847: written by Amos Daniel, 1863, not translated or summarized (illegible handwriting)

7. Labrador text in German (see Brigitte Sonne translation in preface)

8. Second text from Labrador, in Inuttut:
   [NKS 2488, III nr. 289; remains untranslated]

Notes

1. THE HISTORY AND GEOGRAPHY OF THE TALE

1. The sole exception seems to be the Anishinaabe nation oral variant recorded on CD by Kenny Pheasant (n.d.) and a tantalizing fragment from the multilingual Cree elder Snowbird Marten of Fort Chipewyan, Alberta (see Malcolm 1981). Marten spoke Cree, Chipewyan, and English.

2. An extended discussion of the folkloric terms *tale type* and *motif* may be found in Alan Dundes's essay "The Motif-Index and the Tale Type Index: A Critique" (1997).

3. The analogy may break down for the Sun and Moon or Sun-Sister Moon-Brother episode, an episode that has been recorded more often as a stand-alone tale rather than as a sequel to "The Blind Man and the Loon." Additional research needs to be done on the relationship between such tales as these and how they interface.

4. A notable exception to this generalization is Kenny Thomas Sr.'s episodic cycle of Yaamaagh Telcheegh (Thomas 2005).

5. Several other Eskimo folk narratives portray the loon as a magico-religious personage closely associated with the visionary spirit world. See especially Diamond Jenness's "The Loon's Brides" (1924) or "The Loon and the Raven" tale type.

6. The geographic distribution of these regional groups (i.e., oicotypes) does not necessarily coincide with the range and habitat of the game animals with which they are associated.

7. The archaeologist Owen Mason, who has made a career of excavating sites in northwest Alaska, has pointed out to me that the assemblage of artifacts at Ipiutak, including the loon with the ivory eyes, while contemporaneous with early Thule culture, are fairly unconnected to Thule culture and the Thule migration (pers. comm.).

8. I borrow this conceit from the Gwich'in story of Vasaagìhdzak, who famously carried around a sack full of songs. See Johnny Frank's story in Mishler (2001, 44–45). Also in keeping with this notion is the Indian name of the Gwich'in fiddler Bill Stevens, Ch'adzaa Aghwaa (He Carries the Dance) (Mishler 1999).

9. For a better understanding of this hunting method using "a swim bladder" for a float see, for example, http://tea.armadaproject.org/zellinger/8.20.2000 .html.

10. Something similar occurs in Maggie Gilbert's Gwich'in version of the story, when she talks about the blind man's substitution of *tr'ìnjàa* (woman) for *sha'at* (my wife). See chapter 4, lines 132–36 and the ensuing discussion.

2. THE WRITING OF THE TALE

1. Compiled by Birgitte Sonne over a ten-year period, the Sonnesbase currently contains 2,292 documents compiled in an askSam text database file called SAGN99.ask. Each document in the base contains a folk narrative text or text summary, many of which are from unpublished archival collections. The entire database and the askSam viewer may be downloaded free of charge from Birgitte's web page, http://tors.ku.dk/biblioteker2/eskimologi/datasamlinger/sonnesbase/. Written almost entirely in Danish, these texts may now be quickly copied and processed by Google Translate into many other languages.

2. Okak is the name of a Labrador coastal village founded by the Moravian missionary Jens Haven in 1776. It was destroyed by the 1918 Spanish flu epidemic and largely abandoned the next year. Hebron was a Labrador community located in the Bay of Kangertluksoak, founded in 1831 and hard hit by influenza and typhoid in the early 1860s. It was abandoned in 1959.

3. See, for example, http://www.newadvent.org/bible/tob002.htm#1.

4. Curiously, Oosten also used the same Iglulik story in his doctoral thesis (1976, 49–53) where he changed the title but reprinted Rasmussen's text almost verbatim, dropping only a few Inuktitut words. He also reprinted Nâlungiaq's Netsilik variant from Rasmussen (1931). In neither case are the Native storytellers acknowledged by name.

5. A complete list of these semi-literary variants may be found in Appendix B, Part II.

3. THE TALE BEHIND THE TALE

1. A short biographical sketch of Henry Tate may be found online at http://www.abcbookworld.com/?state=view_author&author_id=7567

2. See my review of Judy Thompson's book on Teit in the *Alaska Journal of Anthropology* (Mishler 2007).

3. These unpublished Rasmussen texts are identified as Sonnesbase documents SB 324, told by Jonasine Nielsen of Saattoq; SB 1375, by an unnamed storyteller at Angmassalik, published in Danish only; SB 1496, told by Cecilie Olsen (Sisê) of Sisimiut; SB 1544, told by Arnaluk, described as "an old woman of about sixty [years of age]" of Appat (it was recorded in 1903–4 and published in English in 1908); SB 1608, told by Silas of Ilimanaq; SB 1732, by an unnamed storyteller at Neria; SB 1895, told by Gert Lyberth of Maniitsoq; SB 2176, told by Matînarujuk of Nuuk; SB 2224, told by Gaba Olsen (Gâba) of Kuuk; and SB 2274, told by Kuania of Illuluarsuit.

4. THE TELLING OF THE TALE

1. The bracketed words in these first two lines are understood. —Lincoln Tritt (LT) Other understood words or sounds are shown in brackets, and bracketed numbers represent line numbers. —Craig Mishler (CM)

2. A wall clock chimes here. —CM

3. *Reh* has no referential meaning. —Fannie Gemmill (FG) *Reh* is equivalent to a period. It punctuates. —Caroline Tritt-Frank (CF) This line of quoted words is Maggie's own expansion of the story. It stands out as her own because of the missing tag, vàràhnyàa. —Kenneth Frank (KF)

4. Maggie is apparently using hand gestures here. —FG

5. A dog starts barking outdoors, intermittently. —CM

6. Again, Maggie seems to be gesturing. —FG

7. When she says *yik'į* (arrows) here, it is understood that she means both bow and arrows. —FG and KF

8. *Chehtsi'* is a shrimp-like freshwater bug that is eaten by fish and by waterfowl. It is about an inch long. —KF Chehtsi' are not true insects but amphipods, a kind of crustacean known as *Gammarus lacustris*, more commonly called scuds. The irony here is that such creatures would be perfect food for the loon, the blind man's power animal, but they are not regarded as suitable for human consumption. —CM

9. This is the femur or thigh bone of the moose, known as *ghwaa* or *ch'aghwaa*. —KF

10. Here too, *dik'į'* (arrows) means both his bow and arrows. —KF

11. In other words, he could now see perfectly well. —CM

12. I love the way she uses high and low tones in this line. —CF

13. See note 9 earlier.

14. This series of CBC Radio One Gwich'in language broadcasts, as of this writing, does not yet include "The Blind Man and the Loon." For more on the series, which started in 2009 and was rebroadcast in 2010, see http://www.cbc .ca/aboriginal/2009/10/legends-project-6.html.

15. Petitot's early variant (1886), recorded from Sylvain Vitoedh, is only in French, but significantly reports "un orignal" (moose) as the prey animal. This moose appears again on the second page of the bilingual edition of the tale (Petitot 1888, 246), immediately following the text shown above in Image 4.

5. THE ART OF THE TALE

1. A photo of this snow sculpture has been posted on a private web page at http://almosthuman.ca/jambalaya/pictures/2002-02-winterlude/pic33.html.

2. This interpretation, which remains anonymous, may be viewed at http:// gallery.ca/cybermuse/enthusiast/acquisitions/1999-2000/sharky_text_e.jsp.

6. THE MEDIATED AND THEATRICAL TALE

1. This film may be viewed online at http://www.youtube.com/ watch?v=DfUmSFVncPk or see a short clip at http://avtrust.ca/master works/2001/en_film_2.htm.

2. For more on the Nicola Athabaskans, search for the "Nicola-Similkameen" entry in the online *Canadian Encyclopedia* at http://www.thecanadianencyclo-pedia.com. The Lower Nicola Indian Band belongs to the Nlaka'pamux Nation of Interior Salish and has its own web site: http://www.lnib.net.

3. It is unknown whether the choreography for this ballet has survived. There is some information on Willy Blok Hanson at the Dance Collection Danse archives in Toronto. For additional insights, see Jack Chambers's extended essay, "Loon's Necklace: Calvin Jackson and the Conquest of Canada, 1950–1956" (2008).

4. How the Loon Got Its Necklace. Narration, string quintet, percussion. Ms. RCI 388 (Czech Quar, R. Coneybeare narrator). Toronto: Canadian Music Centre, 1971. See also www.musiccentre.ca/apps/index.cfm?fuseaction=score.FA_dsp_details&bibliographyid=1479&dsp_page=1.

5. Elinor Benjamin is the webmaster for the Storytellers of Canada/Conteurs du Canada and is profiled at: http://www.sc-cc.com/directory-pages/benjamin-elinor.html and http://www.bookcentre.ca/directory/elinor_benjamin.

6. A published variant of the Ant Woman and the Blind Man in the Ahtna language may be found in Billum (1979, 49–50), listed here in appendix B.

7. The Anishinaabemowin recording is offered for sale online at http://www.anishinaabemdaa.com/cdrom.htm. There is a one-minute preview of "The Loon's Necklace."

8. Personal communication to the author from David Smith, University of Minnesota–Duluth, December 21, 1988.

9. The archived *NatureWatch* podcast may be listened to or downloaded from the Web at: www.trumix.com/podshows/526008.

10. For a complete listing of all these media variants, consult appendix B, part 3.

7. THE POWER OF THE TALE

1. Kenny's performance of the tale of the Blind Man and the Loon lasts thirteen minutes and thirty-nine seconds, compared to Maggie Gilbert's telling, which is a little over eleven minutes. However, Kenny actually continues on for another twenty-one minutes, adding more episodes to the Yaamaagh Telcheegh cycle.

2. An orphan can be defined as a child who has lost either one or both parents to death. In virtually all Eskimo variants of the story of the Blind Man and the Loon, we never hear what happened to the young blind man's father. It is an open question as to whether he died or simply separated from his wife at an earlier date.

3. Asen Balikci, in his ethnographic work with the Netsilik Eskimo (1963,395), observed that there are rigid meat sharing rules at Eskimo winter camps which may not be as strongly enforced in their summer camps. He sees these rules for sharing meat as promoting bonds between unrelated extended families.

4. A number of other Eskimo folk narratives portray the loon as closely associated with the visionary spirit world. See especially Diamond Jenness's "The Loon's Brides" (1924) and the widely-known tale of the Raven and the Loon painting each other (Fienup-Riordan 1994, 124–25).

5. See especially the online file "Species Used for Subsistence Purposes" at the Alaska Department of Fish and Game: http://www.subsistence.adfg.state.ak.us/geninfo/publctns/cpdb.cfm and the "Resource by Region" section of the Community Subsistence Information System database located at: www.subsistence.adfg.state.ak.us/CSIS. Also see the results of the Nunavut Wildlife Harvest Study of 2004 posted at: www.nwmb.com/english/resources/harvest_study/NWHS%202004%20Report.pdf.

6. An early source documenting Inuit loon hunting and edibility is Vilhjalmur Stefansson ([1922] 2001, 457).

7. See chapter 4, lines 159–64.

CONCLUSION AND AFTERWORD

1. See Engelbart's extended essay "Boosting Our Collective IQ" at: www.dougengelbart.org/pubs/books/augment-133150.pdf.

2. *American Heritage Dictionary of the English Language.* 4th ed. Boston: Houghton Mifflin, 2007.

3. Catharine McClellan has used the critical term *masterpiece* appropriately to describe and recognize one of the tales in her own field collections from the Yukon, *The Girl Who Married The Bear: A Masterpiece Of Indian Oral Tradition* (1970).

APPENDIX C

1. Source: Knud Rasmussens Arkiv (Det kongelige Bibiliotek)—Knud Rasmussen's Archive—The Royal Library, Copenhagen. [KRKB 1, 7(19). Dagbøger fra den litterære Grønlandsekspedition 1902–04/The Diaries of the Danish Literary Greenland Expedition (1902–04)]. Told by Cecilie Olsen/Sísê/Sissili (Sisimiut/Holsteinsborg).

2. The skin of a seal, cut in thin slices to make a string. —KPJ

3. This parenthetical sentence may be a clarification by the writer of the story. —CM

4. Source: Knud Rasmussens Arkiv (Det kongelige Bibiliotek)—Knud Rasmussen's Archive—The Royal Library, Copenhagen. [KRKB, 1, 4(12), Dagbøger fra den litterære Grønlandsekspedition 1902–04/The Diaries of the Danish Literary Greenland Expedition 1902–04, no.10]. Told by Matînarujuk/Matiinarujuk (Nuuk /Godthåb).

5. Apparently, she was standing up in shallow water on a beach. —CM

6. Source: Knud Rasmussens Arkiv (Det kongelige Bibiliotek)—Knud

Rasmussen's Archive—The Royal Library, Copenhagen. [KRKB, 1, 7(20), Dag-bøger fra den litterære Grønlandsekspedition 1902–04/The Diaries of the Danish Literary Greenland Expedition 1902–04]. Told by Kuania/Kuannia/Kuaannia (Illuluarsuit: Sydøstgrønland?).

7. I/we couldn't read the word between the two words *Najaminut* and *aal-laruteqqippaa*. It was impossible; most of the letters in that word were not readable. —KPJ

8. The end of the last sentence and the end of this story are both missing in the original. —KPJ

9. A piece of skin clothing. —KPJ A kind of parka. —CM

10. A piece of skin to make a whip out of. —KPJ

11. It says "gentagelse" in Danish, which means "repeating." —KPJ Apparently, this was inserted by Knud Rasmussen as shorthand for repeating the earlier words spoken by the geese, namely, "Place yourself in front of us, and then we will spread our wings and wave them." —CM

12. This is a jump from third person narrative (he) to first person narrative (I). —KPJ

13. The solid line here in brackets apparently represents a tiny drawing of the beluga breaking the surface of the water. —CM

14. This last phrase in italics is in Danish, apparently Rasmussen's note to himself. —KPJ

15. See note 8.

APPENDIX D

1. The mussels she feeds her son create a direct detailed connection with the variant Knud Rasmussen collected in Greenland seventy-five years later from Cecilia and Frederik Olsen. See the text of SB 1496 in appendix C. —CM

2. An ulo or ulu is a woman's knife, shaped with a semicircular blade. It is very efficient for cutting fish or butchering animals. —KPJ and CM

3. An amaut is a parka worn by Inuit women. It has a large pouch behind the neck for carrying a baby. —KPJ

4. The word used here is *qivittoq*, which means leaving society, going into exile. —KPJ

5. *Toorneq* means a spirit, a helper to the shaman. —KPJ See my extended discussion of these spirits in chapter 7. —CM

6. *Igneq* is a creature who is half-human, half-animal. This sentence is difficult to understand in the original. —KPJ

7. A harpoon-float is called an *avataq*. —KPJ See my discussion of its ethno-graphic and ethnohistoric significance in dating the story in chapter 1. —CM

8. The final sentence of the manuscript is very difficult to read and understand. —KPJ

References

Aarne, Antti. 1964. *The Types of the Folk-Tale: A Classification and Bibliography.* Translated and enlarged by Stith Thompson. FF Communication No. 3, 2nd Revision. Helsinki FFC No. 184. Helsinki: The Finnish Academy of Science and Letters.

Amittu, Aisa. 1998. My Life. *American Indian Art Magazine* 23 (3):109.

Anderson, Wanni W. 2009. *The Dall Sheep Dinner Guest.* Fairbanks: University of Alaska Press.

Anderson, Wanni W., and Ruth Tatqaviñ Sampson, eds. 2003. *Folktales of the Riverine and Coastal Iñupiat.* [Kotzebue AK]: Northwest Arctic Borough.

Andrew, Frank, Sr./Miisaq. 2008. *Paitarkiutenka: My Legacy to You.* Edited by Ann Fienup-Riordan. Seattle: University of Washington Press.

Bakhtin, Mikhail. 1981. "Discourse in the Novel." In *The Dialogic Imagination: Four Essays,* edited by Michael Holquist, translated by Caryl Emerson and Michael Holquist, 259–422. Austin: University of Texas Press. First published 1934.

Balikci, Asen. 1963. "Shamanistic Behavior among the Netsilik Eskimos." *Southwestern Journal of Anthropology* 19 (4):380–96.

Bastian, Dawn, and Judy Mitchell, eds. 2004. "Blind Boy." In *Handbook of Native American Mythology,* 54–55. New York: Oxford University Press.

Bennett, John, and Susan Rowley, eds. 2004. *Uqalurait: An Oral History of Nunavut.* Montreal: McGill–Queen's University Press.

Benveniste, Émile. 1953. "Le Vocabulaire de la vie animale chez les Indians du Haut Yukon." *Bulletin de la Societé de Linguistique de Paris* 49:79–106.

Bergsland, Knud, ed. and trans. 1987. *Nunamiut unipkaanich/Nunamiut stories.* Told in Iñupiat Eskimo by Elijah Kakinya and Simon Paneak. Barrow: North Slope Borough Commission on Iñupiaq History, Language, and Culture.

Berlo, Janet Catherine. 1993. "Autobiographical Impulses and Female Identity in the Drawings of Napachie Pootoogook." *Inuit Art Quarterly* 8 (4):4–12.

Berman, Judith. 1994. "George Hunt and the Kwak'wala Texts." *Anthropological Linguistics* 36 (Winter):483–514.

Bierhorst, John, ed. 1997. *The Dancing Fox: Arctic Folktales.* New York: William Morrow.

Binford, Lewis R. 1983. *In Pursuit of the Past: Decoding the Archaeological Record.* New York: Thames and Hudson.

Birket-Smith, Kaj. 1918. "The Greenland Bow." *Meddelelser om Grønland* 56 (1):3–25. Copenhagen.

——. (1924) 1976. *Ethnography of the Egedesminde District with Aspects of the General Culture of West Greenland*, translated from the Danish by Aslaug Mikkelsen. New York: AMS Press. First published 1924.

——. 1953. *The Chugach Eskimo*. Copenhagen: Nationalmuseets publikationsfond.

——. 1959. *The Eskimos*. Rev. ed. London: Metheun. First edition published 1936.

Bissell, Keith. 1974. *How the Loon Got Its Necklace: A Legend of the Salish Tribe of Indians from the Interior of British Columbia* (sound recording). Montreal: Radio Canada International, 33 ½ rpm. Copy at the University of Texas Fine Arts Library, Austin.

Blondin, George. 1990. *When the World Was New: Stories of the Sahtú Dene*. Yellowknife NWT: Outcrop, the Northern Publishers.

Blue, Annie. 2007. *Cungauyaraam Qulirai: Annie Blue's Stories*. Edited by Ben Orr and Eliza Cingarkaq Orr. Fairbanks: Alaska Native Language Center.

Boas, Franz. (1888) 1964. *The Central Eskimo*. Sixth Annual Report, Bureau of American Ethnology, 1884–1885. Reprint, Lincoln NE: University of Nebraska Press. First published 1888.

——. 1891. "Dissemination of Tales among the Natives of North America." *Journal of American Folklore* 4:13–20.

——. (1895) 2002. *Indian Myths and Legends from the North Pacific Coast of America: A Translation of Franz Boas' 1895 Edition of Indianische Sagen von der Nord-Pacifischen Küste Amerikas*. Translated by Dietrich Bertz. Edited and annotated by Randy Bouchard and Dorothy Kennedy. Vancouver: Talonbooks. First published 1895, in German.

——. 1904. "The Folk-lore of the Eskimo." *Journal of American Folklore* 17:1–13.

——. 1910. *Kwakiutl Tales*. Vol. 2. New York: Columbia University Press.

——. 1916. *Tsimshian Mythology*. Thirty-first Annual Report, Bureau of American Ethnology, 1909–1910. Washington: Bureau of American Ethnology.

——. (1927) 1940. "Religious Terminology of the Kwakiutl." In *Race, Language, and Culture*, 612–18. New York: Free Press. First published 1927.

Bouchard, Randy, and Dorothy Kennedy. 2002. "Editors' Introduction" to Boas, *Indian Myths and Legends*, 21-49.

Bringhurst, Robert. 1999. *A Story as Sharp as a Knife: The Classical Haida Mythtellers and Their World*. Vancouver: Douglas & McIntyre; Lincoln: University of Nebraska Press.

Brown, Dave. 1985. "Brown's Beat." *Ottawa Citizen*, September 10, C1.

Burch, Ernest S., Jr. 1979. "Indians and Eskimos in North Alaska, 1816–1977: A Study in Changing Ethnic Relations." *Arctic Anthropology* 16 (2):123–51.

——. 1988. "The End of the Trail: The Work of the Fifth Thule Expedition in Alaska." *Études/Inuit/Studies* 12 (1–2):151–70.

"Calvin Jackson, Pianist, Dies; Wrote 'Molly Brown' Score." 1985. *New York Times*, December 8, A52.

Caswell, Helen. 1968. *Shadows from the Singing House: Eskimo Folk Tales*. Rutland VT: Charles Tuttle.

Chambers, Jack. 2008. "Loon's Necklace: Calvin Jackson and the conquest of Canada, 1950–1956." *Coda* 340 (August/September):26–31, 33–48, 60–61.

Charlie, Andy. 1997. "Iingilnguq Tunutellgek-llu: The Blind Boy and The Two Arctic Loons." In *Ellangellemni: When I Became Aware*, edited by Eliza Cingarkaq Orr, Ben Orr, Victor Kanrilak, Jr., and Andy Charlie Jr., 6–25. Fairbanks: Lower Kuskokwim School District and the Alaska Native Language Center.

Cleaver, Elizabeth. 1984. "Idea to Image: The Journey of a Picture Book." *The Lion and the Unicorn* 7/8:156–70.

Coffin, Tristram, ed. 1961. *Indian Tales of North America*. Austin: University of Texas Press.

Crawford, Allison. 2007. "My Grandmother Used to Tell Me That Story." *UT pop-culture: Newsletter of the University of Toronto Psychiatric Outreach Program* 6:2–4.

Crawley, Frank Radford "Budge." 1949. *The Loon's Necklace*. 16 mm film, 11 minutes. Chicago: Encyclopedia Britannica Educational Corporation. Released in French as *Le Collier Magique*, 1950. Restored and made into a video in 1981.

Creed, John. 1984. "Inupiat Elder Continues Healing Arts." *Tundra Times*, November 21, 3–4.

Crockford, Susan. 2008. "Be Careful What You Ask For: Archaeozoological Evidence of Mid-Holocene Climate Change in the Bering Sea and Implications for the Origins of Arctic Thule." In *Islands of Inquiry: Colonisation, Seafaring and the Archaeology of Maritime Landscapes*, edited by G. Clark et al., 113–31. Canberra: Terra Australis 29, ANU E Press.

Dégh, Linda. 1969. *Folktales and Society: Story-telling in a Hungarian Peasant Community*. Translated by Emily Schossberger. Bloomington: Indiana University Press.

———. 1994. *American Folklore and the Mass Media*. Bloomington: Indiana University Press.

Dorais, Louis-Jacques. 1990. "The Canadian Inuit and Their Language." In *Arctic Languages: An Awakening*, edited by Dirmid Collis, 185–289. Paris: UNESCO.

Dorsey, George A., and Alfred L. Kroeber. 1903. *Traditions of the Arapaho*. Chicago: Field Museum Columbia, Publication 81. A.S., Vol. 5:282–93.

Dumond, Don. 1969. "Toward a Prehistory of the Na-Dene." *American Anthropologist* 71:857–63.

———. 1987. *The Eskimos and Aleuts*. Rev. ed. London: Thames and Hudson.

Dundes, Alan. 1997. "The Motif-Index and the Tale Type Index: A Critique." *Journal of Folklore Research* 34 (3):195–202.

Dunning, J. 1985. *The Loon: Voice of the Wilderness*. Dublin NH: Yankee Books.

Dwyer, Corinne. "The Loon's Necklace." In *Loon Legends: A Collection of Tales Based on Legends*, 7–23. Illustrated by Mark Coyle. St. Cloud MN: North Star Press, 1988.

Dwyer-Shick, Susan. 1974. Review of *The Loon's Necklace. Ethnomusicology* 18 (3):487–88.

Egede, Hans. 1818. *A Description of Greenland*. London: T. & J. Allman. Electronic version online at Google Books. First published in Danish as *Den gamle Grøn-lands nye Perlustration,* 1741; first English translation 1745.

Ekblaw, Walter Elmer. 1928 (1961). "The Material Response of the Polar Eskimos to their Environment." In *Annals of the Association of American Geographers*, 18 (1). Reprint, New York: Krauss Reprint Corporation.

Farrand, Livingston. 1900. "Traditions of the Chilcotin Indians." *Memoirs of the American Museum of Natural History* 4:35–36, 52.

Fienup-Riordan, Ann. 1994. *Boundaries and Passages: Rule and Ritual in Yup'ik Eskimo Oral Tradition*. Norman: University of Oklahoma Press.

Finley, Carol. 1998. *Art of the Far North*. Minneapolis: Lerner.

Finnegan, Ruth. 2004. "Quote Marks Past and Present: The Multiplexities of Display." Invited Plenary Address, American Folklore Society Annual Meeting, Salt Lake City.

———. 2011. *Why Do We Quote? The Culture and History of Quotation*. Cambridge: Open Book Press. Available online at Google Books.

Ford, James A. 1959. *Eskimo Prehistory in the Vicinity of Point Barrow, Alaska*. Anthropological Papers of the American Museum of Natural History 47: Part 1. New York.

Frink, Lisa, Brian Hoffman, and Robert Shaw. 2003. "Ulu Knife Use in Western Alaska: A Comparative Ethnoarchaeological Study." *Current Anthropology* 44 (1):116–22.

Gilbert, James. 1991. Interview with Caroline Tritt-Frank and Mary Tritt in 1990. Translated by Mildred Peter. In *Nakai' T'in'in: "Do It Yourself": A Plan for Preserving the Cultural Identity of the Neets'aii Gwich'in Indians of Arctic Village*. Arctic Village AK: Arctic Village Council. Copy at Fairbanks North Star Borough Public Library.

Gilbert, Trimble. 1991. Interview with Teresa Thomas on October 13, 1986. 43 pp. In *Nakai' T'in'in: "Do It Yourself": A Plan for Preserving the Cultural Identity of the Neets'aii Gwich'in Indians of Arctic Village*. Arctic Village AK: Arctic Village Council. Copy at Fairbanks North Star Borough Public Library.

Grimm, Jacob. (1815) 1999. "Circular Concerning the Collecting of Folk Poetry." In *International Folkloristics: Classic Contributions by the Founders of Folklore*, edited by Alan Dundes, 1–7. Lanham MD: Rowman & Littlefield. First published 1815.

Guggenheim, Hans. 1971. "Review of *The Loon's Necklace*." *American Anthropologist* 73(6):1478–80.

Gulløv, Hans C., and Robert McGhee. 2006. "Did Bering Strait People Initiate the Thule Migration?" *Alaska Journal of Anthropology* 4 (1):254–63.

Hall, Edwin S., Jr. 1975. *The Eskimo Storyteller*. Knoxville: University of Tennessee Press.

Haqpi, Michael. 1993. "'Carvings are not just carvings—they tell a story': An Interview with Simon Tookoome of Baker Lake." *Inuit Art Quarterly* 8 (2):6–7.

Hare, G. P., S. Greer, R. Gotthardt, R. Farnell, V. Bowyer, C. Schweger, and D. Strand. 2004. "Ethnographic and Archaeological Investigations of Alpine Ice Patches in Southwest Yukon, Canada." *Arctic* 57 (3):260–72.

Haring, Lee. 2003. "'Who Were You Talking To?' Diasporic Folktales." *Journal of Folklore Research* 40 (2):149–73.

Heine, Michael, Alestine Andre, Ingrid Kritsch, and Alma Cardinal, eds. 2007. *Gwichya Gwich'in Googwandak: The History and Stories of the Gwichya Gwich'in*. Tsiigehtshik and Fort McPherson: Gwich'in Social and Cultural Institute.

Hessel, Ingo. 2006. *Arctic Spirit: Inuit Art from the Albrecht Collection at the Heard Museum*. Vancouver: Douglas & McIntyre.

Hill, Miriam. 2002. "Kimmirut Artists Compete in Ottawa Snow Sculpture Competition." *Nunatsiaq Online Magazine*, February 8. http://www .nunatsiaqonline.ca/stories/article/kimmirut_artists_compete_in_ottawa_ snow_sculpture_competition/.

Hills, Peggy, ed. 2006. "How the Loon Got Its Necklace" (vocal performance.). 12 min. 34 sec., compact disc audio recording. *The Storyteller's Bag*, Mississauga ON: Chamber Music Society of Mississauga.

Hoedeman, Co. 1975. *Lumaaq, an Eskimo Legend*. 7 min. 55 sec, b & w animated film. Drawings by Davidialuk. Ottawa: National Film Board of Canada.

Holtved, Erik. 1951. *The Polar Eskimos: Language and Folklore*. Vols. 1–2. København: C. A. Reitzels.

———. 1967. *Contributions to Polar Eskimo Ethnography. Medelelser Om Grønland* 182 (2):1–180. Copenhagen: C.A. Reitels Forlag.

Honko, Lauri. 2000. "Text as Process and Practice: The Textualization of Oral Epics." In *Textualization of Oral Epics*, edited by Lauri Honko, 3–56. Berlin: Mouton De Gruyter.

Hughes, Charles. 1960. *An Eskimo Village in the Modern World*. Ithaca: Cornell University Press.

Hymes, Dell. 2003. *Now I Know Only So Far: Essays in Ethnopoetics*. Lincoln: University of Nebraska Press.

Ipellie, Arnaitok [Arnaittuq Aipili]. 1997. "Lumaajuq." *Inuktitut Magazine* 81 (1997):63–68.

Jakobsen, Merete Dement. 1999. *Shamanism: Traditional and Contemporary Approaches to the Mastery of Spirits*. Oxford: Berghahn Books.

Jenness, Diamond. 1924. "The Loon's Brides." In *Report of the Canadian Arctic Expedition, 1913–1918*, 13 part A: 52–53. Ottawa: F. A. Acland.

Jensen, Anne M. 2007. "Nuvuk Burial I: An Early Thule Hunter of High Status." *Alaska Journal of Anthropology* 5 (1): 119–22.

Johnston, Thomas. 1976a. *Eskimo Music by Region: A Comparative Circumpolar Study*. Mercury Series, Paper No. 32. Ottawa: National Museums of Canada.

———. 1976b. The Eskimo Songs of Northwestern Alaska. *Arctic* 29 (1):7–19.

Jones, Raymond, and Jon Stott, eds. 2006. *A World of Stories: Traditional Tales for Children*. Don Mills, Ontario: Oxford University Press.

Kaalund, Bodil. 1983. *The Art of Greenland: Sculpture, Crafts, Painting*. Translated by Kenneth Tindall. Berkeley: University of California Press, 1983. First published 1979.

Kalifornsky, Peter. 1991. *A Dena'ina Legacy: K'tl'egh'i Sukdu: The Collected Writings of Peter Kalifornsky*. Edited by James Kari and Alan Boraas. Fairbanks: Alaska Native Language Center.

Kankaanpää, Jarmo Kalevi. 1996. "Thule Subsistence." PhD diss., Brown University. Ann Arbor: University Microfilms.

Kiyuklook, Herbert. 1987. "Hunting Walrus the Eskimo Way." In *Savoonga*, vol. 2 of *Sivuqam Nangaghnegha: Lore of St. Lawrence Island*, edited by Anders Apassingok et al., 181–85. Unalakleet: Bering Strait School District.

Klein, Tom. 1985. *Loon Magic*. 2nd ed. Ashland WI: Paper Birch Press.

Kleivan, Inge, and Birgitte Sonne. 1985. *Eskimos—Greenland and Canada*. Iconography of Religions, 8 (2). Leiden: E. J. Brill.

Koranda, Lorraine. 1972. *Alaskan Eskimo Songs and Stories*. Booklet and LP audio recording. Seattle: University of Washington Press.

Kragh, Peder. 1875. *Udtog af Missionair P. Kraghs Dagbog*. Haderslev: Th. Sabo.

Krauss, Michael E. 1982. *In Honor of Eyak: The Art of Anna Nelson Harry*. Fairbanks: Alaska Native Language Center.

Krauss, Michael, and Victor Golla. 1981. "Northern Athapaskan Languages." In *Subarctic*, edited by June Helm, 67–85. Vol. 6 of *Handbook of North American Indians*. Washington: Smithsonian Institution.

Kreutzman, Jens. 1997a. *Jens Kreutzman: Fortællinger & Akvareller*. Edited and translated by Kirsten Thisted. Nuuk: Atuakkiorfik.

———. 1997b. *Oqaluttuat & Assiiliat*. Edited by Kirsten Thisted and Arnaq Grove. Nuuk: Atuakkiorfik.

Kroeber, A. L. 1899. "Tales of the Smith Sound Eskimo." *Journal of American Folklore* 12 (46):166–82.

Kroeber, Karl. 1998. *Artistry in Native American Myths*. Lincoln: University of Nebraska Press.

Krohn, Kaarle. 1971. *Folklore Methodology Formulated by Julius Krohn and Expanded by Nordic Researchers*. Translated by Roger Welsch. Austin: University of Texas Press.

———. 1999. "The Method of Julius Krohn." In *International Folkloristics: Classic Contributions by the Founders of Folklore*, edited and translated by Alan Dundes, 37–45. Lanham MD: Rowman & Littlefield. First published 1891.

Larsen, Helge. 1969. "Some Examples of Bear Cult among the Eskimo and Other Northern Peoples." *Folk* 11:27–42.

Larsen, Helge, and Froelich Rainey. 1948. *Ipiutak and the Arctic Whale Hunting Culture*. Vol. 42 of Anthropological Papers of the Museum of Natural History. New York: Museum of Natural History.

Latocki, Barbara, ed. 1983. *Baffin Island: The Winnipeg Art Gallery, July 23–September 25, 1983*. Winnipeg: Winnipeg Art Gallery.

Laugrand, Frédéric, Jarich Oosten, and Francois Trudel, eds. 2005. *Apostle to the Inuit: The Journals and Ethnographic Notes of Edmund James Peck. The Baffin Years, 1894–1905*. Toronto: University of Toronto Press.

Leechman, Douglas. N.d. Typescript entitled "The Loon's Necklace." 4 pp. MS-120, box 26, folder 12. Douglas Leechman Collection, British Columbia Archives, Victoria.

———. 1931. "The Loon's Necklace . . . and Whence It Came: A Legend of the Pioneer Days in British Columbia." *Forest and Outdoors* 27 (1):24–25.

———. 1942. "The Loon's Necklace." *The Civil Service Review* 15 (4):372–459. Copy on file in Douglas Leechman Collection, British Columbia Archives, MS-1290, box 19, file 11, Victoria.

———. 1952. "Folk-lore of the Vanta-Kutchin." Ottawa: *National Museum of Canada Bulletin* 126:81–82.

———. 1956. "The Loon's Necklace: A Legend of the Interior Salish." In *Native Tribes of Canada*, 258–64. Toronto: W. J. Gage.

———. 1964. "The Loon's Necklace: A Legend of the Interior Salish." In *Canadian Reflections: An Anthology of Canadian Prose*, edited by Philip Penner and John McGechaen, 247–52. Toronto: Macmillan Company of Canada.

Leechman, J. D., and M. R. Harrington. 1921. *String Records of the Northwest*. New York: Museum of the American Indian, Heye Foundation.

Lindner, Banjo Dan. 1992. *The Loon's Necklace*. Compact disc audio. South Strafford VT: Banjo Dan Lindner.

———. 1994. *The Catamount Is Back: Banjo Dan's Songs of Vermont, Vol. II*. Compact disc and cassette audio. South Strafford VT: Banjo Dan Lindner.

Lundström, Håkan. 1980. "North Athabascan Story Songs and Dance Songs." In *The Alaska Seminar*, edited by Anna Birgitta Rooth, 126–64. Uppsala: Almqvist & Wiksell.

Lynch, Kathleen, compiler and illustrator. 1978. *Northern Eskimo Stories*. Anchorage: Anchorage Community College Adult Literacy Laboratory.

MacDonald, John. 1998. *The Arctic Sky: Inuit Astronomy, Star Lore, and Legend*. Toronto: Royal Ontario Museum and Nunavut Research Institute.

MacLean, Edna Ahgeak. 1990. "Culture and Change for Inupiat and Yupiks of Alaska." In *Arctic Languages: An Awakening*, edited by Dirmid Collis, 158–84. Paris: UNESCO.

Maher, Ramona. 1969. *The Blind Boy and the Loon and Other Eskimo Myths*. New York: John Day.

Malaurie, Jean. 1955. "The French Geographical Expedition to Thule, 1950–1951: A Preliminary Report." *Arctic* 8 (4):202–14.

———. 1985. *The Last Kings of Thule*. Translated from the French by Adrienne Foulke. Chicago: University of Chicago Press, 1985. Originally published as *Les derniers rois de Thulé*, 1955.

———. 2003. *Ultima Thule: Explorers and Natives in the Polar North*. New York: W. W. Norton.

Malcolm, Andrew H. 1981. "Through Canada's North by Dogsled." *New York Times*, Travel Section, September 13.

Mary-Rousseliere, Guy. (1980) 1991. *Qitdlarssuaq, the Story of a Polar Migration*. Translated by Alan Cooke. Winnipeg: Wuerz Publishing Co. First published 1980, as *Qitdlarssuaq: L'histoire d'une migration polaire*. Montreal: Presses de l'Université de Montreal.

Mason, J. Alden. 1910. "Myths of the Uintah Utes." *Journal of American Folklore* 23:299–363.

Mathiassen, Therkel. 1927. *The Thule Culture and Its Position within the Eskimo Culture*. Copenhagen: Gyldendalske Boghandel, Nordisk Forlag.

Maud, Ralph. 1989. "The Henry Tate-Franz Boas Collaboration on Tsimshian Mythology." *American Ethnologist* 16 (1):158–62.

———. 1993. *The Porcupine Hunter and Other Stories: The Original Tsimshian Texts of Henry W. Tate*. Vancouver: Talonbooks.

———. 2000. *Transmission Difficulties: Franz Boas and Tsimshian Mythology*. Vancouver: Talonbooks.

Mayokok, Robert. 1960. *Eskimo Stories*. Nome AK: Nome Nugget.

McCartney, Allen P. 1980. The Nature of Thule Eskimo Whale Use. *Arctic* 33 (3):517–41.

McClellan, Catharine. 1970. *The Girl Who Married the Bear: A Masterpiece of Indian Oral Tradition*. Publications in Ethnology No. 2. Ottawa: National Museum of Man.

———. 1975. *My Old People Say*. Publications in Ethnology No. 6, vol. 2. Ottawa: National Museum of Man.

———. 1987. *Part of the Land, Part of the Water: A History of the Yukon Indians.* Vancouver: Douglas & McIntyre.

McGhee, Robert. 1977. "Ivory for the Sea Woman: The Symbolic Attributes of a Prehistoric Technology." *Canadian Journal of Archaeology* 1:141–49.

———. 1996. *Ancient People of the Arctic.* Vancouver: University of British Columbia Press.

McKennan, Robert A. 1959. *The Upper Tanana Indians.* New Haven: Yale University Department of Anthropology.

———. 1965. *The Chandalar Kutchin.* Montreal: Arctic Institute of North America.

Melnyk, George. 2004. *One Hundred Years of Canadian Cinema.* Toronto: University of Toronto Press.

Melville, Herman. (1851) 1922. *Moby-Dick; or, The White Whale.* Boston: The St. Botolph Society. First published 1851.

Melzack, Ronald. 1977. "The Origin of the Narwhal." In *Why the Man in the Moon Is Happy and Other Eskimo Creation Stories*, 26–33. Toronto: McClelland and Stewart.

Merkur, Dan. 1985. *Becoming Half Hidden: Shamanism and Initiation among the Inuit.* Stockholm: Almqvist & Wiskell International.

———. 1991. *Powers Which We Do Not Know: The Gods and Spirits of the Inuit.* Moscow: University of Idaho Press.

———. 2005. *Psychoanalytic Approaches to Myth: Freud and the Freudians.* New York: Routledge.

Metayer, Maurice. 1972. *Tales from the Igloo.* Edmonton: Hurtig Publishers.

Mills, Alice. 2003. *Mythology: Myths, Legends, and Fantasies.* Edited by Janet Parker and Julie Stanton. Lane Cove, Australia: Global Book Publishing.

Mishler, Craig. 1981. "'He Said, They Say': The Uses of Reporting Speech in Native American Folk Narrative." *Fabula* 22 (3–4):239–49.

———. 1986. *Born with the River: An Ethnographic History of Alaska's Goodpaster and Big Delta Indians.* Report of Investigations #86-14. Fairbanks: Alaska Division of Geological and Geophysical Surveys.

———. 1988. "The Blind Boy and the Loon: A Native American Tale Type." Unpublished paper presented at the American Anthropological Association Annual Meeting, Phoenix.

———. 1999. Compact audio disc liner notes for *Gwich'in Athabascan Fiddle Music*, by Bill Stevens. Fairbanks AK: Bill Stevens.

———. 2007. Book review of Judy Thompson's *Recording Their Story: James Teit and the Tahltan. Alaska Journal of Anthropology* 5 (1):159–60.

———. 2008. "Folk Art Meets Folk Tale: The Blind Man and the Loon." Unpublished paper presented at the American Folklore Society Annual Meeting, Louisville, Kentucky.

Mishler, Craig, ed. 2001. *Neerihiinjìk: We Traveled from Place to Place: The Gwich'in Stories of Johnny and Sarah Frank.* 2nd ed. With audio compact disc. Fairbanks: University of Alaska Native Language Center.

Moir, John. 2000. "Émile Petitot." *Dictionary of Canadian Biography.* http://www.biographi.ca/EN/ShowBio.asp?BioId=41771

Momaday, N. Scott. 1969. *The Way to Rainy Mountain.* Albuquerque: University of New Mexico Press.

Moore, Pat, ed. 1999. *Dene Gudeji: Kaska Narratives.* Watson Lake, Yukon: Kaska Tribal Council.

Morice, Adrien. 1892. "Notes Archaeological, Industrial, and Sociological on the Western Denés, with an Ethnographical Sketch of the Same." *Transactions of the Canadian Institute* 6:171–72.

Morrow, Phyllis, and Toby Volkman. 1975. "The Loon with the Ivory Eyes: A Study in Symbolic Archaeology." *Journal of American Folklore* 88 (348):143–50.

Murdoch, John. 1892. *Ethnological Results of the Point Barrow Expedition.* Ninth Annual Report of the Bureau of Ethnology. Washington DC: Government Printing Office.

Nelson, Edward. 1899. *The Eskimo about Bering Strait.* Eighteenth Annual Report of the Bureau of American Ethnology. Washington DC: Government Printing Office.

Norman, Howard. 1990. "How the Narwhal Got Its Tusk." Told by Pioopiula to Michael and Severance Rosegood. Translated by Severance Rosegood. In *Northern Tales: Traditional Stories of Eskimo and Indian Peoples,* 83–86. New York: Pantheon Books.

Nungak, Zebedee, and Eugene Y. Arima, translators. 1969. *Unikkaatuat Sanaugarngnik Atyingualiit Puvirngniturngmit: Eskimo Stories From Povungnituk, Quebec.* National Museums of Canada Bulletin 235, Anthropological Series 90:48–51. Reprinted as *Inuit Stories-Povungnituk-Légendes Inuit* by the NMC in 1988.

Nutaraaluk, Lucassie. (2001). [Untitled]. In *Interviewing Inuit Elders,* 66–67. Vol. 4 of *Cosmology and Shamanism,* edited by Bernard Saladin D'Anglure. Arviat: Nunavut Arctic College.

Oosten, J. G. 1976. "The Theoretical Structure of the Religion of the Netsilik and the Iglulik." PhD diss., Meppel, Netherlands. Krips Repro.

———. 1983. "The Incest of Sun and Moon: An Examination of the Symbolism of Time and Space in Two Iglulik Myths." *Études/Inuit/Studies* 7(1):143–51.

Oosten, Jarich, and Frédéric Laugrand. 2006. "The Bringer of Light: The Raven in Inuit Tradition." *Polar Record* 2 (3):187–204.

Oozeva, Conrad. 1987. "Hunting in Gambell Years Ago." In Gambell, vol. 1 of *Sivuqam Nangaghnegha: Lore of St. Lawrence Island,* edited by Anders Apassingok et al., 129–43. Unalakleet: Bering Strait School District.

Petitot, Émile. 1876. *Monographie des Dènè-Dindjié.* Paris. Available at Early Canadiana Online.

———. 1878. *Monograph of the Dènè-Dindjié Indians.* Translated by Douglas Brymner. Ottawa. Available at Early Canadiana Online.

———. 1886. *Traditions Indiennes du Canada Nord-Ouest.* Paris: Maisonneuve Frères. Available at Early Canadiana Online.

———. 1888. *Traditions Indiennes du Canada Nord-Ouest: Texts originaux and traduction litterale.* Alençon: E. Renaut-De Broise. Available from Google Books.

———. 1890. *Accord des mythologies.* Paris: Émile Bouillon.

Petrone, Penny. 1992. *Northern Voices: Inuit Writing in English.* Toronto: University of Toronto Press.

Polette, Nancy. 2006. *Books Every Child Should Know: The Literature Quiz Book.* Westport CT: Libraries Unlimited.

Rainey, Froelich. 1947. "The Whale Hunters of Tigara." *American Museum of Natural History Anthropological Papers* 61 (Part 2).

Rasmussen, Knud. 1908. *The People of the Polar North: A Record.* Edited by G. Herring. Compiled from the Danish originals. Part 1: The New People: Polar Eskimo. London: Kegan Paul, Trench, Trübner and Company.

———. 1927. *Across Arctic America: Narrative of the Fifth Thule Expedition.* New York: G. P. Putnam's Sons. Reprint, Fairbanks: University of Alaska Press, 1999.

———. 1929. *Intellectual Culture of the Iglulik Eskimos.* Translated from the Danish by W. Worster. Vol. 7, part 1 of *Report of the Fifth Thule Expedition, 1921–24.* Copenhagen: Gyldendalske Boghandel Nordisk Forlag. Reprint, New York: AMS Press, 1976.

———. 1930. *Observations on the Intellectual Culture of the Caribou Eskimos.* Translated from the Danish by W. E. Calvert. Vol. 7, part 2 of *Report of the Fifth Thule Expedition, 1921–24.* Copenhagen: Gyldendalske Boghandel Nordisk Forlag. Reprint, New York: AMS Press, 1976.

———. 1931. *The Netsilik Eskimo: Social Life and Spiritual Culture,* part 1: The Netsilingmiut. Vol. 8 of *Report of the Fifth Thule Expedition, 1921–1924.* Copenhagen: Gyldendalske Boghandel Nordisk Forlag. Reprint, New York: AMS Press, 1976.

———. 1932. *Intellectual Culture of the Copper Eskimos.* Translated from the Danish by W. E. Calvert. Vol. 9 of *Report of the Fifth Thule Expedition, 1921–24.* Copenhagen: Gyldendalske Boghandel Nordisk Forlag. Reprint, New York: AMS Press, 1976.

Reichard, Gladys. 1921. "Literary Types and Dissemination of Myths." *Journal of American Folklore* 34 (133):269–307.

Remie, Cornelius. 1988. "Flying Like a Butterfly, or Knud Rasmussen among the Netsilingmiut." *Études/Inuit/Studies* 12 (1–2):101–27.

Ridington, Robin. 1996. "Voice, Representation and Dialogue: The Poetics of Native American Spiritual Traditions." *American Indian Quarterly* 20:467–89.

Rink, Hinrich. 1859. *Kaladlit Okalluktualliait: kalâdlisut kablunâtudlo* [Legends from Greenland]. In Kalaallisut and Danish. Godthaab. Available online from Google Books.

———. 1866. *Eskimoiske Eventyr og Sagn*. Kjøbenhavn: C. A. Reitzels Boghandel. Available online in Danish from Google Books and the Internet Archive.

———. (1875) 1997. *Tales and Traditions of the Eskimo*. Edinburgh: William Blackwood and Sons. Translation of Rink's *Eskimoiske Eventyr og Sagn*, 1866. Reprint, Mineola NY: Dover Publications, 1997. Available online from Internet Sacred Texts and Google Books.

———. 1877. *Danish Greenland: Its People and Its Products*. Edited by Robert Brown. London: Henry S. King. Reprint, AMS Press, New York. Available online from Google Books.

———. 1887a. *Sagn og fortaellinger fra Angmagsalik*. Collected by G. Holm. Edited with annotations by H. Rink. Kjøbenhavn: F. Dreyer. Available online from Google Books.

———. 1887b. "Elements of the Greenland Traditions and Tales." In *The Eskimo Tribes: Their Distribution and Characteristics, Especially in Regard to Language with a Comparative Vocabulary and a Sketch-Map*, 2:107–13. Copenhagen: C. A. Reitzels; and London: Williams and Norgate. Available online at Google Books.

Roch, Ernst, ed. 1975. *Arts of the Eskimo: Prints*. Barre MA: Barre Publishers.

Rooth, Anna Birgitta. 1976. *The Importance of Storytelling*. Uppsala: Almqvist & Wiksell.

Rubin, Don, ed. 1982. *Canada on Stage: Canadian Theatre Review Yearbook, 1981–1982*. Toronto: CTR Publications.

Ruppert, James, and John Bernet, eds. 2001. *Our Voices: Native Stories of Alaska and the Yukon*. Lincoln: University of Nebraska Press.

Saladin d'Anglure, Bernard. 1990. "Nanook, Super Male: The Polar Bear in the Imaginary Space and Social Time of the Inuit of the Canadian Arctic." In *Signifying Animals: Human Meaning in the Natural World*, edited by Roy Willis, 178–95. London: Unwin Hyman.

Saltman, Judith, and Gail Edwards. 2004. "Elizabeth Cleaver, William Toye, and Oxford University Press: Creating the Canadian Picturebook." *Papers of the Bibliographical Society of Canada* 42 (1):31–64.

Savard, Rémi. 1966. *Mythologie esquimaude: Analyse de textes nord-groenlandais*. Québec: Université Laval, Travaux divers/Centre d'études nordiques.

Savoie, Donat, ed. 1970. *The Amerindians of the Canadian North-west in the 19th Century, As Seen by Émile Petitot*. Vol. 2. Ottawa: Department of Indian Affairs and Northern Development.

———. 1996. "Émile Petitot." In *Lobsticks and Stone Cairns: Human Landmarks in the Arctic*, edited by Richard Davis, 153–54. Calgary: University of Calgary Press.

Seidelman, Harold, and James Turner. 1994. *The Inuit Imagination: Arctic Myth and Sculpture.* New York: Thames and Hudson.

Silook, Roger S. 1976. *Seevookuk: Stories the Old People Told on St. Lawrence Island.* N.p. Copy on file at the Loussac Public Library, Anchorage.

Silver, Shirley, and Wick R. Miller. 1997. *American Indian Languages: Cultural and Social Contexts.* Tucson: University of Arizona Press.

Simeone, William E., and James W. VanStone. 1986. "'And He Was Beautiful': Contemporary Athapaskan Material Culture in the Collections of the Field Museum of Natural History." *Fieldiana Anthropology,* n.s. (19):1–108. Available online at the Internet Archive.

Simpson, John. (1855) 1988. "Observations on the Western Esquimaux and the Country They Inhabit . . ." Vol. 2, appendix 7 in *The Journal of Rochfort Maguire,* edited by John Bockstoce. London: The Hakluyt Society. First published 1855.

Snyder, Gary. 2007. *Back on the Fire: Essays.* Berkeley: Counterpoint.

Søby, Regitze Margrethe. 1988. "Some of the Works of Knud Rasmussen as yet Unpublished." *Études/Inuit/Studies* 12 (1–2):193–204.

Sonne, Birgitte. 1982. "The Ideology and Practice of Blood Feuds in East and West Greenland." *Études/Inuit/Studies* 6 (2): 21–50.

———. 1988. "In Love with Eskimo Imagination and Intelligence." *Études/Inuit/Studies* 12 (1–2):21–44.

Spencer, Robert F. 1959. *The North Alaska Eskimo.* Bureau of American Ethnology, Bulletin 171. Washington DC.

Spencer, Robert F., and W. K. Carter. 1954. "The Blind Man and the Loon: Barrow Eskimo Variants." *Journal of American Folklore* 67 (263):65–72.

Stefansson, Vilhjalmur. 2001. *Writing on Ice: The Ethnographic Notebooks of Vilhjalmur Stefansson.* Edited by G. Pálsson. Hanover: University Press of New England.

Swanton, John. 1908. "Haida Texts—Masset Dialect." *Memoirs of the American Museum of Natural History* 14 (2):353–62.

Teit, James A. 1900. "The Thompson Indians of British Columbia." Edited by Franz Boas. *Memoirs of the American Museum of Natural History,* 2 (4). New York.

———. 1917. "Kaska Tales." *Journal of American Folklore* 30 (118):427–73.

———. 1921. "Tahltan Tales." *Journal of American Folklore* 34 (133):223–53.

Thalbitzer, William. 1941. *The Ammassalik Eskimo: Contributions to the Ethnology of the East Greenland Natives.* Copenhagen: Reitzels Forlag.

Thisted, Kirsten, ed. 1997. *Jens Kreutzman: Fortællinger & Akvareller.* Nuuk: Atuakkiorfik.

———. 1998. "The Collection of Greenlandic Traditions." In *The Epic: Oral and Written,* edited by Lauri Honko et al., 207–19. Mysore: Central Institute of Indian Languages.

———. 2001. "On Narrative Expectations: Greenlandic Oral Traditions about the Cultural Encounter between Inuit and Norsemen." *Scandinavian Studies* 73 (4):253–96.

Thomas, Kenny, Sr. 2005. *Crow Is My Boss: The Oral Life History of a Tanacross Athabaskan Elder.* Edited by Craig Mishler. Norman: University of Oklahoma Press.

Thompson, Judy. 2007. *Recording Their Story: James Teit and the Tahltan.* Vancouver: Douglas & MacIntyre; Seattle: University of Washington Press.

Thompson, M. Terry, and Steven M. Egesdal, eds. 2008. *Salish Myths and Legends: One People's Stories.* Lincoln: University of Nebraska Press.

Thompson, Stith. 1953. "The Star Husband Tale." *Studia Septentrionalia* 4:93–163. Reprinted in *The Study of Folklore*, edited by Alan Dundes, 414–74. Englewood Cliffs NJ: Prentice Hall, 1965.

———. 1955. *Motif-Index of Folk Literature.* Vol. 4. Bloomington: Indiana University Press.

———. (1929) 1967. *Tales of the North American Indians.* Bloomington: Indiana University Press. First published 1929.

Titus, Walter. 1972. "Blind Man and the Loon." Tape recorded in English and Lower Tanana by Karen McPherson at Minto, Alaska, on August 31, 1972. Oral History Collection, Rasmuson Library, University of Alaska, Fairbanks. Tape H91-12-68.

Toye, William, and Elizabeth Cleaver. 1977. *The Loon's Necklace.* Toronto: Oxford University Press.

Turner, Edith. 2006. *Among the Healers: Stories of Spiritual and Ritual Healing around the World.* Westport CT: Praeger.

Van Deusen, Kira. 2009. *Kiviuq: An Inuit Hero and His Siberian Cousins.* Montreal: McGill–Queen's University Press.

von Sydow, Carl Wilhelm. (1932) 1999. "Geography and Folk-Tale Oicotypes." In *International Folkloristics: Classic Contributions by the Founders of Folklore*, edited by Alan Dundes, 137–51. Lanham MD: Rowman & Littlefield. First published 1932.

Vuntut Gwitchin First Nation and Shirleen Smith. 2009. *People of the Lakes: Stories of Our Van Tat Gwich'in Elders/Googwandak Nakhwach'ànjòo Van Tat Gwich'in.* Edmonton: University of Alberta Press.

Wallis, Velma. 1993. *Two Old Women: An Alaskan Legend of Betrayal, Courage, and Survival.* Fairbanks AK: Epicenter Press.

Wilgus, D. K. 1973. "The Text Is the Thing." *Journal of American Folklore* 86 (341): 241-252.

Workman, William. 1974. "The Cultural Significance of a Volcanic Ash Which Fell in the Upper Yukon Basin about 1400 Years Ago." In *International Conference on the Prehistory and Paleoecology of Western North American Arctic and Subarctic*, edited by Scott Raymond and Peter Schledermann, 239–61. Calgary: University of Calgary Archaeological Association.

Worthy, Barbara, ed. 2003. "Lumaajuuq The Blind Boy." In *Inuit Legends, Volume 2*. Set of two audio compact discs, in English and Inuktitut. Canadian Broadcasting Corporation.

Zolbrod, Paul. 1995. *Reading the Voice: Native American Oral Poetry on the Written Page*. Salt Lake City: University of Utah Press.

Index

Page numbers in *italics* refer to black-and-white illustrations. References to color illustrations in the gallery also appear in italics and are labeled *fig. 16, fig. 17*, and so forth.

acoustic elements, 87–88
Affanasi, Chief, *15*
Alix, Claire, xv, 22
Alutiq, 12–13
Amaunalik, 61–62, *63*
Amittu, Aisa, 105
Amittu, Tilly, 105
Amittuq, Davidialuk Alasua, 100–101, 106, 108, *fig. 25*
amulets, 106, 147
Andre, Eliza, 90, 132
d'Anglure, Saladin, 21, 50, 141, 147
Anishaabemowin, 130
Anishinaabemdaa (audio recording), 130–31
"The Ant Lady," 129, 220n6
Arnâluk, 54, 218n3 (chap. 3)
archaeology, and dating of tale, 18–25
Arctic Village, xx, xxvi, 14, 44, 67–68, 70–71, 77
Arnaktauyok, Germaine, 99, 101, *fig. 22*
Arnaquq-Baril, Alethea-Ann Aggiuq, 125–26
Aron of Kangek, 94
arrows, 22, 143
art, tale-inspired. *See* folk art
Ashoona, Pitseolak, 102–3
audio recordings, 129–32

auditory elements, 87–88
Aulajijakka: Things I Remember #5, *fig. 20*
Avdla, 32

Back River, 57
Bakhtin, Mikhail, 91
Balikci, Asen, 220n3
ballet, 126–27
Barbeau, Marius, 123
bear arrows, 22
bear skin, 101
beluga, 11, 13, 20, 23; in film, 130; human transformation into, 4, 7, 140, 160; in tale-inspired art, 102–4, 106–7; in tale texts, xiv, 194, 200–201, 207–8, 213, 222n13
Benjamin, Elinor, 128–29
Beynon, William, 123–24
Birket-Smith, Kaj, 12–13, 22, 50, 145, 147
Bissell, Keith, 127, 129
bladder, harpoon, 20–22
The Blind Boy and the Loon (film), 126
Blind Man and the Loon (Regat), *fig. 21, fig. 28*
Blindman Sees Loon (Sebastian), 100, *fig. 23*
blind mythtellers, 90–91
Blondin, George, 7–8
Blue, Annie, 12, 64–65, 83, *fig. 16*
Boas, Franz, ix, xi, xvi; collection of, 39–40; Group H variant and, 16; sources of, 50–51; Toye variant and, 46

bone grease, 87–88

bows, 22. *See also* arrows

Bringhurst, Robert, 44, 51, 65, 90–91

Bruce, Ellen, 90

Burch, Tiger, 18, 61

Canadian Broadcasting Corporation, 123

Carter, W. K., 22, 41, 137, 144

cartography, storytelling as, 154

Caswell, Helen, 43, 46

censorship, 45, 122

ceremonial masks, 123

Charlie, Andy, 126, 150–51

Chinook Jargon, 40

classic, tale as, 155–56

Cleaver, Elizabeth, 45, 47, 94, 96, 151

collecting, xx–xxi

collectors of the tale, 50

commercial media variants, 183–84

context(s), ix, xi, xxiii–xxiv, xxvi, 41, 51, 56, 69–70, 86, 135–37, 153–54

Copper Inuit, 55

copyright protections, 43–44

Crawley, F. R. "Budge," 120–21, 123–24, 151

Crawley, Judith, 120–21

Crawley, Michal Anne, 123

Crockford, Susan, 22

Cut Nose, 17

Dandy Jim, 52, *53*, 122

de Laguna, Frederica, 50

Daniel, Amos, 32–33

Danish, xiii–xv, xviii, 17, 20, 30–31, 33, *35*; archives, 185; collectors of the tale, 50; language, xvi, xxv, 17, 27, 30, 32–33, 35–36, 54, 56, 94, 197, 218n1 (chap. 2), 218n3 (chap. 3), 221–22; missionaries, 28–29, 40, 145

dating "The Blind Man and the Loon," 18–25

Dégh, Linda: on folklore in electronic world, 119; on scholarly traditions, xxiii; on storytellers, 49, 65

dentalium necklace, xxiv, 14, *15*

Dick, Charlie, 14

diffusion, 17–19

disabled, contributions of, 138–39

dog traction, 23

Dorsey, George, 2, 17, 50

drag float, 20–22

Dwyer, Corrinne, 46

Dwyer-Schick, Susan, 124

"The Early Days Indians," 83

Egesdal, Steven, 136

Ekblaw, Walter, 141

English, 36–37, 88–89

Erick, Ernest, 69

Eskimo oicotypes, 10–13

Eskimo subtype: healing in, 152; kinship theme in, 138; language groups representing, 2; morphology and geography and, 1; overview of, 3–5; polar bear taboo in, 142; violence in, 149–50

ethnography and areal studies, xxii–xxiii

ethnopoetics, xxii

family, as theme of tale, 137–39

Farrand, Livingston, 14, 50, 121

Fienup-Riordan, Ann, 64

films based on the tale, 120–26

Finnegan, Ruth, 108

folk art: analysis of, 106–8; categories of, 97–106; history of, 93–96; list of works, 109–18; overview of, 108–9; samples of, 96–97

folklore: collecting, xxi; in electronic world, 119; Grimm on, xix; as hypertext, 153–54; Krohn on, xxiv; social dynamics of, 155; traditions of, scholarship, xxii–xxiii
Frank, Caroline, xvii, 70–71, 77, 219n3, *fig. 18*
Frank, Johnny, 18, 44, 83
Frank, Kenneth, xvii, 44, 70–71, 77, 87, 135, 219n3, *fig. 18*
French, 37–39, *38*
full tale type, 6–8

geese: sight restored by, 10, 33, 159, 222n11; in tale texts, 206, 211–12
geology, morphology and, 1–3
Gilbert, James, 67, 68–69, 70, 89, *fig. 17*
Gilbert, Maggie, x–xi, xvi–xvii, xx, xxii, xxvi, 14, 39, *68, fig. 17*; analysis and commentary on telling of, 82, 217n10, 219n4, 219n6, 220n1; character voices of, 83–84; English in telling of, 88–89; English translation of, 77–82; Gwich'in text of, 71–76; life of, 67–68; memorial potlatch for, 68–69; performance context of, 69–70; poetic justice and symmetry of, 152; religious dimensions in tale of, 145; structure of telling of, 89–90, 161; variant of, 143; voice of, 86–88, 91; voice of tradition and, 84–86
Gilbert, Trimble, 67–68, 70
Gilday, Carla Rae, xvii, 96, 101, *fig. 24*
Goose, Agnes, 109
Goose, Louie, 132

Greenlandic: Holtved and, 62; Rasmussen and, 40, 54–55, 191–209; reporting speech in, 34; Rink and, 29–30, 33; storytellers and, 65; variants told in, 185–87
Grimm, Jacob, xix
Group A (Greenland Polar Bear Group), 9, 10, 11–12, 19
Group B (Lumaaq Polar Bear Group), 9, 10, 11–12, 93
Group C (Northwest Alaska Polar Bear Group), 7, 9, 10, 11–12, 18
Group D (Southwest Alaska Group), 9, 12–13
Group E (Black and Grizzly Bear Group), 9, 14, 16
Group F (Caribou Group), 9, 13, 14–16
Group G (Moose Group), 9, 13–14, 16, 90
Group H (Buffalo Group), 9, 14, 16–17
Guggenheim, Hans, 124
Gwich'in Indians, xxii, 18
Gwich'in language: Maggie Gilbert's telling in, 71–76; Petitot and, 37–39; prosody, 70; reporting speech in, 34, 85; sound recordings in, 90; textual standardization and, 44; traditional tales in, 84

Hall, Edwin, 6–7, 43, 50
handicapped, contributions of, 138–39
Hare, 17, 37
harpoon bladder (float), xiv, 19–22, 122, 205, 214, 217n9, 222n7 (app. D)
harpoon(s), xiv, 4–7, 10–13, 19, 20–23, 102, 106–7, 125, 152, 160, 201, 208, 213

Harry, Anna Nelson, 16
healing and healing ritual: in tale-inspired art, 99–101; through revenge, 148–49
heteroglossia, 91
Historic-Geographic method, 3
Hoedeman, Co, 124–25
Holm, Gustav, 50
Holtved, Eric, xv, xxv, 50, 61–62, *63*, 139
Honko, Lauri, 42
How the Loon Got Its Necklace (musical piece), 127
Huwakzuk, *61*
Hymes, Dell, xxii, 85, 90
hypertext, tale as, 153–54

Igjugârjuk, 58
Iglulik, 41–42
Ikinilik, 57, *60*
Indian subtype: justice in, 152; kinship theme in, 138; language groups representing, 2; morphology and geography and, 1; overview of, 5–6
Internet variants of tale, 132–33
Inuit: disabled among, 138–39; folk art and, 93, 96–97, *98*, 108–9
Inuit Legends (audio recording), 130
Inuktitut: in *Inuit Legends*, 130; reporting speech in, 34
Iñupiat Eskimos, 18, 147
Ipellie, Arnaitok, 11, 66
Ipiutak loon skull, 18–19
Itugssarssuat, 62
Ivaluardjuk, 41–42, 54–55, *59*

Jackson, Calvin, 126–27
Jakobsen, Merete, 141
Jenness, Diamond, 50, 95, 217n5, 221n4 (chap. 7)

Jeremiaasen, Karolina Platou, xvi; transcriptions and translations by, 191–214
Johnnieapik, 102
Johnston, Thomas, 146
Jones, Raymond, 46, 151
Jørgensen, Sofie, 54
justice, social, as theme of tale, 148–52

Kalaallisut. *See* Greenlandic
Kalifornsky, Peter, 14, *66*, 83, 150
Kappianaq, George, 103
Kiakshuk, 102
Kibkârjuk, 57–58, *61*
Killiktee, Ooloopie, 103
kinship, as theme of tale, xxvii, 24, 89, 109, 137–38, 148, 153, 155
Kleivan, Inge, 142
Komoartuk, Ekidluak, 102
Kragh, Peder, 29–30, 32, 36, 65, 185, 211, 215
Krauss, Michael, xvii, 16, 24, 50
Kreutzmann, Jens, 32, 36, 65, 185, 215
Kroeber, Alfred, x, 2, 17, 50
Kroeber, Karl, 85
Krohn, Julius, 3
Krohn, Kaarle, xxiv, 3
Kuania, 54, 218n3 (chap. 3), 222n6 (app. C)
Kwakiutl, 51

lamps, stone, 10, 19, 22–23, 55, 58, 148, 214
Leechman, Douglas, 14, 42, 47, 120–23, 127, 130
The Legend of the Blind Boy (Sharky), *fig. 26*
Legend of the Loon that helps the Blind Man See (Tukalak), 100

linguistic area hypothesis, 1
The Loon Gives Lumaq His Sight (Arnaktauyok), *fig. 22*
loon(s): decoration of, xxiv, 14; hunting, 150; markings of, xxiv; symbolism of, 143–44; in tale texts, xiii–xiv, 199
The Loon's Necklace (ballet), 126–27
The Loon's Necklace (film), ix, 14, 45, 94, 120–24, 126, 130, 151, *fig. 29*
"The Loon's Necklace" (musical composition), 131–32
The Loon's Necklace (play), 127–28
Loucheux, Sylvain Vitoedh, 37–39, *38*
Lowie, Robert, 50
Luke, Abraham, xx, 143
Lumaaq, an Eskimo Legend, 106, 124–25
Lumaaq group, 11. *See also* Group B
Lumak (Amittuq), 106, *fig. 25*
Lund, Jakob, 32–33
Luumajuq, 11
Lyberth, Gert, 54, 58, 218n3 (chap. 3)
Lynge, Hans, 10

MacDonald, Larry, 123
Maher, Ramona, 46
Makari, 12–13
Malaurie, Jean, 50, 62–64, 101, 107, 145, 149
Märchen, European, 46
mask(s): of blindness, 105; ceremonial, 123; Old Hamilton loon, *fig. 27*
Mason, Owen, xv, 217n7
Mathews, Robin, 128
Mathiassen, Therkel, 22–23
Mayer, John, xxv
Mayokok, Robert, 106–7

McClellan, Catharine, 14, 50, 144–46, 221n3 (concl.)
McGregor, Walter, 16
media, folklore in: audio recordings and radio broadcasts, 129–32; commercial media variants, 183–84; films, 120–26; Internet variants, 132–33; overview of, 119–20; theatrical and performing arts, 126–29
medicine man, 5, 73, 79, 89–90, 120–21, 141, 145, 157
medicine power, xxvii, 16, 141, 145–46
Melnyk, George, 122
Melzack, Ronald, 46
Merkur, Dan, 147–48
migration(s): Thule, 19–20; of written texts, 28–29
Miller, Wick R., 85
Mills, Alice, 43
Momaday, N. Scott, 43
Morice, Father A. G., 14, 17, 173
morphology, geology and, 1–3
Morrow, Phyllis, 18–19
motif(s): of Eskimo subtype, 4; of full tale type, 6–7
movies, 120–26
Murdoch, John, 22

Nacktan, Lena, 16
Nâlungiaq, 56–57, *60*
narwhal: human transformation into, 4, 7, 10–11, 102–3, 137, 140, 160; origin of the, xix, 46, 51, 107; in tale-inspired art, 102–3, 107; in tale texts, 213
NatureWatch (radio program), 132–33
necklace, dentalium, xxiv, 14, *15*
Nenana, 131
Netsilik Eskimo, 23, 56–57, 140

Netsilingmiut, 56–57

Netsit, 55–56, *59*

Nicola River, 120–21

Nielsen, Jonasine, 10, 54, 218n3 (chap. 3)

Norton, Nora Paaniikaaluk, 7, 12

Nunavik, 10, 11

Nunavut Animation Lab: Lumaajuuq (film), 125–26

Nutaraaluk, Lucassie, 11, 21–22

oicotypes: defined, 2–3; emergence of, 3; Eskimo, 10–13; importance of regional, 2; Indian, 13–17; regional, with hypothetical diffusion, *9*; variants and, 8–10. *See also* Group A–Group H

Old Crow, 90

Old Hamilton loon mask, *fig. 27*

Old John Lake, 18

The Old Man and the Loon (Gilday), 101, *fig. 24*

Olsen, Cecilie (Sísê/Sissili), 54, 218n3 (chap. 3), 221n1 (app. C)

Olsen, Gaba, 54, 218n3 (chap. 3)

"One-eyed Susie," 52, *53*

Oosten, Jarich, 41–42, 218n4

Out of the Sea (Saila), 107

performing arts, 126–29

Peter, Jo Ann, *68*

Peter, Linus, *68*

Peter, Martha, *68*

Peter, Titus, 67, *68*

Petitot, Émile, 17, 37–39, 50, 90, 219n15

Petrone, Penny, 41–42

Pitsiulak, Donny, 103

Pitsiulak, Lypa, 103–4

polar bear: cult, 148; illustrated in tale-inspired art, 94, 97–99, 102; killed by bow and arrow, 22–23, 62; killed by spear, 46; pants, 61–62; rites and taboos regarding, 140–42, 148; in tale texts, xiii, 61, 94, 193, 198–200, 205–7, 212–13; as tale trait, 4, 11, 14

Pootoogook, Kananginak, 97–99, *fig. 20*

psychology of tale, 147–48

Pualuna, 62–64

Pudloo, Eyesiak, 103

Qitdlarssuaq, 19–20

quotative, 85. *See also* reporting speech

Qupiqrualuk, Aisa, 99, 106, 107, 115

radio broadcasts, 129–32

Rasmussen, Knud, ix–x, xvi, xxvi, 149; collection of, 10, 23, 40–41, 50; Greenlandic variants of, 191–209; on harpoon bladders, 20; manuscript collections in Danish archives, 185; religious dimensions in tale of, 145, 149; sources of, 52–61; variant collected by, 10, 23

redaction(s), 36–37, 43, 47, 94, 122, 128, 155

Regat, Jacques, xvii, 96, 99, 101, 104–5, *fig. 21*, *fig. 28*

Regat, Mary, xvii, 96, 99, 101, 104–5, *fig. 21*, *fig. 28*

religious dimensions of tale, 144–47

Remie, Cornelius, 57

reporting speech, 34, 84–85, 87

revenge, 148–52

Ridington, Robin, on Americanist writing, 82

Rink, Hinrich, 29–37; diffusion and, 17; Rasmussen and, 41; on

revenge, 149; tale versions of, xiii–
xv, 215; textual standardization
and, 44. See also *Tales and
Traditions of the Eskimo* (Rink)
rites, concerning polar bear, 140–43

Saila, Pitaloosie, 107
Savard, Rémi, 141, 148
seal bladder, 20–22
seal poke, 20–22
Sebastian, Robert E., xvii, 96, 100,
124, *fig. 23*
Seidelman, Harold, 139
Selawik AK, Eskimo variant, 7
semi-literary variants, 42–46, 179–83
shamanism, 144, 147
Sharky, Toonoo, 104, *fig. 26*
Shulus, 120–21
Silver, Shirley, 85
Simpson, John, 138–39
Smith, David, 132
snow sculpture, 103
Snyder, Gary, 119
Søby, Regitze, 58
social dynamics of folktales, 155
social justice as theme of tale, 148–52
social voice, 84
Sonne, Birgitte, xvi, 30, 32, 142, 149,
218
Sonnesbase (database of
Greenlandic tales), xvi–xvii, 10,
28, 30, 167, 169, 185, 215, 218
Spencer, Robert F., 22, 41, 50, 137, 144
spirit helpers, x, 89, 109, 145–46
standardization, textual, 44
Steenholdt, Wittus Frederik, xvi, 18,
29, *31*, 32, 65, 155, 185, 211–15
Stefansson, Vilhjalmur, 139
stone lamps. *See* lamps, stone
storytellers: blind, 90–91; Boas's
sources, 50–51; Holtved's

sources, 61–62; Malaurie's
sources, 62–64; overview of,
49–50, 65–66; Rasmussen's
sources, 52–61; Teit's source, 52
The Storyteller's Bag (audio
recording), 129–30
storytelling, as cartography, 154
Stott, John, 46, 151
subtype. *See* Eskimo subtype; Indian
subtype
Sun-Sister Moon-Brother incest tale,
11, 137, 147–50, 217n3
Swanton, John, xvi, 50, 90

taboos, concerning polar bear,
140–43
Tales and Traditions of the Eskimo
(Rink), 94, *95*
tale type, 3, 6–8
Tanacross, xx, 2, 16, 89, 136, 138,
143, 146, 150
Tate, Henry, 46, 51
technology, Thule, 20–23
Teit, James, 50, 52, 89, 122, 145,
218n2 (chap. 3)
textual standardization, 44
Thalbitzer, William, 139, 140–41
theatrical and performing arts,
126–29
themes, of tale, 137–40
"they say," 84–85. *See also* reporting
speech
Thisted, Kirsten, xv, 33, 54
Thomas, Kenny, Sr., xx, 88–89, 136,
150, 217n4, 220n1, *fig. 19*
Thompson, Stith, 6
Thompson, Terry, 136
Thule, 61–62
Thule culture, 20–23, 217n7
Thule migration, 19–20
Titus, Walter, 87, 131

Togiak, 64–65

Toye, William, 45–46, 94

tradition, voice of, 84–86

trait(s): conventional tale, 97; in Eskimo oicotypes, 4, 10–13; of Indian oicotypes, 13–17; manifested in tale, 8; paradigm of tale, 157–61

transformation as theme of tale, 139–40

Tsigehtchic, 90

Tsimshian, 51

Tukalak, Lukassie, 100

Turner, Edith, 135

Turner, James, 139

Ullulaq, Judas, 102

ulus, 19, 23, 102, 107, 212–13, 222n2

Unka, Ellen, 132

values, of tale, 137–40

Vandeegwizii, Old John, 18

variants: bibliography of, 163–89; elements present in all, 7–8; Rasmussen's Greenlandic, 191–209; regional group, 8–10; of Rink, 215; of Steenholdt, 211–14

Victor, Paul-Émile, 50

violence: omission of, 45; as theme of tale, 148–52

voice(s): in Maggie Gilbert's telling, 83–84; of tradition, 84–86

Volkman, Toby, 18–19

von Sydow, Carl, ix, xxiii, 2

Wade, Patricia, 129

walrus, 4, 11, 13, 20, 23; hunting accidents, 21; as tale trait, 160

water bugs, 143–44, 219n8

witchcraft, xxvii, 34, 45, 144, 149

Worthy, Barbara, 130

writing of "The Blind Man and the Loon": Émile Petitot collection, 37–39; Franz Boas collection, 39–40; Hinrich Rink collection, 29–37; Knud Rasmussen collection, 40–42; migration of written texts, 28; overview of, 27–29; semi-literary variants, 42–46

Yamaagh Telcheegh, 136–37, 150

Yup'ik, 4, 64, 83, 104, 126, 146

Yup'ik Eskimo area, 2, 12, 150–51